W9-CLD-208

APR 98

PHILOSOPHY AND EDUCATION:
ACCEPTING WITTGENSTEIN'S CHALLENGE

Philosophy and Education

VOLUME 6

PHILOSOPHY AND EDUCATION:
ACCEPTING WITTGENSTEIN'S CHALLENGE

Edited by

Paul Smeyers and James D. Marshall

Reprinted from *Studies in Philosophy and Education,*
Volume 14, Nos. 2–3, 1995

DISCARD

KLUWER ACADEMIC PUBLISHERS
DORDRECHT / BOSTON / LONDON

A C.I.P. Catalogue record for this book is available from the Library of Congress

ISBN 0-7923-3715-8

Published by Kluwer Academic Publishers,
P.O. Box 17, 3300 AA Dordrecht, The Netherlands.

Kluwer Academic Publishers incorporates
the publishing programmes of
D. Reidel, Martinus Nijhoff, Dr W. Junk and MTP Press.

Sold and distributed in the U.S.A. and Canada
by Kluwer Academic Publishers,
101 Philip Drive, Norwell, MA 02061, U.S.A.

In all other countries, sold and distributed
by Kluwer Academic Publishers Group,
P.O. Box 322, 3300 AH Dordrecht, The Netherlands.

Printed in the Netherlands

TABLE OF CONTENTS

Preface

We met in London at the second INPE conference in 1990. One of us commented on the other's paper and as a result and of later correspondence Paul suggested to Jim that there was a need for a collection on Wittgenstein and education. It has taken three years, with many faxes, E-mails and telephone calls. There were also discussions in Varna in 1992 and major work in Leuven in 1992 and 1993. We spent some time thinking about potential contributors and what we would have hoped for in such a collection. We are certain about the quality of the contributions, but the reader can judge about the structure.

Jim would wish to thank Paul and *KU Leuven* for their generous hospitality during the production of the collection. In return Paul would wish to thank Jim for his long distanced patience.

The result we hope has been worth the effort.

We would especially like to thank Betty Vanden Bavière for her production of the manuscripts.

We would also wish to thank C.J.B. Macmillan and D.C. Phillips, Kluwer's external reviewers, for their helpful advice. Finally we thank Kluwer in the person of their Editor, Peter de Liefde, for his patience and guidance.

James D. Marshall
Paul Smeyers

Studies in Philosophy and Education **14**: 125, 1995.

The Wittgensteinian Frame of Reference and Philosophy of Education at the End of the Twentieth Century

An Introduction to *Philosophy and Education: Accepting Wittgenstein's Challenge*

PAUL SMEYERS AND JAMES D. MARSHALL

University of Leuven, Belgium and University of Auckland, New Zealand

If the ability to inspire a wealth of exciting philosophy in others is the mark of a great philosopher, then Wittgenstein is one. His 'deep thoughts' as well as his abstruse (cryptical) style, have inspired scholars not only within the different fields of 'pure' philosophy, but from disciplines as diverse as theology and mathematics and including disciplines such as psychology, sociology and education. Our concern is mainly with education. Regrettably understanding of Wittgenstein within philosophy of education has been until very recently, rather superficial. Notwithstanding references to the early work and to the later position in a handful of books and articles, it is clear that education has not grasped the full potential of Wittgenstein's philosophy. The themes that were developed by Wittgenstein challenge our understanding of education, and of philosophy of education. To take up the challenge posed by Wittgenstein is the focus of the present volume.

After a brief introduction to Wittgenstein's philosophy and a general outline of the state of the art of philosophy of education, the rationale of the structure of the volume is elaborated and brief introductions to the different chapters are given.

Readers familiar with Wittgenstein and/or the state of the art of philosophy of education can start with either of these parts or directly with the introduction to the chapters. Notes are given at the end of each chapter, but all the references are compiled together at the end of the volume. The list of references starts with a set of abbreviations that is used for referring to Wittgenstein's works. Square brackets are used for additions for clarifications in quotations by the author of the chapter.

WITTGENSTEIN'S PHILOSOPHY

Yet another introduction to Wittgenstein's work can only be justified if a lack of knowledge of his position, can arguably be defended amongst the envisaged readership. Such is undoubtedly the case for the discipline of education, and for philosophy of education. But there is another reason why it is necessary to go into some basic Wittgensteinian ideas. His philosophy is not only very rich, but

3

Studies in Philosophy and Education **14**: 127–159, 1995.

it also generates different perspectives, some of which are mutually exclusive. Though it cannot be the intention of the editors to pin down either for the contributors or for the readers of this volume, *the one and only* interpretation, it is nevertheless necessary to make clear in which way we understand and have been impressed by this philosophy, *in so far* as it is relevant for education and philosophy of education. In doing that, a concept of education must intrude and permeate the account. But as Wittgenstein himself argued, we have to start from the concepts we use, we need 'friction' (PI, I, # 107). Obviously, only a limited number of issues can be dealt with, others can be touched upon and some cannot even be mentioned.

Below we will discuss consecutively the 'theory' of meaning, the importance of basic propositions, and the 'form of life' and understanding of human action. Finally, some of his ideas concerning ethics and philosophy itself will be elaborated. The relevance of the elaborated basic insights to education will only be mentioned in passing, but these will, we trust, become clear. At the end of this part, some implications for education are proposed.

One final remark may suffice to characterise the general frame-work that has been used. It is customary to differentiate between the earlier and the later philosophy of Wittgenstein. No attempt will be made in this introduction to do justice to the numerous differences nor to the similarities between the two periods. While the main inspiration will be sought in the posthumously published *Philosophical Investigations* (1953), the ideas can be traced back to the decade following the 1922 publication of the *Tractatus Logico-Philosophicus*.[1]

'MEANING' AND 'ACTING'

In the determination of the meaning of a word, the context fulfils, according to Wittgenstein, a crucial role. The idea of a 'language-game' is used to express this. The meaning of a sentence, like that of a word or phrase, is internally related to the criteria of our understanding. These are of two main types: *explaining* the sentence, word or phrase, and *using* it correctly. The form of explanation typical for sentences is that of paraphrase: the sentence to be explained is replaced by another sentence that disposes with a problematic expression, an opaque construction, or an uncertain use. The use of sentences has two major characteristics which can be understood as subdivisions of our understanding. The focus in one is the ability to produce a sentence in appropriate circumstances; in the second that we react to a sentence in a way appropriate to the circumstances. Both indicate that a 'language-game' is part of an activity or of a 'form of life'. This latter concept was crucial to overcoming the difficulties of the earlier calculus model of language. This suggests that it is possible to interpret the rules of the language in such a way that an interpretation cannot be wrong and, moreover, that a rule determines independently of its use whether an expression has been used correctly. Section 242 of the *Philosophical Investigations* reads therefore:

"If language is to be a means of communication there must be agreement not only in definitions but also (queer as this may sound) in judgements" (PI, I, # 242).

and in section 241 this agreement is called an agreement not in opinions but in 'forms of life'.

The paradigm example of a 'language-game' given by Wittgenstein is the game of chess. Chess shows that rules are not 'grounded', and that rules cannot be justified by any reference to reality. Furthermore, the rules are autonomous and 'arbitrary', in the sense that they could have been different. In a 'language-game' the following can belong: certain words, expressions, gestures, a particular context and a constitutive activity. Only within a 'language-game' will we be able to justify a certain inference, a certain behaviour; within a 'language-game' we can speak of justification and lack of justification, of evidence and proof, of mistakes and groundless opinions, of good and bad reasoning, of correct and incorrect measurements.

"What counts as an adequate test of a statement belongs to logic. It belongs to the description of the language-game" (C, # 82).

Within a system of thinking and acting there occur, up to a point, investigations and criticisms of the reasons and justifications that are employed in that system. We bring this inquiry to an end when we come upon something that we regard as a satisfactory reason, and that we do so shows itself in our actions. The end, Wittgenstein says,

"... is not certain propositions' striking us immediately as true, i.e. it is not a kind of *seeing* on our part; it is our *acting*, which lies at the bottom of the language-game" (C, # 204).

It is by our actions that we fix a boundary of the 'language-game'.

We are initiated into 'language-games'. Wittgenstein insists upon the importance of the way this initiation proceeds, and on its relevance to establishing meaning. In section 77 of the *Philosophical Investigations* he writes:

"In such a difficulty always ask yourself: How did we *learn* the meaning of this word ("good" for instance)? From what sort of examples? in what language-games? Then it will be easier for you to see that the word must have a family of meanings" (PI, I, # 77).

Not only does the meaning of a word turn on the context in which it is learned, but, obviously, there are different contexts in which the word is used, or to put this more technically, there are different 'language-games'. The meaning of a word will be different according to the context. More precisely, there is no such thing as *the* meaning of a word, there is only *a* (and this realised in this present context) meaning of the word, and usually in that particular context the meaning of a word is clear to the participants. As was indicated (cf. PI, I, # 77) Wittgenstein therefore suggests that in order to understand the meaning of a word we look at the particular situations in which the word is learned. Not surprisingly such a way of thinking has raised questions about relativism, as different contexts provide different meanings for a word. If we think from the opposite direction it seems to a certain extent true. At the same time, one could argue that whatever words we use to realise are themselves in turn context-dependent. And as different contexts are at least in principle not inconceivable, it might be possible to think of a number of them. But can we *really* imagine them, one can and should ask? Furthermore, the meaning of an expression seems constantly to slip away, so that it is difficult to decide, it is argued, what exactly has been said. In these interpretations – for which the dense nature of Wittgenstein's writings must to some degree be held responsible – the 'language-game' is understood more as a game with words instead of being inherently connected with reality.

Wittgenstein's 'theory' of meaning advocates neither a position of pure subjectivity nor of pure objectivity. From the beginning, what one could call an element of risk, is present in the way communication is conceived. However, the consistency of meaning Wittgenstein argues for is free of essentialism. Though every situation is in some sense new, the different meanings of a concept are linked with each other through family-resemblances. In order to be understood, the present use may not be radically different from the former ones. It is within the *normal* context that the meaning of a concept is determined. The others *and* I proceed in this way. There is no absolute point of reference (neither internal nor external) for them, or for me. The community of language speakers forms the warrant for the consistency of meaning. Analogously the meaning of an action can be decided from the 'third person perspective'. And in turn 'intention' finds its proper place in the context of action.

Wittgenstein also conceives action as in the main part being non-reflective. Human behaviour is conceived as a constant stream of reactions which only very rarely, and in such cases only for a moment, are stopped by deliberate reflection. To answer a question, as to follow a command, does not contain usually an anterior step in which the situation is analyzed. To act is not first to think and consequently to do something. It is to do something in a certain manner (which doesn't mean that one cannot reflect upon it afterwards).

In what I do it will become clear what I stand for, the things that I value, and the way that I go on and 'follow a rule'. To say that what I do is voluntary in this sense, does not mean that I have reflected upon it, nor does it imply that if I reflect upon it, I can take a stance outside of reality. It only means that the things I do cannot be considered as random activities which are just 'done' by me without being conscious of them or engaging with them. It goes without saying that different meanings can be ascribed to my actions, that my action can have more than one meaning, and also that I can deceive myself. But in normal circumstances, I take it for granted that the intention of what one does, has not been searched for by the actor.

Crucial, as has been indicated already, is the social determination of meaning and understanding. The meaning of a concept is not the result of what I intend, but is determined and carried, by the community to which I belong. To understand a concept means to be able to paraphrase it and to act accordingly. In both the 'third person perspective' is predominant. But language is first the language of the others. It determines the way that I can speak: otherwise I risk being unintelligible. 'Concepts' and 'actions' are necessarily and inseparably interwoven with each other and belong to a 'language-game'. That, and all other 'language-games', are 'grounded' in a 'form of life'.

'FORM OF LIFE'

With the concept of the 'form of life', Wittgenstein indicates what he considers to be the bedrock of our 'language-games'. It can be marked off, in so far as it can be spoken of, as all of the most fundamental propositions on the ethical, epistemological, metaphysical and religious level. They are given. Precisely because of their givenness, justification comes to an end. These unjustified and unjustifiable patterns of human activities can be seen as the complicated network of rules which constitute language and social life. This 'given' is a whole: it is the 'language-and-the-world'. We cannot place ourselves outside of it. Examples of basic propositions are for instance Moore's well known sentences 'I am a human being', or 'There are physical objects', to which Wittgenstein refers in sections 4 and 35 of *On Certainty* (1969). Further examples are sentences saying that one has two hands, and that all human beings have parents (C, ## 157 & 240). The 'certainty' of the 'form of life' is not carried by knowledge but is a priori for that knowledge. These propositions are unmoving foundations (C, # 403); exempt from doubt (C, # 341); they stand fast (C, ## 151 & 235); and are absolutely solid (C, # 151). They 'ground' all my activities 'wrongly' expressed by the words 'I know' (cf. C, # 414). Our acting is embedded in a matrix of certainty that precedes our knowledge (the matrix of knowing-and-doubting and knowing-and-'making a mistake'). The ordinary certainties are the roads on which we walk without hesitation. They are not the only possible ones, and not perhaps the correct ones (not even those which have worked in experience). But they are the roads on which we are, and we have no reasons for leaving them: "I have no grounds for not trusting them. And I trust them" (C, # 600).

Differences concerning these basic propositions will cause us to call another person a fool and a heretic, Wittgenstein argues in *On Certainty* (# 611). And in the following section we read:

> "I said I would 'combat' the other man, – but wouldn't I give him *reasons*? Certainly; but how far do they go? At the end of reasons comes *persuasion*. (Think what happens when missionaries convert natives)" (C, # 612).

If we try to doubt everything, Wittgenstein argues, we would not get as far as doubting anything: "The game of doubting itself presupposes certainty" (C, # 115). A shared 'form of life' is a prerequisite for objectivity itself and the existence of a common world is its logical presupposition. To describe this common world from an uncertain ground is impossible. The 'form of life' can be seen as the complex network of the constituent rules of the social life and of the language which we use. As we cannot place ourselves outside it, we cannot talk *about* it, but can only recognise it as the theoretical boundary. For this reason it cannot be taken as a basic ground or ultimate foundation for absolute objectivity or truth. What we call objective and true is determined by this 'boundary': "If the true is what is grounded, then the ground is not *true*, nor yet false" (C, # 205).

These and other remarks, for example in *Remarks on Frazer's Golden Bough* (1979), have given further fuel to the relativism debate. Can different cultures, it is asked, be compared at all? Can people act as they please within a certain culture? Or is the contrast between two fundamentally different cultures never so radical? Can one at least understand someone else's perspective to some limited extent without accepting it? Are people so different from each other that they can no longer understand one another, and that they can't reach agreement any more? Is it then all the same whatever we do? Can no criticism whatsoever be made of the position of women in the Arab world or can no criticism be made of the activities of the Nazis in the Second World War? So it seems, at least at first sight. It looks as if Wittgenstein's position urges us to accept the radically different before we can understand it or 'see the point' of it. Furthermore, that we *can* see it seems not to be in our hands but rather to be a matter of being persuaded.

Wittgenstein's opposition to the craving for generality should restrain us from claiming that dialogue between people belonging to different cultures is impossible, but it should also restrain us from insisting that dialogue is always possible. He seems to say something like this: "I can't but think and/or act in this way". He doesn't grant the same status to what others think compared to us (neither on the epistemological nor on the ethical level) without, however, at the same time being willing or able to affirm the correctness (in the strong sense) of his own position. This ironical result, as it is called by Sayers (1987), can be understood in the following way: for Wittgenstein it is not necessary to arrive at an ultimate standard and/or ultimate foundation of rationality. Such a 'craving for generality' or looking for 'foundations' seems to him to be superfluous. In our opinion this must be the conclusion not only for his stance concerning epistemology, but also for his metaphysics and ethics. The wrong questions were and are still being asked – a typical philosophical mistake, according to Wittgenstein.

Concerning the problem of relativism Winch argues in *Trying to Make Sense* that the task of reason in certain cases is not to arrive at a position which has to be accepted by both parties, even if they are both willing to reach agreement. What seems to be important is to try to understand the position of the other party, including the difficulties that go with it. Winch writes:

> "There is no ground whatsoever *a priori* for expecting the emergence of some position free of difficulties which everyone would be able to accept. But that does not mean at all that there is no difference between someone who accepts and lives by a position with clear understanding of its strengths and weaknesses, of where it may lead him, of what the alternatives are, and someone who does not understand these things" (Winch, 1987, p. 189).

Winch also draws our attention to the fact that Wittgenstein's notion of agreement as a condition of being able to communicate does not presuppose that an agreement should be reached about *everything* if communication is to be possible at all. This seems to be an idea closely linked to the meaning of 'following a rule'. One cannot indicate all the cases which possibly belong to the area of application of a certain rule by (the phrasing of) the rule itself. 'To follow a rule' means to be able to go on in a certain way. As Malcolm puts it:

> "We go on all agreeing, following rules and applying words in new cases – without guidance. Other than the past training, there is no explanation. It is an aspect of the form of life of human beings. It is our nature. To try to explain it is like trying to explain why dogs bark" (Malcolm, 1986, p. 181).

This 'going on' is quite evidently socially sanctioned.

Through the theses of the social determination of meaning and understanding we can grasp in what way an investigation of the use of language clarifies our concepts. The crucial role is fulfilled by the context. To understand a concept one has to describe the context in which it is used; different cases of its use are placed together. Furthermore to understand such speaking and acting is first to be able to participate in these activities, to go on, to follow the rule – and only secondarily (and to a certain extent, not even necessarily) to be able to talk about them. This ability 'to go on' limits in a strong sense those who can understand a practice to those who can participate in it.

UNDERSTANDING HUMAN ACTION

Wittgenstein strongly opposes the view that understanding to which the 'Geisteswissenschaften' should adhere must be that of the natural sciences. On the very last page of the *Philosophical Investigations* one reads:

> "The confusion and barrenness of psychology is not to be explained by calling it a 'young science'; its state is not comparable with that of physics, for instance, in its beginnings. (Rather with that of certain branches of mathematics. Set theory.) For in psychology there are experimental methods and *conceptual confusion*.... The existence of the experimental method makes us think we have the means of solving the problems which trouble us; though problem and method pass one another by" (PI, II, p. 232e).

The confusion in psychology is the result of the confusion between the problems it has to study and the method that has to be followed, Wittgenstein argues. The confusion is caused by the experimental method (borrowed from physics) which tries to explain human behaviour by analysing the connection between dependent and independent variables.

Some insightful remarks can be found in his *Remarks on Frazer's Golden Bough* (1979) and secondly in his *Lectures and Conversations on Aesthetics, Psychology and Religious Belief* (1966). Concerning Frazer's 'assembling of facts' Wittgenstein comments:

> "I *can* represent this law, this idea, by means of an evolutionary hypothesis, or also, analogously to the schema of a plant, by means of the schema of a religious ceremony, but also by means of the arrangement of its factual content alone, in a '*perspicuous*' representation.... This perspicuous representation brings about the understanding which consists precisely in the fact that we 'see the connections'. Hence the importance of finding *connecting links*" (GB, p. 69).

This method is identical formally with the philosophical method in which a perspicuous representation of a number of cases of X is given. According to Wittgenstein representation makes it possible. Similarly, in the human sciences to reach an understanding consists in seeing connections. To look for a further explanation seems to be to Wittgenstein something different from 'placing things side by side', and is in his view wrong.

Concerning the explanation of the magical he claims:

> "The very idea of wanting to explain a practice – for example, the killing of the priest-king – seems wrong to me" (GB, p. 61).

Somewhat further it reads:

> "I believe that the attempt to explain is certainly wrong, because one must only correctly piece together what one *knows*, without adding anything, and the satisfaction being sought through the explanation follows of itself. And the explanation isn't what satisfies us here at all" ... "Here one can only *describe* and say: this is what human life is like" (GB, p. 62–63).

In the 'Geisteswissenschaften', the human 'sciences', one must try to understand human conduct, try comprehending the reason(s) for our actions. The understanding that is offered, has to be of the same kind as the understanding of the praxis, the descriptions of the everyday language. First, in order to talk about the same issues as those who are involved one has to describe the situation in such a way that they are able to recognise it for themselves. Second, for whatever kind of understanding that is offered, at least rules of translation are necessary to relate (make understandable, and/or define) the technical language to the ordinary language (cf. also Winch, 1958, p. 89). Understanding thus always goes back to the understanding of the practitioners. Wittgenstein further advises to refrain from formulating theories, because they are not capable of bringing forward the heterogeneity of cases and always presuppose more homogeneity than in fact can be found. He also suggests that not everything is explainable or understandable and he draws our attention to different kinds of understanding. Particular concerns are: 'what is important for a human being', and 'what is relevant without being useful for something else'.

> "Kissing the picture of one's beloved. That is *obviously not* based on the belief that it will have some specific effect on the object which the picture represents. It aims at satisfaction and achieves it. Or rather: it *aims* at nothing at all; we just behave this way and then we feel satisfied" (GB, p. 64).

The important difference between understanding and explaining can further be indicated by the difference in the effects they have for those involved.

> "Compared with the impression which the description makes on us, the explanation is too uncertain. Every explanation is an hypothesis. But an hypothetical explanation will be of little help to someone, say, who is upset because of love. – It will not calm him" (GB, p. 63).

The tasks of research in the human sciences are therefore to be found in interpretation, which according to Wittgenstein means one must "place things side by side" (cf. Moore, 1955, p. 19). Incidentally, Wittgenstein accepts that different approaches are possible. Concerning the interpretation of a dream he says it is

"... fitted into a context in which it ceases to be puzzling" (LA, p. 45) but one can also form a hypothesis:

> "On reading the report of the dream, one might predict that the dreamer can be brought to recall such and such memories. And this hypothesis might or might not be verified" (LA, p. 46).

"To place things side by side" brings up the relationships between the a priori and the a posteriori and between 'what is the case' and 'what ought to be the case', i.e. the normative. Also in the later philosophy of Wittgenstein, he maintains the earlier position that "... the limits of *language* (...) mean the limits of *my* world" (TLP, # 5.62). However, since Wittgenstein later gave up the 'picture theory of language', this would now mean something different. 'Language' and 'the world' are no longer separated from each other but are one: 'language-and-the-world'. Though 'the world out there' is in a certain sense there irrespective of and prior to our language, it is in another sense only there *for us* (the shift from *my* to *us* indicates a second major difference with the earlier position), from being spoken of afterwards. To put this in a Heideggerian way – and there are of course a number of fundamental similarities between his and Wittgenstein's position – it can be worded as follows. Only in so far as people speak of certain things do they, i.e. the things, come into existence, they are brought in the openness, and they become 'beings'. Before that they were *not non-existent* but literally (in a non-Aristotelian way) *not existent*, not conceived. In this sense what is the case, what we can speak about (the a posteriori), which exemplifies what is important to us, what is relevant to us, what impresses us, determines future meaning (what can be spoken about, the a priori) in a radical manner.

An analogous relationship can be noted between 'what is' and what 'ought to be' the case. Wittgenstein stresses over and over again that justification comes to an end. We exhaust our justifications and are then confronted with 'what we do' (cf. PI, I, # 217). Far from being arbitrary, this is basic to the human condition. As facts are only facts within a 'theory', we cannot speak about values except as present in particular situations. Facts bring forward our 'language-games', our 'form of life'. They bring, as far as this is possible, 'the bedrock' into the open. In this sense our utterances about what is the case, though conceptually laden, are submitted to the influence of 'what is the case' in the way that they are shaped. The separation of 'what is there' and 'what is said' by means of a conceptual apparatus, cannot be made radically. Without concepts one cannot speak about 'what is there' and in any case concepts without instantiations are empty. This interwovenness implies that there are limits upon what can be said 'by us'. As was indicated earlier, 'what is said by us', reveals 'what is important for us' and exemplifies 'what has made an impression on us', which brings values and normative issues to the forefront. In this sense 'what is there for us' is linked with 'what has value for us'. The situation in which we find ourselves and which has led to this particular use of the concepts that are at stake has left its mark upon both. Also both are the focus of reflection by those involved and confront them in certain cases with an appeal for engagement.

Both relationships (the a priori/a posteriori and the relationship between 'what is' and 'what ought to be' the case) are conceived by Wittgenstein as 'in constant evolution', the speed of it to be indicated by the changing of the banks of the river (cf. C, # 99). In a very radical way Wittgenstein asserts that one cannot step outside the 'form of life', that one cannot judge it using external (and/or eternal) criteria, and that in this sense what we care for cannot be justified along supra-human terms though, again, that doesn't mean that it's all the same whatever we do.

'ETHICS'

It will be clear that Wittgenstein's criticism of the longing for crystalline purity does not only concern epistemology, but also has far-reaching implications for the domain of ethics. The ethical problem confronts us with the claims of other persons. To say that the meaning of 'good', and of 'human', is not once and for all determined, does not mean that it doesn't matter what we do. Precisely because we have options it is not always evident that we will follow this or that option. The 'choice' of this or that, leads at the same time unavoidably to a regret for what is not chosen. Our acting belongs to a whole in which we generally act *evidently*. This only means that we are able to justify (technically by reference to the 'language-games') why we act in a certain way, but are not at the same time able to give an ultimate, exhaustive justification. In the same way Wittgenstein argues that we cannot determine the length of the standard metre or the time on the sun (cf. PI, I, ## 50 & 350). Furthermore, it is not only impossible to give an exhaustive justification for the intrinsic reasons mentioned, it is also impossible because there are other meaningful (sometimes even irreconcilable) areas of our lives which are not totally separated and isolable from one another.

Convincing someone on the ethical level is not (simply) a matter of giving them reasons. It is more like a practice in which other people are interactively involved. Being moved by a person seems to be crucial here. It will be recalled that Wittgenstein quoted Goethe: "Im Anfang war die Tat (In the beginning was the deed)" (C, # 402). To reach understanding, and agreement, one should first of all try to involve one's opponent in a particular 'language-game'. As Edwards says:

"... by playing it to understand its *telos* from within; to feel for himself (sic) its attractions; and thus to recognise the game's internal standards of excellence" (Edwards, 1982, p. 157).

The actual participation is important before the opponent can be engaged. A new way of acting is therefore the first requirement.

Far from being an advocate for nihilism Wittgenstein holds a subtle balance between the Enlightenment and the full blown post-modernist position. In an interesting study *The Authority of Language. Heidegger, Wittgenstein, and the threat of Philosophical Nihilism*, Edwards (1990) asks whether it is possible to give up the philosophical view of who we are without at the same time undermining the liberal-democratic forms of political life that the view has nourished. He argues that though Wittgenstein's account of language turns out to be an attack on the Enlightenment picture of the self, outlining that at the bottom of our linguistic community we find obedience and not free choice, appropriate reactions and not autonomous decision, yet, nevertheless, Wittgenstein's view may avoid any taint of authoritarianism.

Edwards argues that the possibility of our conscious self-direction in accordance with some rule finally rests not on our capacity to see the rule clearly and then to opt for it, but rather it depends on our capacity to be moved by the rule in a particular way, to respond to it, not to 'act on our own' (cf. 1990, p. 180). According to him one's selfconsciousness is not immediately self-given, rather it depends for its very possibility on the satisfaction of certain empirical conditions that are utterly beyond one's control. Concerning these conditions Edwards indicates one's embodiment, the immediate unlearned presence of the 'natural expression' of sensation and of being surrounded early on by other creatures such as myself, with a certain set of attitudes toward the feelings naturally manifested in my 'Äusserungen' (utterances, spontaneous expressions). He reminds us that 'nonsense' for Wittgenstein is a term that is used for the criticism of a 'form of life' from the perspective of another 'form of life'. He also reminds us of the fact that the sound human understanding Wittgenstein hungers after, is not a prize guaranteed to those who spend their lives thinking about it. If, Edwards argues, we can come to see our agreement in 'form of life', as the background for all authoritative affirmations, for all the specific overt agreements we make with one another, then we can account for the possibility of those agreements in a way that preserves their wonderfulness and their Pathos. But at the same time this refuses to become onto-theological, i.e. using for instance an Aristotelian idea of the essence of a human being or an analogous religious concept.

> "Because it is not idealised, it is not a nature that can at a stroke solve our ethical and intellectual problems; it will not tell us what to think or what to do. But it can assure us that as we try to decide these things, our efforts, successful or unsuccessful, are nourished by the common world – the 'scene for our language-game' – that we share with others" (Edwards, 1990, p. 233).

The first person, the 'I', is not 'the limit of the world'. It is not a metaphysical or a transcendental subject, causally and epistemologically independent of the world one surveys, rather it is one that is part of that world,

> "... a world understood as a holistic community of agents and speakers, a world made possible by our natural agreement – i.e., our normal coincidence – with one another in what we are inclined to do and say" (Edwards, 1990, p. 234).

The answer of the individual to what appeals to him, can be conceived as a kind of primary taking up of responsibility, but it can also be spelled out towards the others (cf. De Dijn, 1991, p. 342). The real ethical attitude, De Dijn argues, is the realisation of the acceptance of the vulnerability and of the defencelessness of what is valuable: the effective respect of the transcendent and of what is valuable, beyond the limit where it appears in its own glitter and value.

In this sense neither the individual, nor the community is regarded separately and as the locus of responsibility. Neither does this locus reside somewhere in between them. The individual 'answers' the transcendent appeal (from the other or more broadly the intersubjective structure, or the symbolic order in Lacan's terms) to take responsibility and engages him- or herself. A structure of the individual-subject-and-the-others thus comes forward. Wittgenstein's ideas seem to suggest to us that though one cannot give sufficient reasons to ground 'the framework', that doesn't mean that one can step outside of it. To be initiated into that frame-work is not merely something that could more or less systematically be done through education by other human beings. Wittgenstein's position seems to imply that it will always and unavoidably take place, irrespective of specific aims.

THE NATURE OF PHILOSOPHY

For Wittgenstein the aim of philosophy is to reach an overview, a perspicuous representation of a certain part of our language, as it "... earmarks the form of account we give, the way we look at things" (PI, I, # 122). This 'Uebersicht' can only be reached by an investigation of the way in which sentences and expressions are used and of their rule-governed connections. As Winch in *The Idea of a Social Science* (1958) rightly observes, it is not a second order philosophy that is aimed at:

> "We cannot say...that the problems of philosophy arise out of language *rather than* out of the world, because in discussing language philosophically we are in fact discussing *what counts as belonging to the world*. Our idea of what belongs to the realm of reality is given for us in the language that we use. The concepts we have settle for us the form of the experience we have of the world.... there is no way of getting outside the concepts in terms of which we think of the world... The world *is* for us what is presented through those concepts. That is not to say that our concepts may not change; but when they do, that means that our concept of the world has changed too" (Winch, 1958, p. 15; cf. also PI, I, # 121).

Nor does philosophy try to make explicit metaphysical propositions, as it occupies itself with grammatical propositions which show us language as it is used in the unity of the-language-and-the-world. For Wittgenstein, metaphysical propositions belong to the domain of 'nonsense'. They are 'senseless', as one tries, by means of language, to make explicit what belongs to the 'grammar' of the language, i.e. the context to which the expression belongs and which makes clear what can be done with it (cf. PI, I, # 122). Philosophical problems arise when 'meaning as use' is ignored – for at the basis of philosophical problems is a false understanding of language. This becomes clear for example, in thinking about essences. Wittgenstein shows it is a 'mistake' to think that something common has to be presupposed in order to use a general term. (In other words, it is wrong to think with Plato, that all cases of 'democracy' or of 'intelligence' must share a common essence.)

> "The confusions which occupy us arise when language is like an engine idling, not when it is doing work" (PI, I, # 132).

Elsewhere he says:

"We have got on to slippery ice where there is no friction and so in a certain sense the conditions are ideal, but also, just because of that, we are unable to walk. We want to walk: so we need *friction*. Back to the rough ground!" (PI, I, # 107).

Philosophical problems arise "when language *goes on holiday*", when language does not fulfil any more the function that it has in everyday life. And philosophers behave often

"...like little children who scribble some marks on a piece of paper at random and then ask the grown up "What's that?" (CV, p. 17e)

Philosophy, for Wittgenstein, is therapy; for by seeing how language actually works, philosophical problems disappear and philosophical questions come to an end. The aim is to teach someone to pass from a piece of disguised nonsense to something that is patent nonsense (cf. PI, I, # 464), as the 'repressed nonsense' is made explicit. By means of concrete examples a perspicuous representation is given. Philosophy is an expression of practical understanding. It brings into our consciousness the relevant elements and creates, and grounds in some sense, the phenomena which are its object.

A philosophical problem is for Wittgenstein also someone's real and concrete problem; it is a problem that is posed by someone. Schweidler (1983) argues that, according to Wittgenstein, a philosopher is someone who has gone through a particular process in which he has 'grounded' in a new way his attitude to the world. The philosophical wonder is characterised by its complete lack of clarity concerning its own ground. The philosophical problem leads one away from the usual speaking and thinking and creates a particular kind of puzzlement. The philosopher knows neither more nor less than someone else, but he isn't satisfied. "I don't know my way about", is Wittgenstein's typical characterisation of a philosophical problem (cf. PI, I, # 123). The mistake of metaphysics is to not recognise the puzzlement. The metaphysician wants to give clarity at a different level and wants to return to the pre-problematic position. This doesn't work so long as he asks *what* he is puzzled about, instead of asking *why* he is puzzled. "It is the form of this question which produces the puzzlement" (BB, p. 169). Therefore it is our attitude that has to change in order to overcome the puzzlement. This is not a psychological matter, nor a matter of ceasing to ask questions one cannot answer, but it does require a change in outlook and attitude.

It has been argued already that philosophy does not just deal with language, but with the confusions to which its 'misuse' can give rise. To regulate the use of words is not the philosopher's aim. The task of philosophy consists in

"...assembling reminders for a particular purpose" (PI, I, # 127). Before this he gives the following characterisation: "What *we* do is to bring words back from their metaphysical to their everyday use" (PI, I, # 116).

Philosophy can offer only a certain kind of understanding of non-philosophical propositions; and an understanding that certain kinds of propositions are not legitimate. Philosophical questions will be resolved and this will put the philosophical worries to an end. Not the subject, nor the result, but the *nature* of the philosophical questions and their solutions constitute their character.

15

Philosophy is first of all an activity. There are no theories in philosophy, as theories presuppose hypotheses that can be tested evidentially. Theories can be changed in view of new facts and can become more or less accurate in predicting certain phenomena. In philosophy there are no new facts, thus no theory. Neither does philosophy offer foundations, as if we would not be able to go on without it. From its insistence on 'knowing one's way around', philosophy is a guide in the town of language.

"The real discovery...", Wittgenstein argues, "...is the one that makes me capable of stopping doing philosophy when I want to. – The one that gives philosophy peace, so that it is no longer tormented by questions which bring *itself* in question" (PI, I, # 133).

Elsewhere it reads:

"...the difficulty – I might say – is not that of finding the solution but rather of recognising as the solution something that looks as if it were only a preliminary to it" (Z, # 314).

In the sense of therapy there is progress in philosophy, but in the sense that it is an activity everyone has to do for themselves. It is not something that can be done once and for all but must be a continuous activity, constantly renewing and revitalising itself. But there must be a conscious decision not to ask further, and to renounce the idea of rising above the world of daily life. Wittgenstein's method is to remind us of the particular and of the limits of justification, for that is the only way one can approach philosophical problems. To combine freedom and restraint meaningfully, one has to stop questioning by an intentional act, as to seek further 'grounding' will remove the immediate being tied to the facts, and will end up in the interwovenness of language-and-the-world. "The difficulty here is, in not trying to justify what admits of no justification", Wittgenstein writes (PG, p. 101); elsewhere he says:

"If I have exhausted the justifications I have reached bedrock, and my spade is turned. Then I am inclined to say: "This is simply what I do." (PI, I, # 217).

In his aversion to 'justification', in his dealing with the question why there cannot be a further justification, the philosopher realises the Wittgensteinian concept of philosophy. Confronted with the question why this is the answer, one can only say that this is how we act: "What people accept as a justification – is shown by how they think and live" (PI, I, # 325). So the aim of philosophy can be said to be "To shew the fly the way out of the fly-bottle" (PI, I, # 309).

In section 144 of the *Philosophical Investigations* Wittgenstein describes the result of a philosophical investigation as follows:

"I wanted to put that picture before him, and his *acceptance* of the picture consists in his now being inclined to regard a given case differently: that is, to compare it with *this* rather than *that* set of pictures. I have changed his *way of looking at things*" (PI, I, # 144).

Elsewhere he writes "As if you had invented a new way of painting; or, again, a new metre, or a new kind of song" (PI, I, # 401). Giving reasons in philosophy is analogous according to Wittgenstein, to giving reasons in aesthetics. There can be a discussion, but that has more to do with sensitising the 'opponent' to appreciate a work of art differently, than with reaching conclusions (cf. Moore, 1955).

Where he describes his method he speaks of giving examples. Therefore it is sometimes argued that Wittgenstein is of the opinion that philosophy ought really to be written as a poetic composition (cf. CV). In this sense philosophical propositions offer new criteria for the use of certain concepts (cf. Lazerowitz, 1977, 1984), and new ways of looking at things. This position explains why a philosopher who has been shown the 'correct' usage of language does not give up his stance. It explains why the 'fly cannot be shown the way out of the fly-bottle' as it is its prison only at a superficial level. At a deeper level it is a home it has built for itself. In a philosophical proposition what is valuable for someone takes the shape of what longs to be true; the truth happens there. To put this phrase in a Heideggerian way – by being brought into the openness of what could not appeal before.

SOME IMPLICATIONS FOR EDUCATION

From a Wittgensteinian position 'education' can be conceived as a dynamic initiation into a 'form of life' (cf. Macmillan 1984, Smeyers 1992). From this position parents are seen as the 'first educators' and from this responsibility, the responsibility of the state concerning schooling can be 'derived'. Children are important to parents – what they are, and what they achieve, doesn't leave them indifferent. These educators offer the child the truths by which they live: what moves them, what appeals to them, what supports the idea of 'human being' they offer to the child hoping that she or he will participate. This is an initiation into what is self evident, or the initiation into the 'form of life', as Wittgenstein puts it. Their offering of, and making present the horizon of meaning, is at the same time a taken or accepted responsibility, or the intentional aspect of the process of child-rearing. 'Aims of it' can be conceived as summarised formulations, as elucidations of the idea of human kind, as anticipations from the point of view of the parent, which are embedded in the 'form of life'. This is not to say that having certain basic propositions is merely the result of an external process that happens to us. In the end, through a number of experiences, what matters is the acceptance of an offered meaning. The subject is embedded in the culture in a certain way. He or she is immediately grasped in the human order, structured by certain relationships, and identified by language. The notion of 'form of life' is therefore pre-eminently *the* pedagogical notion, as it also relates to the concept of a person. In the personification of the parents is shown what it means to live a human life. It is into this that the educandus is beckoned.

Whilst it is not a 'second order' activity, Wittgensteinian philosophy of education would try to make explicit the 'grammar' of the educational language and its presuppositions. It will not offer new facts, nor hypotheses that can be tested. There would be no attempt to offer general justifications through ordinary language, nor to lay out necessary and/or sufficient conditions for the use of certain concepts. What it would offer is a discussion of the nature of an educational question. This philosophy of education fully accepts the fact that there is not one interpretation, but only *an* interpretation. Its normative impact is recognised; it can only determine the valid questions and the criteria for their answers. On the rightness of its interpretation there may be discussion, but only in so far as it can persuade others. Besides its task in indicating the incorrectness of certain arguments and the impossibility of accepting certain presuppositions, there is then the task of offering an interpretation that convinces others: the explication of reasons that carry one's 'engagement'.

In so far as meaning is involved it will be clear that attention will be given to the particular aspect of a situation (cf. Cuypers, 1992; Kazepides, 1991; Marshall, 1985; Smeyers, 1992). This cannot be separated from the quest for justification. What falls outside one's actions and one's language is not intelligible and thus cannot be justified. Only through educational practice will it become clear 'what is there for us' and 'what is valuable for us'. Urging people to choose between 'facts' and 'concepts' is, according to Wittgenstein, therefore blatantly nonsensical. In this matter, as is the case more generally for Wittgensteinian epistemology and ethics, there is no either/or. It is always language-and-the-world, always the individual-and-the-others. Philosophy of education therefore cannot remain indifferent to developments within the educational context, but must take a stance. To offer nothing is itself to take a stance. In the acceptance of this lies the strength of this kind of philosophy of education. It finds its place in the varied landscape of what moves and puzzles the educators, who are not so much interested in the formation of human beings for a *particular* society, of manipulating that process, but in making explicit, clearing out in the setting of the sun, the different forms of the human condition.

Philosophy of Education: The State of the Art

Philosophers have always been interested in education, but for some, education has occupied a key position in their social and/or political philosophy. Clear examples of the latter are Plato, Hobbes, Rousseau and Dewey (1916). Philosophy of education as known in the English speaking world was developed by John Dewey, but languished, if not slumbered, until an alleged 'revolution', and the advent of what came to be called analytic philosophy of education. In Western Europe philosophy of education's concerns were traditional and Enlightenment based, as in the thought of Kant and Herbart. They were concerned with the transition between child and adult. This reformulated Enlightenment programme, and its critiques, have dominated philosophy of education in Western Europe.

In what follows we will present a state of the art and summary of the subject, Philosophy of Education in the English speaking world, including an account of the 'revolution' in philosophy of education, and a discussion of the development and the state of the art in Western Europe. Of necessity these will be brief and the reader is referred to, for example, the recent Pergamon Encyclopedia (Husén & Postlethwaite, 1994). By the term 'English speaking philosophy of education' we are referring in the main to the (academic) pursuit of philosophy of education in Great Britain, North America, Australia and New Zealand. By 'Western Europe' we are referring to its pursuit in Germany, Austria and countries to the west of these two, but excluding Great Britain, though we will be concentrating on sources from Germany, the Netherlands and Belgium.

ENGLISH SPEAKING PHILOSOPHY OF EDUCATION

In the 1950's and 1960's in the English speaking localities there were three ways at least of approaching philosophy of education. To a certain extent these approaches reflected the age, background in education, and philosophical expertise of teachers and academics working in the area of philosophy of education.

In one approach students were encouraged as prospective educators, to have a sound philosophy. Underlying this belief can be seen the traditional view that philosophy is *foundational* for education, that in some way it was able to arbitrate upon questions of truth and values, although it was not always articulated in such a formal manner. This foundational position occurs also in the Western European approach to philosophy of education. Or sometimes colleagues meant that students should be wise educators drawing upon sound principles to inform their educational practice in classrooms. Here the notion of wise judgement is important because, expressed more formally, or in a more philosophical manner, this is an approach to the practice of education in a *pragmatic* manner, where philosophy is seen as a wisdom, as in the writings of Jean Piaget (1971), John Dewey(1938), and, more recently, Richard Rorty (1982a). Usually, however, all that was meant was that philosophy was sound practical commonsense backed by liberal humanistic, or religious principles, and the best available offerings of psychology, sociology and history. This wise principles approach, whilst permitting 'honest' philosophy seldom had the underlying philosophical strengths of philosophy of education in Western Europe (see below) and was, at its worst, pretentious moralising with titbits for teachers.

In a second approach, students were introduced to the ideas and works of the Great Educators; here, for example, they met *The Republic* and *The Emile*. But whilst these are philosophical texts in most senses of the word, they tended to be used uncritically in teaching philosophy of education, so that whilst students learned what Rousseau or Plato *said*, they tended not to examine these ideas critically, in their full philosophical milieu, or in their total social and historical contexts. Often the 'exploration' was used to legitimate (or reject) claims to educational orthodoxy.

Finally, and especially in the U.S.A., there was a move towards teaching the '-isms' – sometimes called the comparative approach, whereby philosophy and philosophers were divided into types of theoretical position with recognisable theoretical names, such as 'realism', 'idealism', 'pragmatism'..., and the theoretical and practical implications for the practice of education then 'drawn'. Deduced would be incorrect, as the relationships between any particular '-ism' and principles for practice were far from clear.

19

No doubt this latter approach had particular appeal in North America because, in a similar vein to values clarification in the area of moral-values education, there was little overt intention of promoting a particular version of the 'truth', or any attempt to adjudicate between competing educational claims. As Brubacher (1942) expressed it, the comparative discussion and presentation of the different '-isms' would 'provide an unparalleled opportunity to (the educator) to come to 'his (sic) own' conclusions intelligently and independently'. It is not entirely clear as to why this approach was to give up and die so easily as, potentially, it could have been made philosophically respectable, and charges of dogmatism avoided.

This final point on the third approach applies equally to the others. Each carried within them the potential for a philosophically respectable approach to education. Yet, as practised, they were virtually to disappear in the face of what has been called a revolution, and the emergence of a new paradigm of *doing* philosophy in education – analytic philosophy of education (or APE as James Walker (1984) was to call it). As practised in Western Europe philosophy of education combined features of all of these three approaches. However, within these Western European traditions where philosophy is taken more seriously in education, and where it occupies a prominent part of the general academic curriculum, the limitations and deficiencies of the approaches identified above were less likely to surface – see below.

The 'Revolution' in Philosophy of Education

According to 'orthodox' views there was a revolution in philosophy of education, at least in Britain (see further Marshall, 1988b). A traditional account of this 'revolution' in philosophy of education in the English speaking world is expressed succinctly by R.F. Dearden (1982), who was himself a prominent figure in the (British) revolution:

> "Throughout the 1950's, and in direct response to developments in general philosophy, a new conception of philosophy of education was slowly forming and finding sporadic expression. But all of this was very far from a state of affairs in which it would become natural to think of educational studies as divided into various disciplines, of which philosophy of education would be one. Yet by 1977, Mary Warnock could uncontroversially open her book *Schools of Thought* by saying that 'it cannot any longer be seriously doubted that there is such a thing as the philosophy of education'" (Dearden, 1982, p. 57).

In this brief paragraph Dearden explicitly characterises the *alleged* revolution as being:
(a) a transition from a state of affairs in which philosophy of education's status as a legitimate area of study was in question;
(b) related to corresponding developments in general philosophy (the analytic and linguistic emphases);
(c) a transition towards a state of affairs in which philosophy of education becomes a 'legitimate' academic area of study (a discipline?).
To these characteristics can be added:
(d) that philosophy of education was seen as *foundational* with respect to education, i.e. that it was the arbiter or judge on such matters as truth, value and

meaning, and on the correct ways in which human behaviour is to be explained. (The search for foundations and necessary and sufficient conditions were to be found also in general philosophy.)

Dearden presents us in this paragraph (though not so briefly in his full description of the revolution) with an account which concentrates on academic matters, as though analytic philosophy of education evolved on *rational* grounds, as a result of debate and resolution according to rational criteria. But this would be to ignore the wider social, institutional and educational pressures upon philosophy of education. This 'revolution' must be sited in a much wider 'causal' matrix.

Traditionally philosophy had assumed a foundational role for education. The works of the great educators and their employment in educational institutions reflects this belief. Yet the discourse and practices related to this belief were haphazard, discontinuous and unsystematic. The field was 'ripe' for a coherent and systematic rationalisation of its beliefs and practices. However, it is mistaken to see these changes as merely rational, in the sense that a coherent and rational *reconstruction* can be placed upon the development of philosophy of education in the same way as it has been claimed, happens in science. Some philosophers of science, e.g., Popper (1959), believe that science and its development can be shown to be a rational process. Others however, and notably Kuhn (1962) (who, according to some commentators, argued from a Wittgensteinian position), do not believe this to be the case, and argue that science develops by a series of non-rational jumps or leaps from an established paradigm (set of theories, methodologies, etc), to a new paradigm which is incommensurable with the old paradigm. The type of explanation which is required to explain this shift requires historical, psychological and sociological data which preclude the possibility of a rational reconstruction. A possibility exists then of looking for an explanation of the 'revolution' in philosophy of education in factors other than those related to academic debate, and the identification and resolution of problems on purely rational grounds.

In the U.S.A. two key historical factors for the emergence of philosophy of education as an academic discipline were the formation of the John Dewey Society in 1935 and the Philosophy of Education Society in 1941. The former was established because of what was seen as the pending economic collapse of Western society, and the need for a powerful and positive role for the institution of schooling in the reconstruction of American society. The latter was formed in response to the effect on schools of science, industrialisation, and the changes in economic and political structures of the previous two decades (see e.g., Kaminsky, 1985; Maloney, 1985).

In Great Britain the opportunity was offered by the Robbins Report (1962) which made considerable recommendations for the extension of education and the improvement of teacher training (Peters, 1983). But Robbins was a response to social pressures of the type already mentioned above, of the post-World War II baby boom, and of the increasing demands for education. The London Institute of Education grasped this opportunity, offering courses and training in philosophy of education to meet the demands of the new Bachelor of Education Degrees which Robbins had recommended.

At the same time it was to assume and exercise considerable power.

Professor Richard Peters himself describes how he presented to a crucial conference on British education a view of education as possessing foundations, with philosophy occupying a critical foundational role vis-a-vis the other foundational disciplines. Furthermore, Peters, Hirst and the London 'School', were to exercise massive power over the emerging bureaucratic organisation of philosophy of education. At one time they were lecturing to an audience of 1,000 students, who came from all over the world, and they had virtually cornered the textbook market. The London Institute of Education is an attractive institution for both students and visiting scholars, and it is hardly surprising that the particular view of philosophy of education which is seen as the end product of the revolution should have achieved such prominence.

In this list of 'non-rational' factors we must consider also the driving thrust of professionalism – philosophy of education had to be seen to be an academic discipline capable of respect from colleagues, especially philosophers, and seen to have a coherent research programme in which there were clearly identifiable major problems, methodologies for the 'resolutions' of problems, and some agreement as to the importance of problems and methodologies. The alleged revolution in philosophy of education should be seen and understood in part as an outcome of this drive for professionalism and not a rational change no matter how participants like Dearden saw their role.

For many writing on the emergence of analytic philosophy of education the earlier states of affairs seemed undesirable. There was little agreement, little systematicity, and low regard for philosophy of education within academic circles. It was therefore seen as 'ripe' for revolution and the emergence of a better articulated, disciplined, area of study.

But this state of affairs did not necessarily require a revolution. Better trained personnel working on these undifferentiated 'states' may well have made them more respectable academically – as in Western Europe. However they may have remained as fragmented, and as lacking a common unifying research programme which could have aided professionalism. Whilst they contained bodies of respectable knowledge, established texts and courses of study (including works such as *The Republic* and *The Emile*, the holistic thought of John Dewey, and the innovative practices of Neill and Montessori), they were probably badly taught and by institutions or departments well down the power pecking order. In the new post-World War II educational world *education* as an area of study and, thereby, philosophy of education, had to be seen as very professional. Analytic philosophy of education had the credentials for this political demand (see further, Walker, 1983;1984).

These 'demands' led to such things in the teaching profession as the extension of teacher training, the introduction of Bachelor of Education Degrees, and the requirement that all teachers undergo a period of professional training. In the universities and/or the teacher training institutions, these led to the upgrading of courses, better qualifications of teaching staff and, in general, the 'arrival' of education as an academically respectable and *presentable* discipline. In respect of philosophy of education Dearden was surely correct when he said:

"...there was never a time more ripe for someone to mark out the claims of any newly emerging discipline" (Dearden, 1982, p. 58).

It is clear that philosophy of education in the English speaking world had been languishing, to say the least – and this in spite of C. D. Hardie's (1942) work and D.J. O'Connor's (1957) attack on the state of educational theory. These were not just forays into philosophy of education but competent philosophical critiques of educational theories. They met the philosophical demands of clarity, precision, technicality and professionalism that were being made upon education and its 'disciplines'. But they were not to serve as paradigms for the emerging professionalism of philosophy of education. Why did Scheffler's (1960) *The Language of Education*, and Peters's (1966) *Ethics and Education* apparently succeed where Hardie and O'Connor appeared to have failed?

Each of these earlier works was written from a positivistic philosophical position and should, therefore, have been intellectually in tune with the social and historical conditions that were providing the impetus for the upgrading of education as a 'discipline', field of study...group of foundational disciplines... However that question assumes the validity of academic reasons over other historical and social factors. What was 'needed' was a philosophy of education that met the demands of *professionalism* and not necessarily of academic purity. What was required was a philosophy of education which met the demands identified above but which did not, also, challenge those demands, which was precisely what Hardie and O'Connor had done!

Yet both Hardie and O'Connor exhibited the methodology of general philosophy that was, slowly at first, to permeate philosophy of education. It had its roots in the early work of G. E. Moore (1903), Bertrand Russell's (1916) classical logical work, Wittgenstein's *Tractatus* (1922), the later work of Wittgenstein (e.g., 1953), John Wisdom (1963), J.L. Austin (1962), Gilbert Ryle (et passim), and A.J. Ayer (1935) – clearly not an exhaustive list. But if Scheffler and Peters were to become the most prestigious philosophers within what can be called the analytic movement in Philosophy of Education, they were not the first to adopt this general methodology. Nor should they be seen within philosophy of education as the initiators of the new methodology, as there were others working on analytic projects in philosophy of education. Hardie and O'Connor have already been mentioned but the Archambault (1965) collection establishes this fact historically. In *practice* analytic philosophers of education claimed that they were attempting to clarify the criteria used in the use or application of concepts, by clarifying the rules or conditions under which concepts were used or applied. 'Borrowing' the notion of language as rule governed activity from the work of the later Wittgenstein, though adapted improperly because ultimately they were searching for foundations, and for necessary and sufficient conditions, they adopted the research programme of analysis and clarification.

If Scheffler's *The Language of Education* was to stimulate considerable discussion on the concept of 'teaching', Peters' analysis of the concept of 'education' was to provide an example of conceptual analysis which was to serve as a paradigm. It provided a cutting face for philosophy of education by defining its terrain, and presenting an example of analysis for budding philosophers of education to test themselves upon and, most importantly, in the arenas in which it was to be discussed, provided the respectability that philosophy of education's thrust for professionalism so desperately sought.

In 1972 Abraham Edel, in what has become a classic paper, argued that analytic philosophy of education was at a crossroads. According to Edel (1972) analytic philosophy of education had not fulfilled its promise. Consequently attacks on analytic philosophy came increasingly, and especially from younger scholars concerned with the problems of teaching in periods of intense social transformation, and who could not see guidance coming from philosophy of education in its analytic shape. Analytic philosophy of education was soon standing at the crossroads. It was seen as irrelevant and, consequently, *may* have become marginal. In summary then the traditional view is that within the English speaking world a 'revolution' took place in philosophy of education. Some, however, saw it as an acceptable academic package developed in response to demands upon education that were not merely concerned with intellectual matters.

Our position here would be that, whilst paying lip service to the approach to the philosophy of the later Wittgenstein, analytic philosophy of education's appeals to 'language-games' and conceptual clarity, distorted and subverted the force of the intellectual challenge offered by him to prospective disciplines and to 'theories' of education.

Within North America, whilst not abandoning the gains made by the analytic approach, not only methodologically but also professionally, attempts were made to broaden the field of philosophy of education, but whereas the *Proceedings of the Philosophy of Education Society (U.S.A.)* and *Educational Theory*, have a decidedly different 'feel' about them from the British *Journal of Philosophy of Education*, there is no one clear paradigm which has emerged in either to replace the analytic approach (see *Educational Theory*, 41(3),1991 for a recent summary of the state of the art in North America).

If philosophy of education was at its height in 1981 with the publication of the NSSE Yearbooks' special issue on philosophy of education, and if the division of chapters in the yearbook – into ethics, epistemology, metaphysics, etc. – revealed that philosophy of education had gone 'professional' by becoming, as editor Jonas Soltis seemed to see it, a collection of subfields of subfields of philosophy, then it had also lost touch with educators. The *Harvard Educational Review* symposium of 1981 on the Yearbook made just this point. Philosophers of education by seeking professional legitimacy had given up a place in the cultural conversation on education. By 'seeking' legitimacy in the ideas of philosophy – for example in Rawls, Marx, the phenomenologists and the Frankfurt school – they were no longer communicating with educators. On the contrary it was writers like Illich, Freire, and Bowles and Gintis, who were being discussed in education and not Scheffler, or Soltis, or ... More recently it is Apple, Giroux and McLaren whose works are being widely published and discussed.

However not all of this contested 'ground' has been relinquished. For example philosophers like Harvey Siegel writing on critical thinking, Denis Phillips on objectivity, especially in relation to educational research, and Robin

Barrow on curriculum matters (amongst other things), do have a voice in this conversation on education.

Furthermore forays into modern Anglo-Saxon philosophy and continental philosophy, where there have been sustained attacks upon foundationalism, are self defeating for any professional view of philosophy of education as being able to provide legitimation for educational disciplines through some privileged philosophical access to some form of metaphysical or methodological foundation. In North America philosophers of education are interested in Rorty, for example, and also in Derrida and Foucault. Such thinkers receive a more sympathetic treatment there than in Britain say, but ultimately this would be to attack the professionalism that drove philosophy of education to become a unique 'subject'.

In Australasia a version of Althusserian marxism almost dominated the Philosophy of Education Society of Australasia through the competent work of James Walker (the early Walker), Michael Matthews (1980) and Kevin Harris (1979, 1982). Some of their work and the ensuing debate can be found in *Educational Philosophy and Theory* and *Access*. In Australasia it is interesting that most of the prominent philosophers of education hold high positions within the educational hierarchies that permit them some entry to the conversations on education. However, as the recent 'reforms' in education especially in New Zealand have shown, there was little notice taken of the concerns expressed by academics, philosophers or otherwise, on the future of education.

The marxist tradition of philosophy as critique of *ideology* as introduced into philosophy of education generated considerable debate and a devastating critique of analytic philosophy of education. Yet, perhaps, only in certain quarters of Australasia and the U.S.A. was the strength of this critique acknowledged. It is important to note also that some of the 'actors' now distance themselves from that position (see, e.g., Cooper in Barrow & White, 1993). If the furrows ploughed by Peters are still recognisable in British philosophy of education, the concerns for justification in a pluralistic society have weakened, and philosophical interests have broadened.

However they have not broadened as far as elsewhere. A notion of philosophy of education as a collection of the subfields of the subfields of philosophy still persists. Papers at gatherings of philosophers of education by prominent philosophers, who at best might have been said to be interested in matters educational, have been common since Peters' early days and the early contributions of Gilbert Ryle, amongst others. But if the more traditional concerns of British political and social philosophy are still of concern, see the work of Pat and John White, for example, it is interesting that, in general, North American and continental philosophy, and social and political theory, do not seem to have penetrated the general consciousness of British philosophy of education, – the ideas of Dewey, Rorty and Bernstein, or Sartre, or Foucault, or Habermas, are not on the main agendas. There are of course exceptions. But nor would the work of Western European philosophers of education – discussed in the next section – be widely known, if at all.

It is clear that philosophy of education through the work of Peters and Hirst was very influential in the cultural conversations on education for nearly two decades. It was their work which provided the legitimation both for philosophy of education and, in part, the discipline of education, and for the foundational disciplinary courses (including philosophy of education) that were needed for the expansion of education as an area of legitimate study. But if philosophy of education in the London Institute was once a strong voice in the conversations on education this is now less so. First under attack from sociologists of education and then from the general vocational thrust of education in Thatcher's Britain philosophy of education lost much of its power and influence.

Australian marxism has also declined. It was also foundational in respect of education, buying into that part of the analytic programme, and seeking merely a different foundation. In that respect it too has become subject to the anti-foundationalism of the preceding ten or fifteen years. In response to this Althusserian strand of marxism, and in the hands of James Walker, Colin Evers and Gabrielle Lakomski, a highly technical form of Quinean pragmatism emerged.

It has already been noted that a strong and sustained critique of foundationalism has emerged in recent years in philosophy. For example there are Rorty and Bernstein in North America and Foucault, Derrida, Lyotard and Gadamer from Europe. Philosophy of education is slowly catching up with some of these developments (see the chapters by Peters and Marshall in this collection), but if some of these authors are signalling the end of philosophy then whereto for philosophy of education? As has already been indicated these attacks upon foundationalism have a certain self destructive aspect about them for philosophy of education.

Wittgenstein too must be seen as ploughing some of the furrows for the widespread attack on foundationalism. Nevertheless we believe that Wittgenstein provides *a way out*, or a challenge, which has not yet been taken up as fully as it might be by philosophers of education.

WESTERN EUROPEAN PERSPECTIVES

Now we turn to the different paths which philosophy of education took in Western Europe. At the outset we must note a different history of the 'subject', and different traditions from the English speaking world. These have resulted in the 20th century in different approaches to philosophy of education. In Western Europe there has been a more scholastic approach to philosophy of education, a general lack of interest to date in English speaking linguistic and analytic philosophy – though with some notable exceptions – and a greater interest in and emphasis upon social and anthropological theory and social philosophy.

The issues that are discussed nowadays in philosophy of education in Western Europe, and the particular ways in which they are dealt with, must be understood as part of the history of the subject. Contrary to the post Second World War II English speaking scene, where philosophy of education concerned itself primarily, though not exclusively, with analysis and accounts of schooling, the Western European counterpart occupied itself mainly with problems situated within the broader field of child-rearing including discussions of the concept 'formation' ('Bildung'). Furthermore it is important to realise that continental philosophy of education placed itself firmly within the legacy of 'the' Enlightenment tradition. From this philosophical stance, education was the 'means' to becoming human, i.e. rational. In becoming free from one's inclinations and passions, by putting oneself under the guidance of reason, one's true nature is realised. Construing education as a 'means' to realising one's true nature was not interpreted in a narrow means/end fashion however – in spite of some claims to that effect. Nor should it be seen as highly individualistic and alienating, for being rational was a state of affairs which was universal and which, being the same for everyone, precluded false consciousness and alienation. The educational implications of this Enlightenment tradition, were spelled out mainly by German philosophers of education starting from Kant and Herbart during the 18th and 19th century. Through their work the project of Enlightenment became the project of education.

A good recent illustration of this project is to be found in the work of the Dutch philosopher of education M.J. Langeveld (1946). For Langeveld education is a relation with a specific aim between the adult and the educandus – the achievement of adulthood for the young. The influence adults exert on children will lead them to participate in a dignified life-task-project for themselves. Because adults can be seen as representations of what is objectively good, and because they have already realised this aim dictated by reason, they are in a position to influence children appropriately. Adulthood will be realised when the young person is in authority over the self. This is achieved when one is: able to bind oneself to what one has imposed on oneself; able to maintain steady relationships both morally and practically; not swayed by other people's judgment; and, to put it more positively, has developed values and personal objective standards. Adulthood will involve being able to place oneself under a high moral order or authority and, in being responsible under that order, becoming free. Finally, adulthood involves participation in societal life in a constructive way.

On the other hand the child is conceived as not knowing what is good, as unable to take responsibility, and as generally helpless in the moral sense and begging for guidance. This must be provided by the adult, and the educator becomes responsible by substitution, in a relationship in which trust is the basis of the relationship between educator and educandus. Langeveld's (1946) position can be taken as the paradigmatic position of this educational tradition.

However a radical pluralism has swept the world and this has been the cause of a crisis in education. But it should be noted that the crisis of education, and the parallel crisis of philosophy of education, are part of a wider crisis of rationality itself. The questions whether reason, and reason alone, can decide what should be done, and if, moreover, rational thinking is even possible at all, are at the heart of the matter. For example phenomenology, existentialism, neomarxism, the Frankfurter Schule (that critiqued the use of a rationality which subsumes the particular under the general because of a will to dominate) and others, have criticised the over-ambitious Enlightenment project of rationality. Though the critique of reason by reason belongs itself to the tradition of the Enlightenment, the assumption that our enlightened rationality is adequate, is however called in question – particularly from Nietzsche onwards. Numerous criticisms have been made of the technocratic or means-end reasoning alleged to underlie Kant's philosophy, and of the problems in the notion of 'becoming human'.

A crisis that faces the school is the attempt to unite conflicting educational aims (Hellemans, 1994): between the economical perspective of the educational system (with its emphasis on measurable learning outcomes and its insistence on preparation for the labour-market), and that of providing opportunities for individual development; between personal growth and the transfer of knowledge; between individual development and the social dimension of education. Schools are thus confronted with radically different expectations. Therefore the question as to why schools aren't doing their 'job' any more becomes instead the question; can schools, within the traditional and 'given' conceptual framework, do their job at all?

Furthermore, the claim that modernity has come to an end necessitates the evaluation of the educational programme outlined above, and an evaluation of what might be preserved and what might be discarded.

Not surprisingly this traditional approach or framework of education, as exemplified by the work of Langeveld, has been criticised by 20th century philosopher educators, themselves influenced by phenomenology, existentialism, neo-marxism and the Frankfurter Schule amongst other movements, which have provided bases for these criticisms. Their starting point in education is from the child-centred movement, or reform-pedagogy. For them child-rearing could no longer be characterised by activities pursued by adults in order to bring children to adulthood. Severe doubts were also raised about the concept of adulthood – as examples: what is adulthood?; how do we know when it has been reached?; and, can everyone reach it? From this position the educator (the parent and/or the teacher) is, first of all, the adviser to the child, and the facilitator of what she or he really wants. It is pupils who learn, and who have to master for themselves, starting from their 'real' interests and what they already know. They have to start from what they already know, and from what they perceive as their real interests, and master new material for themselves. It is the child, it is argued, who is from the very beginning responsible for the learning process. Because children know best what is good for them, parents ought not to impose their own values upon their children. Instead they should respect their children's values. As a consequence it is sometimes argued that parents are not even responsible for what their children do as, instead, children are said to be responsible for themselves. Within the Anglo-Saxon context Rogers (1969) and Gordon (1975), more recently, have elaborated similar ideas.

To understand further developments it is essential to make three comments on the developed stance. Firstly, the concept of experience plays a crucial role in this literature. It is doubtful, however, whether this concept can be understood in an organic way whether it is possible that an individual can discover within him or herself what he or she really wants. The closed 'cogito' has rightly been criticised and it is, so it seems, introduced again here uncritically. Values do not arise privately and individually but have to be thought of – from the beginning – as bestowed upon people by 'significant others'. Furthermore, and perhaps even more relevant for education, how could parents and teachers behave as if the values they embrace, have the same significance for them as the values their children accept? This is not to say that a person's values cannot be changed, or that children cannot play a role in the way they are practised, but to think of values as negotiable in the above sense is either a dishonest practice of parents (i.e., parents being subtly manipulative, and only pretending to take the children's values seriously) or else it comes down to denying the true nature of values. Thirdly, it is not clear how parents could avoid initiating their children in the values they live by – parents must inevitably influence their children in very important ways.

As was indicated above, the crisis in philosophy of education reveals itself as a crisis of the problems that have to be dealt with in education because of a shifting concept of education.

Along with the radical critique of the school, the last decade has also produced a radical critique of conceptualising child-rearing using traditional concepts. Furthermore, as society is characterised by ethical and religious pluralism, it is also argued that parents are no longer in a position to initiate their children into a way of life. As society no longer agrees on what is valuable and worth living for, parents can no longer decide upon the values to which children should be introduced. Educators can only indicate possible positions on such matters. To do otherwise can no longer be justified, and to do so is to harm the child. This necessitates a different way of conceptualising education, a way in which it is possible to take into account a different experience of human existence.

Contemporary philosophy of education in Western Europe is characterised by the educational issues introduced above. However at the different centres in which philosophy of education is practised a varied landscape emerges. Some philosophers of education continue to follow the traditional paths as if nothing has really changed. Within the traditional approach representatives of several paradigms can be found: phenomenology; existentialism; transcendental (Kantian) pedagogy; critical rationality; 'geisteswissenschaftlich'-hermeneutic; and, critical-emancipatory. However, in general, the scene is dominated mainly by those who have put these positions in question (see for instance *Zeitschrift für Pädagogik*, 1990, vol. 36, no 1).

A theme present in a large number of discussions, is the relationship between theory and praxis. Some of these authors, particularly in the German literature, see the crisis of educational theory as one of legitimation or justification. One attempt to justify theory is the so-called 'common sense' position (see e.g., Hermann, 1987), in which theory and praxis are reconciled by the use of 'common sense'. But will interest and common sense alone generate problems and solutions? Indeed, what exactly is common sense? This stance has been heavily criticised on these and other grounds.

A second approach is to be found in the *system-theory* of Luhmann and Schorr (1982). A basic assumption is that theory cannot formulate any *rules* which make clear how a practitioner ought to act. Instead educational praxis has to be characterised by the self-sufficiency of the system. An acting human being has to be understood as a self-referential system which, it is argued, is incompatible with a technological kind of approach. This approach does not appear, however, to have addressed the question of justification adequately.

Another approach to the theory-praxis problem is the insistence on 'Allgemeinbildung' (see Klafki in Tillmann, 1987; Pleines, 1987), which could be translated as 'general formation'. One of the aims of 'Allgemeinbildung' is self-determination. Its general character can be justified by reference to Kant's practical philosophy and the recognition of human freedom as an aim in itself. Education is necessary because in practice the learner has not acquired the kind of freedom or self determination underlying the Kantian position. But curricular content that is most suited to self-determination, has to be specified and justified, and this poses considerable philosophical problems. Self determination poses problems of the general and the universal, and of community solidarity. How can general or universal claims be justified from an individualist position of self-determination? An answer offered by Oser (1986) turns upon the work of Kohlberg and the laws of development of general rules in the individual. However, as long as the justification claims are not answered sufficiently, and the relationship between moral acting and moral judgment spelled out satisfactory, this approach will be criticized.

An important stance which dates back to Horkheimer and Adorno is the *critical-emancipatory*. There reason signifies the ability to free oneself from a pre-reflective bond with nature and to be differentiated from it. The capacity of distancing contains the possibility of transforming nature into an object to be dominated. The motive for that is said to be 'the will of self assertion'. The fear of being dominated oneself becomes a will of domination over others. Thus for these authors there is an inner contradiction in reason, which may not be capable of resolution. Habermas, who was critical of the early starting point of the conscious subject, starts from language. He focuses on the emancipation of the individual in an intersubjectivity of unconstrained agreement with others. From his position, though he has not developed himself the implications of his ideas for education, child development is seen as a succession of steps towards greater autonomy and independence through the development of abilities for participation and an increasing interaction in human relationships. However, it is not entirely clear how Habermas can come to terms with the nature of education, as the structure of communicative praxis implies the equality of educator and child. Indeed, from the very beginning both are required to be competent participants. It is here that a number of problems arise for education, not only in as much as a certain level of knowledge is necessary to be a partner in a genuine discussion, but also as an understanding of notions of value seems to be crucial. Within this tradition of critical theory one should see Mollenhauer (1968, 1985) and Peukert (1993) (for further discussion on these issues see Smeyers, 1994).

Finally, a radical reaction to the alleged blind-alley in which education finds itself, has been *anti-pedagogy* (see, e.g., Giesecke, 1987). As knowledge can no longer be claimed to be applicable to a rapidly changing future, it is argued, the justification of present educational activities is called in question. For some philosophers of education this suspicion evolves into a full condemnation of all pedagogy. An education which depends upon preparation for the future for its 'justification' cannot be justified. For them education is but socialisation, marked by a loss of personal responsibility, and manipulation of relationships and communication. However, though a number of philosophers of education were strongly attracted to this position and some still are, it did not receive universal support.

This position anticipated, from the end of the eighties, a full-blown post-modernist debate, in which non-acceptance of, and deconstruction of the foundational conceptual frameworks, whilst looking (desperately) for something radically new, is the focus. The reason for that has to be sought in the kind of rationality that has been developed in the Western world. A rationality that dominates and manipulates instead of being open to new ideas, and new ways of conceiving the world has to be discounted. Reversing this kind of thinking necessitates giving up the present ways in which education is conceived, thereby creating the possibilities for the radically new. However the question as to how the 'radically new' can be conceived without using the concepts of the present, remains unanswered.

On the issue of post-modernism the two broad schools of English speaking and Western European philosophies of education seem to be merging. Somewhat ironically for the tracks that philosophy of education has taken to date, Wittgenstein is emerging in this merger. Already in the U.S.A, Australasia and Europe there is some work. We have selected from these authors, though not all whom we asked, were able to accept the invitation. What follows is new work written exclusively for this collection.

Introduction to the Chapters

Twelve chapters will deal consecutively with general Wittgensteinian ideas, applications to education, and the extension of his ideas into contemporary thought, particularly the modernity/post-modernity debate.

The first three chapters explore in depth some aspects of Wittgenstein's crucially important insights about learning and meaning. The next four examine the relevance of this stance for certain overall educational issues: the liberal education curriculum, the justification of education, the problem of 'newness' (conservatism) and the relevance of experience, and finally personal autonomy as the aim of education. After that three chapters address questions about the discipline of education and some of its subdisciplines: firstly whether the idea of an educational science is sound; followed by what insights can be gained in certain areas of the curriculum, namely in aesthetic and religious education. The final two chapters attempt to show how Wittgenstein's philosophy can engage with contemporary debate.

Considering examples from Wittgenstein's later work, Jim Macmillan examines remarks about 'not learning' from a philosophical and practical perspective. The author denies that Wittgenstein was engaged in empirical investigation or theory-building while supporting the importance of his points as criticisms of various empirical theories of learning and pedagogy.

Wouter van Haaften in his contribution stresses that meaning always comprises not only intersubjective but also subjective elements, and elaborates on their relations. He argues that Wittgenstein's private language argument, and much of linguistic philosophy in his wake, have obscured rather than clarified the many subtleties and potentialities of private meaning. According to van Haaften, private meaning, far from being irrelevant in human communication, plays a key-role both in the constitution of the young person's individuality within the language community, and in the individual's enriching contributions to the shared language and forms of life.

From an extended examination of paragraphs 336 through 343 of Wittgenstein's *Remarks on the Philosophy of Psychology, Volume II*, Luise McCarty and David McCarty motivate a particular kind of answer to the question, "What did Wittgenstein mean by writing – in remark 337 of that work – of a *connection* between teaching and meaning?" On the basis of that answer and on Wittgenstein's behalf, they endeavour to diagnose a number of logical problems hidden in some attempts by philosophers of education to justify courses of educational reform wholesale. Along the way they pause to describe the logical role which facts of education take on in Wittgenstein's writings.

Alven Neiman begins a project of imagining ways in which an acquaintance with Wittgenstein's work might be useful to the practitioner of liberal education. He proceeds by examining a number of plausible applications of a metaphor in which liberal education is compared to philosophy; these thoughts are discussed within the context of an understanding of Wittgenstein's idea of philosophy, as developed in James Edwards' book *Ethics Without Philosophy*. As a result of this discussion he acknowledges three types of 'research programme' available to the liberal educator who is sympathetic to the Wittgensteinian ethos. Neiman concludes with the claim that experiments with these programmes, or telic visions of liberal education, are crucial in an educational world in which an unobtainable objective and outrageous nihilism so often are taken as our only choices in understanding teaching and learning.

In a chapter somewhat critical of Wittgensteinian perspectives, Edwin Brandon attempts to show why our everyday modes of justification cannot be applied in the case of justifying education. The argument rests on the claims that in ordinary cases we correctly assume identity of the person whose different options are in question, whereas the process of education is intended to bring about such substantial changes in a person that this identity breaks down. While

supporting Wittgensteinian claims about the impossibility of ultimate justifications, this chapter contains some criticisms of the appeal to notions such as 'form
of life' when dealing with the usual problems of the philosophy of education.

The rearing by parents of children, and their public education, both involve
initiation, and Western educational literature has consistently conceived schooling and child-rearing in this way. In this sense of initiation parents cannot do
other than introduce the young into what they care for. This weaker type of
justification of these practices is attacked as conserving traditions for their own
sake. Child-centred pedagogy during the Reform-period for instance, but also
more recently, has criticized such 'traditional' positions through the concept of
'experience'. In this chapter Paul Smeyers tries to deal with that concept and its
educational relevance. Initiation into a 'form of life', is necessary. If it needs elements 'of the past', newness is also possible, because it can be thought and is
not incomprehensible, as it can integrate what 'is different' into 'what is'. In this
sense the human condition reveals itself by being bound together with other
human beings, by a givenness in two senses; by a givenness of 'what is there'
and by a givenness of 'what is there for us'.

Personal autonomy is one of the most important educational ideals, if not
the most important one. Although Wittgenstein himself never developed this
ethical or existential theme in his own writings, it is possible to construct a
Wittgensteinian outlook on the nature and importance of personal autonomy. In
the construction of this outlook as well as its defence Stefaan Cuypers offers a
chapter that is based upon two major views in contemporary philosophical
anthropology, namely Harry Frankfurt's *hierarchical model of the self* and
Charles Taylor's *moral psychology*. The main conclusion of such an applied
Wittgensteinian philosophy is that the ideal in educational practice cannot be
personal autonomy of a radical self-determining type, but must be *authenticity*
of which recognition by other people (social dependence) and horizons of significance (*forms of life*) are the possibility conditions.

In the following chapter Paul Standish explores the idea of an educational
science. The idea of a social science is considered as a potential best case for
education. This raises questions concerning the intrinsically linguistic nature of
social phenomena, the social scientist's involvement in a complex background,
and the appropriateness of the large-scale, systematic, and explicit account.
Wittgenstein's holism is elaborated in relation to his conception of philosophy
and the nature of his investigations, and in relation to the understanding of cultural practices, consideration of these being gradually interwoven with an
outline of Wittgenstein's attitude to ethics. Wittgenstein's remarks are found to
offer a spirit which might guide studies in education; in certain respects, they
exemplify appropriate practice in such studies. But they are at odds with the idea
of an educational science.

Nick McAdoo tries to show how one can extract from Wittgenstein an
account of aesthetic education that offers an alternative both to the widely held
view that it is based on a inconsequential subjectivity, and to the equally widely

held view that it is totally determined by the 'deep structures' of class, culture, family pathology and the like. It is one of Wittgenstein's great achievements to show how an aesthetic 'rationality' is possible while at the same time recognising its contingent origins and cultural location. He also considers Wittgenstein's Kantian concern with the 'tremendous' in art and the continuity between his early *Tractatus* view of the aesthetic as that which *shows* itself and the later *Investigations* account of the 'dawning of an aspect'.

The approach to religion taken by Wittgenstein is distinctive, though incomplete and in need of fuller interpretation and evaluation. Its implications for religious education call into question a number of the features and presuppositions of the Liberal Rational conception of that task, so Terry McLaughlin argues. This chapter suggests that the Wittgensteinian perspective lends support to the significance of a confessional approach in certain contexts of upbringing and schooling, and delineates several of the features and problems associated with the view itself.

Michael Peters' chapter provides a provocative interpretation of the later Wittgenstein. First, it is one which disturbs the view of the later Wittgenstein as a place-holder in the analytic tradition, viewing him, rather, in terms of his Viennese origins and the general continental milieu which constituted his immediate intellectual and cultural background. Second, it is a reading which following Wittgenstein's conception of philosophy and recent interpretations regarding Spengler's influence, emphasizes the possibility of both 'post-analytic' philosophy and philosophy of education as forms of cultural criticism. Third, the interpretation here examines the creative appropriation of the later Wittgenstein by Jean-François Lyotard as a basis for establishing an alternative basis for a 'post-structuralist' philosophy of education.

In the final chapter James Marshall looks at two conflicting ways of asking philosophical questions about educational issues, and about the punishment of children in particular. The two approaches are illustrated by reference to the standard account of punishment offered in analytic philosophy of education and by Michel Foucault in his well known book *Discipline and Punish*. The solution offered by Wittgenstein, he argues, places Wittgenstein closer to Foucault than to analytic philosophers of education, particularly those who claim authority from the work of Wittgenstein. Both critique the discourses of the social sciences – Wittgenstein that of psychology in particular, and Foucault that of the human sciences, and they both share the belief that there is a dark side to the Enlightenment message of emancipation through knowledge.

Finally in the epilogue the editors extract from the contributions some possible guidelines for accepting Wittgenstein's challenge.

NOTE

[1] There is a vast literature on Wittgenstein. General introductions to his work that have become classical are for instance Pears (1971) and Kenny (1975); more sophisticated 'commentaries' are:

Baker and Hacker (1980, 1985) and Hacker (1990). Books by Malcolm (1981, 1986, 1993), Rhees (1969, 1984), Winch (1987) and Hintikka and Hintikka (1986) are among others standard to the Wittgenstein scholar. An interesting publication recently published is the collection by Phillips Griffiths (1991) *Wittgenstein Centenary Essays*. General background is provided in Monk's (1989) biography and Janik and Toulmin (1973).

How not to Learn: Reflections on Wittgenstein and Learning[1]

C. J. B. MACMILLAN

Florida State University, U.S.A.

It is well known that when considering a particular concept, language game, or linguistic technique, Wittgenstein often asked "How would one teach this?" or "How is it learned?" What is not so often commented upon is that the latter question is frequently framed negatively: "Who would learn anything from this?" – and the implication is that no one *could* learn anything from the reported remark.

In this paper, I will consider this move in the context of 'pedagogical theory', for educationists should be interested in the answers to Wittgenstein's question as a source of insight into theoretically and practically problematic areas.

Among other things, I shall consider the pedagogical significance of a set of related but disparate comments or moves made by Wittgenstein in his later work. By 'pedagogical significance' I mean nothing very profound, only what might be important in Wittgenstein's work to someone who is trying to think seriously about teaching people in schools and elsewhere; I do not mean to attribute to Wittgenstein a 'pedagogical theory' – or for that matter (at least without argument) any sort of theory.

1. A PEDAGOGICAL CONTEXT: FAILURES TO LEARN

"Why didn't Albert learn *that*?" This should be a teacher's standard question, faced with a student who somehow didn't get what she was teaching him. The answers seem as standard: "He wasn't paying attention". "He is learning-disabled". "He doesn't know how to read". "His parents didn't make him do his homework". "He was hungry". "He is stupid".

The first thing to note about this group of answers is that each one explains the failure to learn by appeal to some characteristic of the student. A second thing to note is that there is an element of blame involved. Albert's not learning is a fault, and the fault is his own.

A second group of answers might look at what the teacher had done (or other features of the 'learning environment'): "He couldn't see the blackboard". "I didn't mention the way in which this connected with his knowledge of history". "I confused him by saying.... " "I didn't cover that in the lecture.... "

Teachers must bear some of the blame for the failure of students to learn, after all – even if they try to find other excuses or causes.

Is there anything of philosophical significance in all this? One is tempted to say that all of these issues are merely empirical, that failures in learning are to be

37

treated like any mundane failure, to be diagnosed by appeal to some sort of empirical or scientific theory, then 'cured' by following through in ways that the theory suggests.

The standard approach to pedagogical problems might be called an 'engineering approach'. It takes as its model something like the problem of a bridge that collapses. Why did the bridge collapse? Answer: The materials of which it was made were not strong enough to take the stresses put upon it. How do we cure it? Find materials which would take such stresses.

Recent reform movements in American schools often seem to assume some such view of the matter: search for the 'knowledge base' of teaching, so that teachers can better diagnose their own successes and failures, so that they can better plan teaching (Shulman 1987, Fenstermacher 1986), and make sure that they have the power to use their knowledge base within the context of schools without undue bureaucratic interference.

This picture is itself confused in much the way that psychology is viewed as confused by Wittgenstein: There are 'methods' but there is also conceptual confusion here, and the methods make us think we can solve the practical problems, but 'problem and methods pass one another by' (PI, II, xiv, p. 232). The philosophical issue then is to see just how this happens – and if there is to be practical value to such a study, there should be some clarification of the concepts that are confused as well as some suggestions for methodological improvement.

Wittgenstein provides not only the slogan for this investigation, but the central examples as well. I shall consider several of these.

2. "THERE ARE PEOPLE WHO SEE", SAYS THE PSYCHOLOGIST

In a splintered set of remarks in *Remarks on Colour*, Wittgenstein considers what might be called the 'logic of information'. (He uses the phrase at ROC, III, # 335; the passages I shall be concerned with begin at ROC, III, # 328 and continue almost to the end of the book – # 341 (350 is the last numbered paragraph.))

> "Could a 'Psychology' contain the sentence: "There are human beings who see"? Well, would that be false? – But to whom would this communicate anything? (And I don't just mean: what is being communicated is a long familiar fact.)" (ROC, III, # 328).
>
> "Psychology describes the phenomena of seeing. – For whom does it describe them? *What* ignorance can this description eliminate?" (ROC, I, # 79).

The implication of the question is that no one could learn anything from a psychologist's description of seeing, that in some way it would not add to one's beliefs or knowledge.

The startling thing about these remarks is that Wittgenstein seems to hold that the sentence, "There are human beings who see", is meaningless [*unsinnig*]:

> "And how can it be meaningless to say "there are humans who see", if it is not meaningless to say there are humans who are blind?

> But the meaning of the sentence "there are humans who see", i.e., its possible use at any rate, is not immediately clear" (ROC, III, # 331).

The implication throughout this passage is that no one could learn anything from our sentence. On the face of it, this seems strange, counter-intuitive. The sentence is structurally sound, not *prima facie* senseless. So surely someone could learn from it. But Wittgenstein seems to be holding that no one could learn anything from that 'Psychology'. Why is this?

It's not that people are stupid, nor that they haven't done their homework or any of the stock educationists' answers. Rather it is this: In order to understand the sentence 'there are people who see', the hearer (learner?) would already have to understand the terms and abilities involved. So he would not learn anything from the remark that he did not already know – it would be irrelevant to any concerns of his, at least insofar as those involve learning something new.

> "If we say "there are humans who see", the question follows "And what is 'seeing'?" And how should we answer it? By teaching [*beibringt*] the questioner the use of the word "see"?" (ROC, III, # 333).

'*Beibringen*', as I have argued elsewhere (Macmillan, 1981), is a term that Wittgenstein uses to emphasize the first learning of a word, usually without any implication of the learner's getting the 'meaning' of the term – the meaning is something else. The parents impart new language in the famous pain example at PI, # 244: "A child has hurt himself and he cries; and then adults talk to him and teach (impart to) him exclamations and, later, sentences. They teach (*lehren*) the child new pain-behaviour."

Tales can be told to make sense of the remark that humans see, and Wittgenstein considers several possibilities: Martians whose first experience of humans was of blind people (ROC, III, # 330); a special technical language of psychologists (ROC, III, # 338); are just two of these. But an *ordinary* person could not learn anything new from the psychologist's sentence, "Human beings see".

> "We learn to use the expressions "I see...", "he sees...", etc., before we learn to distinguish between seeing and blindness" (ROC, III, # 339).

If we have learned to use the expression, it seems, its use out of a special context is meaningless without long tales.

Another remark – from a different context – may help make this point clearer.

> "Someone says irrelevantly "That's a tree". He might say this sentence because he remembers having heard it in a similar situation; or he was suddenly struck by the tree's beauty and the sentence was an exclamation; or he was pronouncing the sentence to himself as a grammatical example; etc., etc. And now I ask him "How did you mean that?" and he replies "It was a piece of information directed at you". Shouldn't I be at liberty to assume that he doesn't know what he is saying, if he is insane enough to want to give me this information?" (OC, # 468).

Parenthetically, it should be remembered that *On Certainty* and *Remarks on Colour* were collections of writings from Wittgenstein's last years; he was working on the problems of colour and certainty at the same time; the overlap should not be surprising.

The point is this: if a hearer couldn't learn anything (new) from a remark, the remark seems at best irrelevant, at worst insane. Or perhaps a philosopher's oddity.

> "I am sitting with a philosopher in the garden; he says again and again "I know that that's a tree', pointing to a tree that is near us. Someone else arrives and hears this, and I tell him: "This fellow isn't insane. We are only doing philosophy" (OC, # 467).

And the implication is that anyone who could use the word 'seeing' would gain no new information from 'Human beings see'. The psychologist's remark is meaningless or irrelevant in a context where his learners are themselves sighted human beings. One can imagine the psychologist's students at that lecture: P: Human beings see. S: Tell me something new. P: ???

How could he go on? A neurological theory, perhaps, that 'explains' seeing in a different way. One is reminded of Socrates in Plato's dialogue *Meno* repeating a Sophist's 'effluent'-loaded theory of seeing with some scorn, along with *Meno*'s admiration of the theory. But no such theory is necessary – at the very least – to explain how we can use the language of seeing. The neurological theory may be necessary for some purposes, but not for explaining the concept of seeing, nor for explaining human experience – except very indirectly.

One further point about this remark before going on to another unlearnable: The fact that a particular sentence or remark is unlearnable is itself a test of its meaning: if no one could learn anything from the remark, it is at best irrelevant and perhaps nonsensical. This is brought out in another context to which I now turn.

3. A LANGUAGE GAME THAT WE CANNOT LEARN?

"We are here describing a language game that *we cannot learn*" (Z, # 339). What possible game can there be that cannot be learned? What is the importance of this paragraph? Here is the game that cannot be learned:

> "If someone were to say: "Red is complex" – we could not guess what he was alluding to, what he was trying to do with this sentence" (Z, # 338).

First note that not learning such a game is no fault of the learner, nor is it a result of bad teaching or poor learning environments. Rather, it is a feature of the game itself that makes learning it impossible.

But it is not the falsity of the sentence that makes it unlearnable or nonsensical, either. One can, after all learn falsities. It is its place in a possible technique, language game, or form of life that is crucial. The attribution of simplicity or complexity to an object is – as Wittgenstein had argued in the *Philosophical Investigations*:

> "... Asking "Is this object composite?" *outside* a particular language game is like what a boy once did, who had to say whether the verbs in certain sentences were in the active or passive voice, and who racked his brains over the question whether the verb "to sleep" meant something active or passive.

We use the word 'composite' (and therefore the word 'simple') in an enormous number of different and differently related ways" (PI, # 47).

The passage (Z, ## 338–339) throws considerable light on Wittgenstein's philosophical methods and position. The following points seem significant: (1) A basic feature of language is that it is *used* and the significance of any language game is the possibility of its being used in human activities. "Red is complex" does not have any such (clear?) use. (2) It also appears here, rather late in Wittgenstein's philosophical development, that he assumes that language games are essential for the understanding of ordinary language.

A digression about language games is necessary. In Wittgenstein's philosophical work, language games had many functions (see Baker & Hacker 1980, 89–99, for one discussion). At times, they seem merely to be inventions for the sake of sometimes whimsical comparisons with ordinary ways of talking, with the goal of showing that philosophical problems arise from misunderstanding linguistic possibilities. At other times, they are invented as a way of simplifying linguistic reality (e.g., the slab game of the first sections of PI), to cut it to its bare bones, as it were. In other cases, it often seems that language games serve as the foundation of an implicit semantical theory (Hintikka & Hintikka, 1986), providing answers to questions about the relation of words and the world. And it can be argued – as by Bloor (1983), for example – that there is an implicit naturalistic theory of knowledge to be winnowed out of Wittgenstein's later works.

By the end of his life, I think, Wittgenstein believed that language games were in fact central in ordinary language, that words and sentences have meaning only as they are part of a recognized language game, itself backed up by *forms of life* and *world pictures*. The opening paragraphs of *On Certainty* show this:

"If you do know that *here is one hand*, we'll grant you all the rest" (OC, # 1)."

Wittgenstein is, of course, puzzling over G. E. Moore's proof of an external world – he sees something fishy in the language used in the proof. In order to get at the fishiness, he suggests that doubt is the central issue, and this in turn leads to

"If e.g., someone says "I don't know if there's a hand here" he might be told "Look closer". – This possibility of satisfying oneself is part of the language-game. Is one of its essential features." (OC, # 3).

Here, the language game of knowing and doubting seems to be what would be found in ordinary language contexts; Wittgenstein assumes that that will provide the meaningful context for the use of the terms, for the purpose of philosophical criticism of Moore's argument.

Remarks on Colour similarly begins with the assumption of language games as a given:

"A language-game: Report whether a certain body is lighter or darker than another. – But now there's a related one: State the relationship between the lightness of certain shades of colour" (ROC, I, # 1).

All of the remarks on colour seem to assume that speaking of language games is entirely natural, a part of ordinary linguistic procedures. I shall not digress further, though, to defend this position.

Pedagogically, the important point about Zettel's game that we cannot learn is that the diagnosis of learning-failure is not limited to the learner and the teacher: some things cannot be learned by *their very nature*. Furthermore, this nature is not easily discovered: it is not in the surface structure of the sentence. Zettel, # 338, contains another example, however, one which might be included in Wittgenstein's summary in 339:

> "But if he says "This chair is complex", we may indeed not know straight off which kind of complexity he is talking about, but we can straight away think of more than one sense for his assertion. Now what kind of fact am I drawing attention to here? At any rate it is an *important* fact. – We are not familiar with any technique, to which that sentence might be alluding" (Z, # 338).

This second example of # 338 does not exactly fit # 339's claim about a language game that cannot be learned; we are aware of many 'techniques' to which the sentence might be alluding. We can learn these techniques, but *which* technique is given not by the sentence itself but (perhaps) by the teacher or text. The relevance to points about simplicity and complexity in TLP and PI should not be missed in this example, of course – this is another place in which Wittgenstein's 'pedagogical turn' serves a philosophical point that is not itself pedagogical. The complexity of an object or something perceived is a function not of the object itself but of its place in a particular language game.

4. BELIEFS ACQUIRED BUT NOT LEARNED

In *On Certainty*, Wittgenstein develops a picture of a person's beliefs about the world as a system of beliefs, some of which are so central that to doubt them would be to throw one's whole way of thinking – and living – into intellectual chaos. These 'stand-fast' beliefs, of the 'form of empirical beliefs' (OC, # 96) are the bedrock of a metaphorical river channel within which we test other beliefs; to challenge one of them – e.g., "My body has never disappeared and reappeared again after an interval" (OC, # 101), or "The world has existed for a long time" – is to throw doubt on the very possibility of doubting itself.

Wittgenstein's assessment of the acquisition of these stand-fast beliefs is that they are not explicitly learned, but rather are picked up or acquired in the course of learning other things.

> "I am told, for example, that someone climbed this mountain many years ago. Do I always enquire into the reliability of the teller of this story, and whether the mountain did exist years ago? A child learns there are reliable and unreliable informants much later than it learns facts which are told it. It doesn't learn at *all* that that mountain has existed for a long time: that is, the question whether it is so doesn't arise at all. It swallows this consequence down, so to speak, together with *what* it learns" (OC, # 143).

But it is not only in learning 'facts' that these other beliefs are acquired; they also come with action:

> "Children do not learn that books exist, that armchairs exist, etc. etc., – they learn to fetch books, sit in armchairs, etc. etc." (OC, # 476).

The point that Wittgenstein is making in these passages is straightforwardly conceptual; 'learning' does not cover all ways of acquiring information and belief. In another passage, the point is extended:

"I do not explicitly learn the propositions that stand fast for me. I can *discover* them subsequently like the axis around which a body rotates. This axis is not fixed in the sense that anything holds it fast, but the movement around it determines its immobility" (OC, # 152).

But it is the nature of the propositions – their place in the system of beliefs – that seems to determine whether or not they are learned or acquired. This seems odd to me; there are several possibilities here of making sense of the point. (a) As the child learns one thing, background information is taken for granted by its teacher, information that is 'swallowed down' along with the explicit learning. This is supported by the remark at 143 (OC) cited above. It suggests that any belief – central or not – might be acquired in this manner. (b) The place of the proposition in the final system of beliefs is determined by the mode of learning (i.e., implicit or explicit). This strikes me as being an empirical claim of a sort that Wittgenstein was unlikely to make in such a context. (c) Perhaps this supports Morawetz's claim "that all fact-acquisition takes place through participation in practices" (1978, p. 11). (Note that Morawetz does not put 'fact-acquisition' into the category of learning.) (d) The belief is one that is presupposed by a practice, a language game, or a world-picture, and cannot be questioned or doubted without making it nonsensical. The temptation is to see the logical priority of such propositions as pedagogical priorities: in order to learn the proposition "Someone climbed this mountain many years ago", one should first learn the presupposed "The mountain existed many years ago". Wittgenstein denies this version of priority: one does not 'learn' the presuppositions of such a game or practice (of historical investigation) *before* learning the individual propositions of the game.

"When we first begin to *believe* anything, what we believe is not a single proposition, it is a whole system of proposition. (Light dawns gradually over the whole.)" (OC, # 141).

In yet another related passage, Wittgenstein seems to divorce learning from instruction:

"It is quite sure that motor cars don't grow out of the earth. We feel that if someone could believe the contrary he could believe *everything* that we say is untrue, and could question everything that we hold to be sure. But how does this *one* belief hang together with all the rest? We should like to say that someone who could believe that does not accept our whole system of verification. This system is something that a human being acquires by means of observation and instruction. I intentionally do not say 'learns'" (OC, # 279).

But why he does not say 'learns' remains something of a mystery; there is in the German '*lehren*' an element of intentionality that seems not to be present in the English 'learn' – and it may be this that explains Wittgenstein's reluctance to say that this is learned: its acquisition is not the result of the individual's intentionally setting out to learn it. English lends itself more readily to talk of 'latent learning' (in the psychological jargon). But it is important to recognize that the conceptual point can be extended to English: there is a sense in which learning should be taken to refer to one mode of acquisition of belief, action, and skill. Full treatment of this point would be beyond the scope of this paper, however.

5. DOUBTING AND NOT-LEARNING

One final example of Wittgenstein's claims that certain things could not be learned; this is given most clearly in *On Certainty*:

> "For how can a child immediately doubt what it is taught? That could mean only that he was incapable of learning certain language games" (OC, # 283).[2]

Finally, we seem to have reached an example in which the blame for not learning is put back upon the child; for it is *his* doubt that leads to the impossibility of his learning; but again, it turns out that the impossibility is not a 'psychological' matter – it is a question of his being able at one and the same time to believe and to doubt the same thing; i.e., this impossibility is a conceptual matter rather than an empirical question.

6. SUMMARY AND CONCLUSIONS

In this paper, I have brought forth several examples of passages in which Wittgenstein uses the fact that some phrase, word, concept, or sentence could not be learned for his own philosophical purposes. Several things should be clear from this exemplification:

First, Wittgenstein's use of the move is not a 'psychological' use. He is not talking about the capacities and abilities of human beings in the way that a psychologist would. This reflects the point made in *Zettel*, where he asks if he is doing 'child-psychology':

> "Am I doing child psychology? – I am making a connection between the concept of teaching and the concept of meaning" (Z, # 412).[3]

Second, the foregoing examples show that Wittgenstein uses the non-learning examples in many ways, for different philosophical purposes. The first example, the psychologist's "Human beings can see" turns out to be a sentence that Wittgenstein cannot imagine a circumstance in which someone could learn anything from its use. Here, the possibility of learning is a criterion of relevance: a speaker who uses a sentence like this (or any sentence?) must assume that his hearer could learn something from it; otherwise, his sentence *in context* does not make sense.

The second example, "Red is complex", suggests a language game that has no sense; Wittgenstein cannot imagine a way in which this sentence could be used in any existing games, nor can he imagine one which uses it. One could not learn to use such a sentence sensibly.

The third example, "swallowing down beliefs", suggests that other modes of acquisition of beliefs may be important in the development of world pictures, forms of life and language games. It is not 'learning' that is the appropriate way of thinking of these other modes of acquisition.

The final example – the impossibility of doubting what one is learning – develops a conceptual relation between learning and doubting that would be easy to miss. It borders on professional ethics, interestingly – for it also brings in a point about the necessity of students' trusting their teachers and texts.

What is the significance of these points for pedagogical theory? Any attempt to draw 'practical' conclusions from Wittgenstein's work is, as everyone knows, fraught with dangers. I do not believe that one can read a pedagogical theory off from Wittgenstein's work, any more than one can read off a theory of colour, of meaning, or of knowledge from his work. But there is some relevance of his remarks in all of these areas. Insofar as there is any directly useful thing in his use of the non-learning move, it is its use in criticism. "Educators should think about this", we might say, as Wittgenstein spoke about explanations and training:

> "The foundation of any explanation is training (educators should think about this)" (Z, # 419, my translation).

But each of the moves sketched in here has reverberations for the pedagogue's standard moves in the explanation of learning failures and successes. The blame, if such there be, does not always fall on the student or on the teacher – it often may be the result of incomprehensible things said in texts, in 'sciences', or by otherwise profound-seeming remarks.

Human beings may see, but we should remember that commenting on it in just that way may prevent more significant learning. Philosophical nonsense hides in grammar. This is too often forgotten in our attempts to develop adequate methods of teaching and education. Wittgenstein provides a welcome antidote to nonsense.

NOTES

[1] This is a longer version of Macmillan, 1989. It was presented at the 14th International Wittgenstein Symposium of the Austrian Wittgenstein Society in Kirchberg am Wechsel.

[2] The German reads: "Denn wie kann das Kind an dem gleich zweifeln, was man ihm beibringt? Das könnte nur bedeuten, dass er gewisse Sprachspiele nicht erlernen könnte". It might better be translated, "For how can the child immediately doubt what someone is imparting to him? That could only mean that he could not learn certain language games".

[3] Again, there is a problem with the translation. The German reads "Betreibe ich Kinderpsychologie? – Ich bringe den Begriff des Lehrens mit dem Begriff der Bedeutung in Verbindung". This might be better translated as "I am bringing the concept of teaching and the concept of meaning into a union".

Wittgenstein and the Significance of Private Meaning

WOUTER VAN HAAFTEN

University of Nijmegen, The Netherlands

Language games are activities of persons within the context of, and based on, a shared form of life. And, as Wittgenstein remarks, "if language is to be a means of communication there must be agreement not only in definitions but also (queer as this may sound) in judgements" (PI, I, # 242). But what should the nature of this agreement be like if communication is to be both possible and enriching for the community?

Wittgenstein emphasised the social nature of our mode of being and, connected to this, the intersubjective character of knowledge and meaning. He reacted against the strong individualistic, and subjectivist, tendencies in the work of Russell and many other empiricists. His contribution in this regard is of great importance and has been widely accepted. It has helped to break the spell of scepticism with respect to our knowledge of the 'external world' and of 'other minds'. It has shown a way out of the *individualist's problem of communality* (cf. Patterson, 1987). The other equally important side to this, however, is the *communalist's problem of individuality*. Wittgenstein, who once wrote: "Only from the consciousness of the *uniqueness of my life* arises religion – science – and art" (NB, p. 79), certainly was highly sensitive to this aspect as well. How can the notion of individuality be safeguarded within the fundamental perspective of our social mode of being? How can individuality *add* to communal meaning?

I think that Wittgenstein, in the various moves of his (anti) private language argument, has given away too much of the *cognitive basis* that is required for *one* main source of individuality, namely subjective meaning with its many subtle idiosyncrasies. Not only intersubjective meaning, but also subjective meaning and even that subjective meaning which Wittgenstein would have called private, play a key role both in our personal experience and in our communication with others. Subjective meaning, comprising both verbal and nonverbal elements, is abundant in interpersonal differences without thereby making communication impossible. On the contrary, precisely these meaning aspects can be most enriching for communication – in ways that Wittgenstein's private language arguments unnecessarily and perhaps unintendedly threaten to preclude, as I shall argue with regard to private knowledge (*section 2*), private rules (*section 3*) and private meaning (*section 4*). Moreover, as I shall try to show in *section 5*, the 'linguistic turn' prefigured by Wittgenstein has played its part not only in systematically concealing these elements of meaning, but also in suppressing the entire issue of possible subjective contributions to meaning itself – thereby severely complicating its discussion. In *section 6*, I indicate how both subjective and intersubjective meanings contribute to the rich relations between

47

Studies in Philosophy and Education **14**: 171–186, 1995.

the individual and the community. The subtle shades of meaning and knowledge, differing from person to person, are partly constitutive of our 'selves' as unique centres of meaning in, and authentic contributors of meaning to, our social forms of life. However, as a starting point for my discussion let me begin by sketching, in *section 1*, the idea Wittgenstein was arguing against: the information processing metaphor.

1. THE SEDUCTIVE INFORMATION PROCESSING METAPHOR

This picture has been current in philosophy for a long time and was particularly pervasive in the writings of empiricists, from Locke to Russell. It also underlies much of modern cognitive psychology and linguistics. And it would most likely be our own intuitive philosophy when thinking about knowledge and communication. It is essentially the idea that we acquire much of our knowledge through sense perception; that the information thus received is processed, organised somehow and then stored; and that the stored bits of information may be connected with words so that we can communicate about what we know through language. The picture suggests that the information a person has, is more directly accessible to himself than it can be to other people: I myself can know without mediation the contents of my mind, I know them first hand, so to speak, while others know them only indirectly. This must be true for our knowledge of objects in the external world, but even more for our inner feelings and emotions. If I am in pain, for instance (an example not only cherished by Wittgenstein but used already by Descartes), I am immediately conscious of it, whereas other people cannot really know what is going on inside me. Another implication of this picture is that I can be more certain about the contents of my mind than about anything else – which made Descartes in the final analysis infer his own existence from his having such cognitions: "cogito ergo sum".

This, roughly, is the central cluster of ideas at issue: attractive, but also giving rise to serious philosophical problems. Most prominent are the problems of scepticism, both about our knowledge of the 'external world', as it came to be called, and about other minds. Also communication would become highly questionable. Yet Russell, for instance, Wittgenstein's most immediate target, was willing to accept what he saw as the inevitable consequences (just as did Descartes – but then after all he could trust God not to be a deceiver). Thus Russell could write: "a man's percepts are *private* to himself: *what I see, no one else sees*; what I hear, no one else hears; what I touch, no one else touches; and so on" (Russell, 1927, p. 114, italics mine). As a consequence, "when one person uses a word, he does not mean by it the same thing as another person means by it". But Russell considered this an advantage: "since different people are acquainted with different objects, they would not be able to talk to each other unless they attached quite different meanings to their words" (1956, p. 195). These are the ideas Wittgenstein does battle with. I cannot survey his many countermoves, but shall go into three main lines of his attack in the next three sections. Let me begin, however, by sketching the general line of my approach.

Wittgenstein was of course right in rejecting Russell's conclusions, but in doing so he may have thrown out the baby with the bath water. Russell claims that *what* we see, *what* we hear, all we really can know must be private internal representations of external reality. As a result, the relation between this internal fund of knowledge and the external world becomes problematic. Wittgenstein reacts by dismissing the information processing metaphor. But it was not necessary for him to do this, and, as I shall try to show in the next sections, that is not what his arguments establish. Russell's conclusions seem to be effected by a *conflation of two uses of the information processing metaphor*. One use is in the context of physiology: information is received by the senses, transmitted by the nerves, and stored in the *brain*. Here the metaphor has a clear spatial connotation, locating the results of the process within our head. The other use is when in ordinary situations we reflect on what we know, and on how we came to know it: we saw something or we heard it from other people, we remember someone's face or the detailed information we got, etc. And now the association with the physiological context has enticed us into similarly localising the *mind*, implying that *what* we see and hear and know and remember is not the familiar things around us but certain replicas hidden inside. Only thus could we come to speak of an 'external world' and of 'other minds' as opposed to what should be known in a more direct, internal way.

Now, in our ordinary reflections on *what* we know we need not abandon the information processing metaphor, provided that the spatial implications of the physiological context are dropped. In particular, we can ponder about *how* we know what we know, and then, irrespective of the intricacies of neurophysiology, say things like: "it appears to *work in such a way that* we know... or can remember...", as is done in fact in cognitive psychology. In this way one may try to do justice, for instance, to facts such as that how we perceive things is not independent of earlier experiences or that there is always a conceptual framework guiding our thoughts and observations, etc., *without* thereby implying that what we see or hear is put away in some private place in our head. For clearly *what* we thus come to know is the concrete things around us or facts about these things; while at the same time it remains true that the information we receive is included in, and may be affected by, the fund of knowledge we dispose of at that moment. As Wittgenstein has forcefully shown, this does not make the contents of our mind private. So far Wittgenstein is right against Russell.

But Russell also had a point. Different persons may of course receive different information even if it is about the same things. This Wittgenstein would not deny. However, Russell was thinking of a particular kind of difference, that can be kept in view only if the information processing metaphor is not dismissed. There are many subtle differences in what we can come to know, both *verbally* in our talking to each other and in reading (etc.) *and non-verbally* in visual and auditive and tactile (etc.) perception, which we are liable to overlook if we only *speak about* what it is we see and hear and know, and refuse to think about what happens when we come to know these things. For example, a deaf person does not know the typical song of a robin, which is an integral part of many other people's knowledge of the bird; even in hearing people this knowledge is not the same for all. But these nuances easily go unnoticed in our normal talk *about* robins. Of course, the differences can be pointed out. But that does not remove them. And only to a certain degree can we put them into words. We can state *that* there are such differences; we can *name* them ("Do you know the song of a robin?" "Yes/no"); but we cannot explain *what* precisely the difference consists in except to somebody who knows the song of the robin. There is nothing to cause concern here, unless it is now suggested that there *is* no relevant difference here *because* we can use the relevant words all the same. Indeed, there are in fact countless such (what in many cases might be called *sub-verbal*) differences in our knowledge, similarly remaining hidden in our speech about the things we know. It is these differences that are my concern in this article. This was also (part of) Russell's point, although he drew the wrong conclusions when he made his highly influential but just as infelicitous distinction between 'knowledge by acquaintance' and 'knowledge by description' (Russell, 1912). I will discuss how Wittgenstein, on the other hand, systematically neglects these differences, as a result of his dismissing the information processing metaphor and his inclination to think about what we know only in terms of what we can *say* we know.

One real source of confusion is of course precisely such expressions as 'what we know': which can be used both for the *same object,* or fact, that you and I know (and can *say* we know); and for your and my *knowledge of* it, which may be (partly) *different.* Moreover, the epistemological obsession with questions of certainty and justification has led to an over-emphasis on propositional knowledge (knowledge *that p*); even to the point that the whole concept of 'knowledge' often got reduced to 'knowledge that'. As a result, all the subtle perceptual *differences* in our knowledge (in the broader sense) that Russell had in mind got lost behind our *identical* propositional formulations of what is known. A more general problem is that even the most nuanced discussions about what we know are necessarily conducted in language and by our using words that may be identical irrespective of their possibility of being related to non-identical (verbal cum non-verbal) cognitive contents. These differences thus threaten to disappear from sight, and this in turn functions as a *reason* in (discursive!) philosophy to limit the concept of knowledge to what can be formulated from the outset. Russell's conclusions are unacceptable indeed, but this *hysteron proteron* should not have been the outcome.

So let us not dismiss in advance the term 'knowledge' in the broader sense, though fully recognising its more specific uses. Then we can distinguish the following relations of inclusiveness between the intersubjective, the subjective, and the private. What I know, and precisely how I know it, may be meaningful to me, it can have personal meaning. Yet this does not imply that this knowledge is subjective. Only those elements or structures in it that I do not have in common with other people are *subjective.* As the information processing metaphor enables us to see, what is subjective in this sense is not fixed. Concepts may be *more or less* subjective. And the subjective may *change over time.* Also it will *differ from person to person.* And *from subject-matter to subject-matter.* For instance, I may be able to 'hear' certain parts of Beethoven's seventh symphony, and you may know the same piece but certainly 'hearing' other features in it, or you may only know the composition by name; and if I am a composer, I may 'hear' *new* music which you do not know but hopefully may come to know. Clearly, for the most part, most of our knowledge is *not* subjective. It is inter-subjectively shared knowledge or it can cease to be subjective. But this fact, however important, does not exclude the possibility of subjective knowledge or meaning. Finally, there may be subjective knowledge or meaning which *cannot* be shared. It is incommunicable (Kenny, 1975, p. 185) and *private* in Wittgenstein's sense. (Private knowledge and meaning would be necessarily subjective; but not the other way round.)

Now, what I want to suggest is, that subjective or even private knowledge and meaning are not only possible but indeed are of crucial importance for the language community, including for education. In the next sections I try to show that Wittgenstein's arguments in the central part of *Philosophical Investigations* do not rule them out; while at the same time these arguments by their very character threaten to hide from view the subtle interpersonal differences in subjective, including private, knowledge and meaning. My primary aim is not, however, to argue that there could be a 'private language', but to show how Wittgenstein's so-called (anti) private language arguments have induced a wrong picture of communication. They have led to a rigidity that Wittgenstein could not have found acceptable.

2. PRIVATE KNOWLEDGE

As a first point, Wittgenstein tries to undermine the general idea articulated by Russell, that only I myself can really know my sensations. This is not even true, Wittgenstein remarks, in the case of such seemingly typically private knowledge as that I am in pain. He tackles this idea along several lines (PI, I, ## 246ff.). To begin with, it is pointed out that other people in fact often do know that I am in pain. This is undeniable, and a good argument against Russell, but clearly this cannot by itself establish that pains might not in principle be entirely private, or that the word 'pain' could not in principle refer to an entirely private content of my mind. Because certain expressions of pain are an integral part of our concept of pain, we often know that somebody is in pain even when we are not told. But this is not sufficient to conclude that such connections of feelings and their expressions are necessary, or that private concepts without such connections cannot exist.

Wittgenstein's next argument against the idea that only I myself could know that I am in pain is remarkable and characteristic. The argument is, that we would never *use the expression* 'I know that I am in pain' (except perhaps as a joke or just to emphasise that I am in pain). However, this linguistic fact about our normal use of the expression 'I know that ...' cannot exclude the possibility of private concepts either. First of all, one may wonder in general about the precise import of the fact that certain things are not normally *said* in ordinary language. But secondly, in this particular case the question may also arise what the use of the expression 'I know that...' does or does not imply for the much broader concept of knowledge. It is striking how often the entire discussion is focused on such first-person utterances (e.g. Hacker, 1990, pp. 46ff.) but they certainly do not constitute the only everyday use of the word 'knowledge' (cf. PI, I, # 116). Indeed, as Wittgenstein remarks, we usually say "I know that *p*" only in situations in which it would also have made sense to doubt that *p* was the case. But, as we do not normally use this expression with regard to our own pains, we need not bother about whether or not it would make sense to say that we doubt if we are in pain. I don't think it would (and Wittgenstein agrees, PI, I, # 288) but the point again is that this cannot be sufficient reason categorically to deny the possibility of private knowledge.

In his focusing on what we can *say* we know, Wittgenstein sometimes goes so far as to reject not only the information processing metaphor but any explanation of how we come to know what we know. Similarly he dismisses the idea that the meaning of a word should in any way be dependent on, what he disapprovingly calls, an internal connecting mechanism. One of his favourite considerations is that the meaning of an expression does not depend on any inner activities at all; because the meaning is: what we answer when asked what it means. In that case, we just give the meaning of the word, without any explanations about 'mysterious procedures'. Moreover, Wittgenstein points out, words like 'meaning' and 'understanding' themselves are not used to refer to mental mechanisms. To understand an expression is not something like consulting a mental dictionary. If somebody says: "Now I see what it means!", he is not reporting an internal happening. And if we want to know whether he has really understood the meaning, we need not inspect his head, but look at how he henceforth uses the term. Such observations about the explanations of words and their meaning are subtle and certainly correct. But they do not, of course, render superfluous, let alone rule out the possibility of, explanations about our capability of using (and of explaining our use of) language. There is a clear distinction here between explaining to somebody the meaning of certain expressions in the language, and explanations, whether or not successful, of how such language use is possible. This distinction should not be blurred in the case of such terms as 'knowledge' and 'meaning'. Observations about our use of these terms can provide no reason to reject *whatever* considerations about 'inner mechanisms' that make this use of the language possible. Even the poorest theory cannot be thus rejected, simply because the argument is misdirected. Wittgenstein may claim not to be interested in this type of explanation, but that does not imply that the 'mechanisms' cannot exist or that they would merely be a piece of irrelevant metaphysics, as he once suggested. In fact all this has nothing to do with metaphysics, but rather with efforts at finding an explanation for processes that somehow must take place for such explanations as Wittgenstein does want to concentrate upon to be possible at all.

The impossibility of private knowledge or private meaning cannot be established along these lines. Meanwhile we have seen how Wittgenstein repeatedly resorts to arguments focusing on *what we (normally) say*, including in the matter of *what happens* when we understand things or say something about them, without questioning how decisive such considerations can actually be. However, this is only one line in Wittgenstein's attack on privacy. We must now turn to what is usually taken to be the heart of his private language argument.

3. PRIVATE RULES

The idea of a private language is introduced in PI, I, # 243, where Wittgenstein asks: "... could we also imagine a language in which a person could write down ... his inner experiences – his feelings, moods, and the rest – for private use?" and he specifies: "The individual words of this language are to refer to what can only be known [sic!] to the person speaking; to his immediate private sensations. So another person cannot understand the language". In # 256 he further explains what he means by contrasting this hypothetical language with the normal language, in which "my words for sensations [are] tied up with my natural expressions of sensation". Wittgenstein's first objection to the possibility of such a language is that it could not be taught to someone else. I come back to this consideration in section 4.

His main objection, however, is formulated in PI, I, # 258 (cf. # 202). This is, that there can be no guarantee for my using the words of that language consistently, that is, according to whatever are supposed to be its rules. Imagine, says Wittgenstein, that I have a private sensation and that I want to keep a diary about it. On each occurrence I shall write down the sign 'S' in my notebook. How, asks Wittgenstein, do I *know* (and that means for him: how can I be *justified* in believing) that it is the same sensation next time? What guarantees my correctly connecting 'S' with that sensation? One reaction could be: "I impress on myself the connection between the sign and the sensation". Wittgenstein retorts: "But 'I impress it on myself' can only mean: this process brings it about that I remember the connection *right* in the future. But in the present case I have no criterion of correctness. One would like to say: whatever is going to seem right to me is right. And that only means that here we can't talk about 'right'". His point is not that I am not allowed to make mistakes. On the contrary, the exception would prove the rule. The notion of doing something correctly presupposes the possibility of failure. In the present situation, however, there can be no failure because the whole idea of doing something correctly *or* incorrectly is thought to have become vacuous as there is no independent criterion: "whatever is going to seem right to me is right" (cf. PI, I, # 279).

This passage has invited many interpretations and speculations, but our question here must be: what precisely is it that is lacking in the hypothetical private language *as compared to* the normal language situation? Then it becomes clear that Wittgenstein's point is not that we could not *have* the relevant sorts of sensation; nor that our memory may sometimes fail us. It has to do with the notion of a criterion or *rule*, which is implicit in our talk of doing things *correctly*.

According to Wittgenstein in the private language situation one condition is not fulfilled for the notion of a rule to make sense: "I have no criterion of correctness". This phrase is ambiguous, however. The reasoning behind it is not that there can be no criterion or rule per se; but that there can be no independent check on my following it ("whatever is going to seem right to me is right") and that *therefore* the whole idea of a rule as such collapses in this case. And then, as a natural consequence, it does not make sense to speak of correct or incorrect, or of making mistakes, either. The crucial difference from the normal (non-private) situation is the lack of any possible form of *independent* testing and, if necessary, correction. I can only fall back on myself, but that, according to Wittgenstein, cannot be decisive for then I may be under the impression that I am using a word correctly, but I cannot distinguish between correct use and my merely thinking that I am using it correctly.

It should be noticed that it is a presupposition of Wittgenstein's discussion that the condition of independence of the 'criterion of correctness' can be met when there are *other people* involved. To see this may help to prevent us from barren philosophical fabrications resulting from irrelevant or simply impossible requirements, e.g. concerning rule following. Often much is made of what is supposed to be impossible in the private language situation without any careful explanation of whether and how the non-private situation by contrast fails to exhibit these problems. What is the crucial contribution of other people? They can alert me if I tend to deviate from an established rule. Now we must realise, however, that both their testing and correcting me, and my being tested and corrected, *presuppose* rather than create the possibility of private consistent rule-following. Intersubjective linguistic consistency or rule-following can only exist provided there is subjective consistency. It is of course miraculous that people can do all this; but the plurality does not detract from the miracle. The intersubjective interventions (and justifications, for that matter) which are allegedly required can only take place, and can only make sense, if the persons involved on both sides are capable themselves of using words consistently (according to what then may be called the meaning rules). Without this private rule-following ability no external check or correction could ever help.

We must certainly acknowledge the importance of intersubjective testing and correcting in the normal (non-private language) situation. I shall come back to this aspect in the next section, in order to indicate more precisely why indeed it is so crucial. However, this does not undermine but only underlines the importance of the private consistency (or ability to follow a rule, if you like, but note how misleading this characterisation can be) that the private language argument was designed to reject. Perhaps this form of primary rule following was excluded by a tacit definition (of 'language'), but it is an undeniable basis for any language to get off the ground. Either the possibility of a private language in this sense is accepted, or there will be no language at all. (In fact, this point, in a slightly different way, was already made by Ayer, 1954, shortly after the publication of *PI*.)

During the last decade the private language argument and the notion of rule following excited renewed interest thanks to various publications, prominent among which was Kripke (1982). They provided new insights into, and interpretations of, the position of the later Wittgenstein (aptly called 'Wittgenstein II bis' by Parret, 1983). The linguistic community has been emphasised even more strongly than before. It is now considered not only necessary for maintaining the rules, but also decisive for what the rules *are*, for what can qualify as meaning at all. Not only is the *consistency* of language use at stake but also its very *constitution*. And the central idea behind this meaning constitution is that the rules of the language have no existence apart from their being expressed in its use by the community. They do not make up a fixed system so that their application could be automatic. And however we might have laid them down, there might always be new situations and cases for doubt, as Wittgenstein showed for the relatively simple case of a rule, '+2', for a series of numbers (PI, I, ## 185ff.). What he wants to elucidate with such examples is that what the rule *is* depends on what the community holds to be the normal use. We can be said to understand what an expression in the language means if we use that expression in ways that are natural for the community. Thus the notion of a rule has become interlocked with the very notion of the linguistic community. The rule is: what is use in the community. In this sense, it is now stressed, there are no independent criteria for the use of an expression.

This idea has been radicalised in Kripke's (1982) original, but to my mind strained, reading of Wittgenstein's private language argument. Language can change at any time, and we can never be sure of using any expression correctly next time. Every application of a word is a leap in the dark. Kripke carries the comparison with the series of numbers to its limit: just as in principle a rule can be formulated for any type of continuation, so this could be done for each new use of the word. "No course of action could be determined by a rule, because every course of action can be made out to accord with the rule" (PI, I, # 201). Thus our knowledge of the language can never guarantee correct use in the future. Kripke's 'sceptical solution' to this 'sceptical paradox' stresses the necessary role of the community: only the community accords concepts to its members, namely as long as these concepts accord with what in the community happens to be accepted as normal. Which would mean that one cannot be said to have any concepts or language outside the community. We need not here go into the heated discussions that were stirred up by this challenging view. At first sight, language now seems to have become entirely dependent on the community. However, even if we accept the somewhat confusing idea that rules can never be detached from their being used, there is nothing in Kripke's argument that necessitates a community as opposed to a single user. Surely, *if* there is a language community using certain expressions, then on his view this community is the only authority on what is their normal use. But from this it does not follow that in a private language situation their use could not be determined by the individual person. On the contrary, on Kripke's reasoning the individual would be the single natural authority! So far, therefore, neither the argument from consistency nor the argument from the constitution of meaning seem to have excluded the possibility of Wittgenstein's hypothetical private language.

4. PRIVATE MEANING

Let us look at one further line of attack. It is raised in the well-known paragraph about the beetle in the box (PI, I, # 293). Everyone supposedly knows what a beetle is by looking at *their* beetle that no one else can see. If the word 'beetle' were to have a use in these people's language, it could not be as the name of a thing, Wittgenstein remarks. "The thing in the box has no place in the language-game at all; not even as a *something*: for the box might even be empty. – No, one can 'divide through' by the thing in the box; it cancels out, whatever it is". If we conceive of the meaning of a word as a name of some particular content in each person's head, not accessible to anybody else, then it could not function in our language. Any such meaning component would be superfluous, an idle wheel. We can, as in algebra, cancel it out on all points. We could not know whether it is the same for everybody, nor even if there is anything at all in the black box. And that would not matter – for language functions irrespective of it.

At first sight, it seems as if Wittgenstein denies that there can be any private contents, e.g. sensations such as pain, at all. But that is not what he means. When asked (PI, I, # 304): "But you will surely admit that there is a difference between pain-behaviour accompanied by pain and pain-behaviour without any pain?" he answers: "Admit it? What greater difference could there be?" – "And yet you again and again reach the conclusion that the sensation itself is a *nothing*". – Wittgenstein: "Not at all. It is not a *something*, but not a *nothing* either! The conclusion was only that a nothing would serve just as well as a something about which nothing could be said. We have only rejected the grammar which tries to force itself on us here". Wittgenstein's point, therefore, is *not* that there are no private sensations – which, for some, rescues him from behaviourism –, nor even that they are private (it would rather be a 'grammatical statement' that they are, cf. PI, I, # 248). His point is that such private contents cannot have a function in the language. They make no difference *whatever* they are. That is why "a nothing would serve just as well as a something about which nothing could be said".

However, this is not very much in line with what we normally want to convey about pain or other 'inner' feelings. How could Wittgenstein come to this con-clusion? We can find a clue in PI, I, # 244, right after he has introduced the notion of a private language in # 243. Wittgenstein then asks: "How do words *refer* to sensations?" This question is soon reformulated as: "how is the connec-tion between the name and the thing set up?" which in turn is identified with: "how does a human being learn the meaning of the names of sensations?" This is telling. Wittgenstein's first point about the idea of a private language concerns the question of how it could be learnt. A private language could never be *taught* to anybody else (e.g., a child). The theme is a recurrent one. So in # 257: "What would it be like if human beings shewed no outward signs of pain (did not groan, grimace, etc.)? Then it would be impossible to teach the child the use of the word 'tooth-ache'".

But now it should be noticed that from this it does not follow that the specific character of the sensations is irrelevant. Even if we could not learn the meanings of words for sensations except through their accompanying outward signs, this certainly does not imply that the sensations themselves are mere idle wheels. Nor does it mean that it makes no difference whether there even *are* any sensations at all 'behind' the groans and grimaces (or whatever). What Wittgenstein has been able to show in these passages is that a private language is impossible *if* conceived as a *communal* language with at the same time *exclusively* private meanings. In that case, he is correct to point out, the meanings of the words could not be taught to the other members of the community. This does *not* imply, however, that a private language of *one single person* would be impossible (unless again this was ruled out by implicit definition of the word 'language', which would have made the whole discussion futile from the outset). The teachability problem would not arise, but such persons would not need first to observe their own behaviour in order to know what their sensations, or what the meanings of their sensation words, are. *Neither* does it follow, therefore, that meaningful subjective or private concepts or parts of concepts are impossible in principle. In other words, Wittgenstein has not excluded the possibility of a private language as such, but only of one almost inherently contradictory variety of it. On the other hand, Wittgenstein has drawn our attention to an important fact, namely, that 'external' factors such as circumstances, accompanying behaviour, etc., are *normally* integral parts of the meanings of our words. Normally, meanings do not exclusively consist of purely subjective elements even in the case of words we typically use for what is going on 'inside'. But there is no reason to conclude that all 'internal' factors could be simply repudiated as idle wheels.

Altogether then, these (anti) private language arguments do not succeed in excluding the private knowledge and meaning components that we were interested in here. I do not claim to have dealt with all the elements in Wittgenstein's rich discussion. But the impossibility of a hypothetical private language can at least not be derived from the fact that (in the normal situation) other people can know that I am in pain; nor from the fact that we do not ordinarily say: "I know that I am in pain"; nor from the fact that in explaining the meaning of a word we do not refer to any explanations about what enables our language use. Next, neither the possibility of private meaning consistency or correct rule following, nor the possibility of private meaning determination or rule constitution have been effectively excluded by the arguments propounded. Finally, as we saw, from the mere fact that a language consisting of words without any external meaning components cannot be taught to other persons, it does not follow that internal, or in that sense private, meaning components are just idle and could just as well be cancelled out.

All this is not to say that a private language would be trouble-free. But then it was not my intent, of course, to rescue a private language. It was only to show that Wittgenstein's arguments *against* it do not hold water if directed at the notion of subjective or private meaning components which I wish to defend. However, I would like to add another positive outcome of this discussion. We can now see something very important, which is constitutive of our *factual*, community-based non-private language use. In *communal* rule-following we

57

can, in addition to the prerequisite capability of private consistency, rely upon intersubjective testing and adjustment. And what is more, intersubjective testing and adjustment are *necessary* in the real situation of a normal, living and evolving language. For the rules of a natural language constantly develop, very gradually and in all sorts of subtle ways, in the common use. It is for this reason that permanent mutual attuning is indeed required. In this sense (different from Kripke) it is correct to say that what the rules are depends on what the community at a certain moment accepts as the normal use. This cannot be deployed as an argument against a private language. But it typically *is* a problem for each living linguistic community. The *common* evolving use of language requires permanent mutual adaptation and adjustment. In a common non-fixed development one cannot just follow the rules according to one's own insight, because the rules themselves change over time. This is characteristic of the interdependence within each living community. However, the mere fact that a private language does not have such problems as are typical of normal languages, cannot without circularity be seen as a shortcoming of the former. Rather, the mutual adjustments constantly required in the normal situation necessitate even more the capacity for subjective consistency. We did not need a private language argument to make this clear, however, for we could have known from the outset that a private language user neither can nor need achieve what is only possible and also only required in the linguistic community. The hypothetical private language is not so much impossible, therefore, but rather might be seen as an extreme, and extremely poor, borderline case.

5. THE SYSTEMATIC CONCEALMENT OF MEANING IN LINGUISTIC PHILOSOPHY

We can learn a further lesson from the foregoing. I would suggest that the manner in which the private language argument is conducted constitutes one example of a peculiar form of *concealment* of meaning which is typical of linguistic philosophy. And it is precisely such kinds of reasonings of Wittgenstein and his followers as we have been studying, that have contributed to the *systematic* character of this concealment. I can explain what I mean only very briefly here (cf. van Haaften, 1975/76) but the general point can be easily seen.

As suggested above, it does not follow from Wittgenstein's arguments that private concepts or (parts of) word meanings cannot exist or be highly specific. The remaining question is, whether they can play a role in communication. In other words, are these subjective parts of meaning doomed to remain private in the normal situation of a communal language? I think this would be a caricature. As soon as language starts functioning these subjective elements also come to play their immensely important role. Precisely because these allegedly private components are so specific, and at least sometimes even unique, they can enormously enrich the communication in the community. For they play a role in the organisation of our experience and may create personal insights and emphases. They colour everything we say! Their role can only be overlooked if communication is somehow conceived of as a simple exchange of rigid pieces of informa-tion, through words as a kind of currency, as coins representing fixed and sepa-rate units of meaning. But that would be an extremely impoverished picture of what is going on in human communication. This is not in accordance with how we experience it to be. It would, for instance, do no justice to what seems so characteristic of communication, namely, our feeling that it can always only be successful up to a point; that it so often seems to succeed *and* fail at the same time. That is so, precisely because of that rich field of subtle and sub-verbal meaning components involved.

In concentrating on meaning as what we say in answer to the question of what a word means, in focusing on *what we say* and allegedly cannot say in ordinary language, these facts about communication are liable to disappear from sight, however. And in subsequently philosophising about the meaning of 'meaning' along the same lines, always departing from *what we say* about meanings of words in general and *what we say* about the meaning of 'meaning' in particu-lar, the concealment of these facts about communication becomes systematic. Thus philosophy helps systematically to obscure what it sought to clarify. It is ironic that Wittgenstein, who has done so much to make us aware of the richness and multifacetedness of language, in this way in fact also made a fundamental contribution to what can only be seen as a grave impoverishment.

Briefly and simplifying, it goes in three steps. First, *my* concept of pain (my knowing what it means) comprises more than what a verbal expression of pain (in whatever terms) conveys. For instance, it encompasses external signs and expressions of pain (Wittgenstein's groans and grimaces). Moreover, it contains not only remembrances of pain experiences of my own, with perhaps one or two very painful cases in particular (the dog that bit me when I was a child); but also my understanding (whatever its status) that somehow you must have similar sen-sations in comparable situations. It includes experiences and associations, but feelings and emotions and valuations as well. And indeed, it may also comprise things we typically *say* about pain, including definitions. All such components may be taken to be part of my concept of pain functioning and resonating in pain-contexts. Second, when we *define* a word, we replace it by other words. In my conceptual framework these substitutes now get included into my concept of pain. But in the definitional moves of interrelating (sets of) words we tend to withdraw from the other parts of the concept. The non-verbal elements in partic-ular do not seem to play a role any more. The same happens in our talking about our experiences. We can still quite well differentiate between the pain as it is or was felt, the words we use to talk about it, and other expressions of the pain; but in talking about it, such distinctions disappear. They get out of sight, *and with them all the related nuances and all their interpersonal differences* (for instance, the felt quality and the anxiety of the dog's bite hide behind the shared words: 'the dog bit me'). Third, when we start philosophising about all this, we talk *about* such definitions and *in terms of* such definitions, thereby making the con-cealment of all that lives under the surface of the words structural and self-con-firming. This drying up of reality into language, this unfortunate 'linguistic turn', is at the same time caused by, and maintained by, and justified by linguistic philosophy. For this is the framework in which we *speak about* the meaning of words and expressions; and in which we *speak about* what can or cannot be the meaning of words like 'meaning' and 'knowledge' and their cognates. In this we are strengthened by the analysis of the concept of knowledge, for instance, in terms of our use of the expression 'I know *that* (with a verbalised proposition following)'. Consequentially an analysis of 'knowledge of' proceeds along the same lines. To give just one example: "There is indeed such a state as an awareness of a thing . . . Even so, the content of any such awareness could be expressed only in terms of what the subject knows about the object, what relevant facts he knows; hence, once again, what a person knows when he has direct awareness of an object is 'knowledge that'" (Hamlyn, 1970, p. 105). Similarly we are reinforced into the same pattern by thinking about meaning in terms of what we *say* when asked what a word means, only willing to think about *what* we know and not about *how* we know it – so that it can now easily be concluded that everybody knows what you mean when you say 'the dog bit me', with the implication that there can be nothing private or subjective to it.

Little wonder then that all this results in a poor picture of communication, of what really *happens* when people use words to communicate. It is along such lines that we are prevented from seeing that communication always is a matter of 'more or less' – even though normally sufficient. What is interesting about communication is precisely that unique persons can nevertheless understand each other, at least up to a point. Only a tacit model of meaning as verbal definition could give rise to so limited an idea of communication as a consequence of which we even saw Wittgenstein discrediting what is involved at the level of the first step above (*proteron*) on the basis of the third (*hysteron*): "a nothing would serve just as well as a something about which nothing could be said".

6. THE CO-CONSTITUTIVITY OF SUBJECTIVE AND INTERSUBJECTIVE MEANING

The private language arguments can retain much of their force against idealism, solipsism, scepticism, and the rest, without being overdrawn into ruling out the information processing metaphor that allows a more nuanced picture of what happens in communication within the linguistic community. Wittgenstein's arguments, with their one-sided emphasis on what can be said, unnecessarily threaten to block our view of what I suggest is one important source of individuality and of the individual person's contribution to communal life. Russell's approach was inspired by the information processing metaphor, but failed because he drew the wrong conclusions from it; whereas Wittgenstein was right in rejecting these conclusions, but was misled into rejecting the metaphor, as a consequence of which he came to neglect subtleties and differences to which he surely was highly sensitive in fact.

Three theoretical positions should be distinguished in discussions about Wittgenstein's private language argument, not two. The first is the *purely subjec-*

tive viewpoint: knowledge and meaning are exclusively subjective in origin; and any intersubjectivity is to be built up from this subjective basis. This is the position Wittgenstein's private language arguments were directed against. The second position is what many have taken to be the only possible alternative if one feels forced to give up the first, viz. the *purely intersubjective* view: knowledge and meaning are necessarily intersubjective; any subjectivity will have to be developed from this intersubjective basis. I think we should clearly opt for a third position, however, namely *co-constitutivity* of subjective and intersubjective meaning. This involves the deep intersubjectivity of the communal form of life that Wittgenstein has drawn our attention to; but also leaves room for subjective meaning, not or at least not entirely constituted from intersubjective resources. Meaning is built up from subjective *and* intersubjective components.

Notice that the three positions are mutually exclusive: the first is exclusively subjective; the second exclusively intersubjective. Only on the third, subjectivity and intersubjectivity are co-constitutive of meaning. And this not with the subjective part hidden somewhere in a private corner, to be considered as irrelevant. On the contrary, the various components of meaning are not really separable because of their thorough interwovenness at all levels. All these interconnected elements play their role in communication, even though some of them would not as such be communicable separately. I suggest that the upshot of the foregoing discussion is, that on the one hand we should not underestimate the importance of the intersubjective constitution of meaning in the normal (non-private) language situation, which Wittgenstein rightly emphasised. But, on the other hand, this pertinent observation should not seduce us into rejecting the possibility and the significance of the contribution of subjective, including private, meaning.

On this third position, agreement in judgements within a shared form of life is a matter of degree. Not because of the fact that we may agree on some judgements and disagree on others, but primarily (queer as this may sound) because we can on each specific judgement agree *more or less*, depending, as we saw, on persons and subject-matter involved. From this vantage point we can now begin to explore the differing forms and degrees of communicability in, for instance, religion – science – and art.

Only thus can we make sufficient room for the individual person as a unique and authentic centre of meaning *within* our common language and shared form of life. Only thus can we get an adequate notion of communication, if that is to be more than the exchange of rigid pieces of information on the model of coins with merely impersonal circulating value. And only thus can we begin to develop an adequate notion of teaching, if that is to be more than the accumulation of the child's accidental share or at best particular blend of otherwise entirely communal bits of knowledge. We can then, for instance, also get a better picture of how in education a child is initiated in a form of life – a process that never does and perhaps never should succeed completely. And we can take account of how different education is, and should be, for example in the fields of religion or science or art (and how different again for poetry or music).

Wittgenstein would certainly agree.

NOTE

I would like to thank professors Ton Derksen (Nijmegen) and Ruth Jonathan (Edinburgh) and the members of the research group in Philosophy of Education in Nijmegen (The Netherlands) for many helpful comments.

Wittgenstein on the Unreasonableness of Education: Connecting Teaching and Meaning

LUISE PRIOR McCARTY AND DAVID CHARLES McCARTY

Indiana University, U.S.A.

Für C.J.B. Macmillan, Doktorvater und Freund

1. TEACHING AND MEANING

At one time, Professor Macmillan was especially exercised with remark # 337 from Volume II of Wittgenstein's *Remarks on the Philosophy of Psychology*. The published translation of this remark reads

> "Am I doing child psychology? I am making a connection between the concept of teaching and the concept of meaning".

At the time of 1985, Macmillan would have contended that the second sentence of the remark was meant to answer negatively the question posed in the first. He opined that the connection to which Wittgenstein adverts is logical rather than psychological and wrote that the "logically connected concepts of teaching and meaning are at stake, not teaching procedures or the psychology of learning" (Macmillan, 1985, p. 414). We do not, at this remove, know what Macmillan may have meant by a 'logical connection' but it is not our object here to criticize Macmillan or his imputation to Wittgenstein of the demand for such a connection. Quite the contrary. We look to endorse the idea that there is a (type of) logical connection between teaching and meaning. We hope to motivate that endorsement from an interpretation of remark # 337 which encompasses circumambient remarks as well. For this, the eight paragraphs # 336 through # 343 of RPP, II are apt. They comprise a tight unit, a philosophical round trip by the end of which we discern the kind of logical connection Wittgenstein may have meant. Unless 'logical' receives such treatment, we will not appreciate, *contra* Macmillan, Wittgenstein's contribution to the psychology of learning. We will not appreciate how simple pedagogical facts such as this: that the words 'probably an armchair' are learnt later in life than 'armchair', may play a suitably logical role. We will fail to see that, if Wittgenstein's thought be credited, there is a perfectly good sense in which education is truly unreasonable: it is not subject to wholesale philosophical justification in terms of the acquisition of concepts to be established anterior to education.

2. ON A LOGICAL CONNECTION

Were we to construe Wittgenstein's logical connection between teaching and meaning propositionally, we might read him as claiming that certain instances of the scheme A below are logically true for particular concepts X and projects p.

63

Studies in Philosophy and Education **14**: 187–200, 1995.

(A) In order to grasp the concept X, one has already to have undergone a process of teaching/learning via p.

'X' is a place for a concept specification and 'p' for a description of a process of teaching. For example, 'X' may be replaced by 'three' and 'p' by 'learning to count by repeating the standard series of numerals and engaging in recognizable counting exercises'. So understood, A seems the sort of thing Wittgenstein asserts, for the concepts 'doubt' and 'calculate', in remark # 343. There, he writes – again in the standard translation – 'A person can doubt only if he has learnt certain things; as he can miscalculate only if he has learnt to calculate'.

Yet problems beset the idea that the logical connection between meaning and teaching gives rise to the logical truth of instances of A. For one thing, no non-trivial instance of A is a theorem of familiar logical systems nor is it an obvious consequence of a theorem. For another, it is no part of the sense, reference or colour of terms such as 'three' that, in order to be understood, they be taught at all. It is not contradictory to exclaim of a child prodigy, 'Nobody seems to have taught him to count 'one, two, three'. He picked it up all by himself'. Thirdly, if logical truths are necessary truths, then no instance of A states a logical truth. For any concept X, one can imagine X grasped as a result of installation rather than impartation. Here is an extreme case: imagine a race of pedagogically spontaneous individuals, a strain of humans very like contemporary Americans. They live – at least on the face of things – much like many Americans, speaking English just as Americans would. These spontaneous folks, however, are beings who are born directly into adulthood: they have no childhood but are born fully grown. You can even imagine them created as adults by God *ex nihilo*. (Perhaps archangels were once pictured in like fashion.) Spontaneous adults suffer no educational preliminaries, *a fortiori* none to speaking or thinking. One might puzzle over the kind of biology or theology that could produce spontaneous adults but there would be little hesitation in attributing to them a grasp of the same concepts we grasp. We can picture communicating with them as readily as we can with the less spontaneous. It follows that no interesting instance of scheme A serves to express a necessary truth or, as Wittgenstein might have said, interesting instances of A lack the form of propositions of logic.[1]

One would like to exhaust other exegetical possibilities before attributing to Wittgenstein a view fraught with objection. So, the question remains: if not logical truths, what did Wittgenstein intend his conjectural reader to take away from remarks ## 336 through # 343 – especially # 337? As mentioned, one line of # 343 suggests that he meant to claim *something* of the sort captured in instances of A. If there is a logical connection running from doubt to prior teaching or learning, what might it be? And how ought we to characterize it?

3. AGAINST HYPOTHETICALISM

In remark # 336 of RPP, II, Wittgenstein worries over the relation between the sentences "That is really an armchair" and "That is probably an armchair". He frets over the prospect that they turn out synonymous. Later, in remark # 343, he looks to be setting out preconditions under which one could work oneself into a state of doubt over the existence of armchairs, that state of doubt being one we can presumably call up more or less at will. He refers to that presumptive state as subject to *Willkür*, an arbitrary will.

For current purposes only, we use the term 'hypotheticalist' to denote those philosophers whose business it was to purvey the idea that every physical object statement is a 'probably' statement and to encourage hyperbolical doubts about chairs. Alfred Ayer, in Chapter Three of his *The Problem of Knowledge* (Ayer, 1956) expressed hypotheticalist views when he contended – with great subtlety – that examination of the concept 'armchair' reveals that any statement like "There's an armchair over there" is a hypothetical one, in epistemological lineage more akin to a generalization like Snell's Law than to an arithmetic truth like '$7 + 5 = 12$'. Ayer believed that to assert that there is an armchair over there is tantamount to asserting that one is probably over there. The peculiar manner by which a hypotheticalist arrives at the conviction that physical object statements are hypotheses is familiar to all philosophy undergraduates. Averments of "There's an armchair over there", made under the best of sensory conditions, are subject to rational doubt in ways that simple arithmetical truths are not – or so undergraduates are told. No matter where we stand relative to the putative armchair and no matter how long we seem to see it, to walk around it, to touch it, a hypotheticalist will insist that it is still perfectly possible that the chair not exist or that the item viewed not be a chair at all. No matter how much 'chairlike sensory data' gets collected, the hypotheticalist would say, it is imaginable that it all be consistent with the supposition that what looks a chair is really a mirage or is composed of a material which will not – once we try sitting on it – support bodyweight. One can, they maintain, always imagine something happening that would convince us that we are not now standing before a real chair. And these (voluntary) imaginings are more than sufficient, the hypotheticalist concludes, to induce in any reasonable person a feeling of doubt over the existence of armchairs.

Included in this overture to hypotheticalism is the presumption that one can *think* oneself at will into a state of doubt about chairs. Once the doubt is recognized, one is also supposed to recognize the existence of physical chairs to be a hypothetical one and any certainty about real chairs to be chimerical. So, hypotheticalists would have it that a crucial epistemic cog in the workings of our language – the feelings which are the supposed semantic values of 'doubt' and 'certainty' – remains under the control of our cognitive faculties, ready to be called up and mobilized at will. Doubt and certainty are thereby supposed to be (founded upon) sensations that we can bring forward on the basis of intellection alone. Just as one is able to make oneself feel angry by reflecting overlong on old slights and insults unreturned, so the hypotheticalist would claim that reasonable feelings of doubt and certainty can be induced at will, as a result of the kind of musings Ayer once rehearsed. The musings are to be subject to volition, to be *willkürlich*, and sufficient to bring us to have feelings of doubt.

4. TEACHING DOUBTING THOMAS

It is against such a hypotheticalist that Wittgenstein's remarks # 336 through # 343 seem to be directed. To follow is a reconstruction of Wittgenstein's thought in these passages, with textual commentary. We begin with remark # 336, in our own translation:

> "Imagine that a child were extremely clever, so clever that one could immediately impart to him the doubtfulness of the existence of all things. From the beginning, he learns: 'That is probably an armchair'.
>
> "And how does he now learn the question: 'Is that also really an armchair?'".

The child Wittgenstein imagines is a lad able, if miraculously, to feel the doubt-fulness of the external world but who is, in other respects, ordinary. We'll call the imagined boy 'doubting Thomas'. If doubt is indeed subject to arbitrary, if intellectualized, discretion, as the hypotheticalist proposes, then a child like Thomas, one of sufficient perspicacity, ought to be able to doubt. For, if what separates blind faith from rational doubt is merely a further series of intellec-tual steps, then the cognitive distance separating the child with unshaken faith in armchairs and one who doubts should be measurable entirely in intellec-tual terms. Hence, were Ayer correct, a doubting Thomas should be a coherent prospect.

In asking, "And how does he now learn the question: 'Is that also really an armchair?'" Wittgenstein sets the reader a challenge: to design a lesson plan for doubting Thomas, a plan to provide him with the 'really a chair' concept, to convey to him the difference between that and 'probably a chair'. To render Wittgenstein's intentions in such prosaic terms – in terms of lesson plans and prospective lessons – is not to pervert them. The idea of a prospective lesson does not lie far from *one* of Wittgenstein's ideas of language-game. When he first introduces the concept 'language-game' in the BB, Wittgenstein writes in a pedagogic vein:

> "Children are taught their native language by means of such games, and here they even have the entertaining character of games" (BB, # 81).

As will be apparent, there is real difficulty in meeting Wittgenstein's challenge. But it is not a difficulty to be laid at Thomas's door: he is a prodigy, after all. Nor should we allow the difficulty to be all ours; we will not find that our imagi-nations are insufficiently fertile to bring forth a variety of lesson plans.

We are to teach Thomas the difference between a thing's probably being a chair and it's actually being a chair. Yet these are concepts we cannot impart to him in any crudely direct fashion, say, via the perennial expedient of pointing to chairs *seriatim* and, after each ostension, enunciating the word 'chair'. Remem-ber that Wittgenstein's Thomas is a clever and committed hypotheticalist. What is he likely to think we are up to in this ostending and enunciating? He must cling to the hypotheticalistic belief that what we keep calling 'chair' is merely probable-chair; all things are to him doubtful. Since he deems us otherwise rea-sonable, Thomas will surely suppose that we are introducing 'chair' as handy abbreviation for 'that's probably a chair'. He reads us as presenting him with a useful shorthand for 'probable-chair', a kind of nickname for it. Nor will matters improve if we involve Thomas himself and instruct him to fetch a chair whenever 'chair' is announced. In that case, Thomas merely modifies his original supposition – that 'chair' abbreviates 'probable chair' – to allow 'chair' to stand as well for the imperative, 'Bring what is probably a chair'. On this reconstrual of 'chair', Thomas can do as well as any when it comes to fetching chairs or, to him, 'probable chairs'. Hence, a lesson plan based upon direct ostension and training will not achieve the desired end.

Our ingenuity is not exhausted. We philosophers teach our undergraduate students the differences between chairs and their appearances not by training them to pick things out in practice but by going theoretical – by teaching them something of the history of philosophy, by conveying the difference between realism and idealism. Such a pedagogic suggestion would be ill-adapted for the ordinary child. But you must remember what an especially clever tyke Wittgenstein imagined Thomas to be. Indeed, this historico-theoretical way of conveying the desired distinction is one Wittgenstein himself notes. At # 338, he writes

> "One man is a convinced realist and another a convinced idealist and teaches his children accordingly. In so important a business as the existence or nonexistence of the external world, they do not want to impart anything false to their children.
> What will one teach them?"

We select suitable 'course materials', perhaps, Berkeley's *Three Dialogues Between Hylas and Philonous* (Berkeley, 1954) and read them to Thomas at bedtime. We help him over Berkeley's dated diction and, as time passes, see that Thomas comes to follow Berkeley's arguments quite well. Yet familiarity with an historico-theoretical distinction does not guarantee a grasp of the everyday idea of physical object. For one thing, it is likely that Thomas now grasps the term 'material object', as used by Berkeley, but takes it to be a term not fit for everyday objects, but, like such mouldy terms as 'quintessence', reserved for disputes of a mouldy sort, ones from quaintly metaphysical bedtime stories. It is not unlikely that he think the role of 'physical object' exhausted in demarcating the intellectual territory of a realist like Berkeley's Hylas from that of the idealist Philonous and used only when imaginary realists and imaginary idealists have their literary showdowns. This is the very worry Wittgenstein himself expresses over teaching 'physical objects' to children. He compares this to teaching a child about fairies and agrees, at paragraph # 338, that children are likely to believe the significance of terms like 'material object' wholly taken up in quaint dispute:

> "On what occasion should they [children who are to learn the distinction between realism and idealism] say 'There are [physical objects]' or 'There are not ...'? Only when they meet people who are of the contrary belief".

Doubting Thomas exhibits a relative maturity that makes it even more likely that he adopt a nonstandard line on his course of reading in historical philosophy. He may come away from his encounter with idealism sharing a view with many of our students: that the debate Berkeley depicts between rival sectarians is of an interest purely academic. He may come to believe that 'realist' and 'idealist' are only conventional denominations for onetime groups holding bizarre and super-stitious views about the natures of those items which are, to Thomas, probable chairs. Indeed, Thomas may want to ask, as Wittgenstein does explicitly in the next paragraph of his treatment – # 339 – "Won't the difference [between those who assert the existence of physical objects and those who deny it] only be one of battle cry?"

The high theoretical road to teaching Thomas did not lead the right way. We should return to the mundane and have a second go. Perhaps Thomas needs to be confronted not with probable or real chairs but with the contrast between probability and reality itself. And this presentation ought to be as dramatic as possible. This is the sort of approach Wittgenstein himself assays in remark # 340. Unfortunately, the translators chose to render Wittgenstein's word '*Spiel*' as 'game' rather than 'play', since it seems to be a play, and not a game, that he has in mind.

> "For doesn't the play [*Spiel*] 'That is probably a . . .' begin with disappointment? And can the first scene be one about possible disappointment?"

We now imagine scripting a simple drama, one illustrating the contrast, with a view to staging it for Thomas. It might be a playlet in which a young woman waits impatiently for her lover's actual arrival, hears a knock at the door, then opens the door and displays obvious signs of disappointment when she finds no one but the postman. For Thomas to grasp the play's idea, he must not only see the play, but he must see the point. He has to recognize the attitude displayed by the actress as one of expectation and, later, one of disappointment. Specifically, he must get the idea that the first scene before him is one of expectation of a lover's real, rather than merely possible, arrival. But that is indeed the rub: this is the very distinction we were already trying to get across and the very one which Thomas seems always to dodge. To distinguish expecting a chair from expecting a probable chair one would already have to be able to distinguish chairs from probable chairs or, *mutatis mutandis*, real and possible arrivals of lovers.

A moment's reflection reveals that no dramatic approach is likely to succeed in putting Thomas in touch with the requisite contrast. Should we juxtapose for Thomas the behaviours and goings-on typical of certainty – confidence and surety in action – with those of doubt or probability – hesitation, checking, looking over the shoulder – the sets of behaviours remain just that: sets of behaviours. They hold nothing within themselves to prohibit Thomas from engaging his talent for probabilistic reinterpretation. Things are no different if we try participant theatre, one wherein Thomas himself gets to play a part and, thereby, learns of real chairs. This participant theatre might be just the kind of thing Wittgenstein had in mind when he wrote, at # 342, of doubting and of playing a language-game:

> "So how does doubt express itself then? I mean: in a language-game and not simply in particular *locutions*. Perhaps in looking at more closely and, therefore, in a seemingly more complicated activity. But this expression of doubt does not always have rationale, goal.

One even forgets that doubting also belongs to a language-game".

What one forgets (and is regularly forgotten by Wittgensteinians who are language-game enthusiasts) is that even a whole language-game is open to reinterpretation. Wittgenstein says so more or less plainly at PI 200. With time, Thomas can learn to follow and to play any game, to join any parade of activities suggestive of doubt or of certainty. He can learn to hesitate, withhold judgment, reconsider, look more closely. He can act all these out. That is yet no guarantee that he sees their points. He is always free to engage a feeling of doubt and to reconceive his actions as appropriate poses. Perhaps he thinks that the 'language-games of doubt and certainty' mark not that distinction – between doubt and certainty – but the distinction between the merely and the highly probable. He can always (re)construe the goal of his actions in line with his doubts. The mere activity of expressing doubt is not sufficient to convey to Thomas the point in doubting that something might be a chair. Indeed, how could we do that without already conveying what it is to be a chair *simpliciter*?

In sum, no lesson plan is likely to bring to Thomas a ken of what it is to be certain about actual chairs. Nothing seems to work since, for Thomas, doubt is a mental state, a feeling which he conjures up as the end product of an intellectual exercise and one which, by hypothesis, he can always bring to the fore. Anything we try to convey to him can itself be made doubtful by calling the feeling up: any ostension, any drama, any activity's putative point. If this is so, then we, together with Wittgenstein, have won through to a significant realization: as a matter of psychological fact, doubting Thomas is cognitively incapable of grasping the concept of real – as opposed to apparent – chair.

5. A WITTGENSTEINIAN ANTINOMY

But wait a minute! This can't be! How could Thomas be deficient in this way? He exhibits no cognitive deficiencies. He lacks no motor skills. We only assumed him to have something extra, something which children of his age do not normally feel: the doubtfulness of everything. In other respects, he is ahead of the game; we suppose him more clever than most. Even reluctant learners among normal children pick up the concept 'chair' and we have not supposed Thomas to be reluctant in any real sense. We can teach him to do anything with and say anything about chairs that ordinary children can. We even teach him to use 'chair' as we do, although he may secretly think it an abbreviation for something else. Anyone observing the bulk of Thomas's behaviour would insist that he comprehends perfectly what we mean by 'chair'. Admittedly, Thomas may well feel something that others do not and he may well say something novel from time to time. But all children do that and it affords no real obstacle to a comprehension of 'chair'.

On the one hand there is reason for thinking Thomas incapable of grasping the distinction between real and apparent chairs. On the other are seemingly convincing reasons for insisting just the opposite: that he can come to read us perfectly well. If our reasoning is cogent, the nub of this seeming antinomy must lie in our original specification of the issue, in our imagining a doubting Thomas, in the very idea that a small child be wholly convinced – in the way of the hypotheticalist – of the doubtfulness of all things. This description must be the root of the contradiction. We hope to show that this was also Wittgenstein's diagnosis of the problem and was expressed in lines already cited from remark # 343, in our own translation:

> "One can only doubt if one has learned the certain (*Gewisses*); in the way that one can only miscalculate if one has learned to calculate".

The standard translation of the first sentence obstructs understanding. It reads 'A person can doubt only if he has learnt certain things'. This is doubly misleading. First, the anaphora linking 'person' to 'he' in the standard translation leads one to suspect that particular individuals – and their idiosyncratic cognitive attainments – afford Wittgenstein's primary concerns. Second, the appearance of 'certain things', instead of 'the certain', tempts one to think that Wittgenstein does mean to assert an instance of scheme A: that a necessary condition for the subsistence of a state of doubt in a person is indeed that *that person* has already gone through *certain definite* stages of learning. But Wittgenstein is not, at least immediately, referring to particular persons and their learning histories. He is referring primarily to what seems far more trite but what turns out to be far more significant: that, in the ordinary course of affairs, being certain is taught us before being doubtful. More carefully put, we might say that Wittgenstein is adverting to the fact that we are first taught to fetch chairs, to field balls and to say 'Hi' with unalloyed confidence, in a way more primitive and simpler than the distinction between confidence and hesitation. The 'certain' that we are taught is that we are taught to act, at first, without the intrusion of doubt. Only later do we come – in appropriate circumstances – to worry, to hesitate over, to doubt of chairs, balls and greetings. Normally there is a reasonable interval of time, in time of learning, between our acquiring the (pre)confidence of 'the certain' and, later, the techniques of doubt. This is the simple fact to which Wittgenstein wants to point. But as simple fact alone, it is only mildly interesting, a mere commonplace. Its significance for Wittgenstein lies in its relation, first, to our *description* of a boy who can learn straight off the doubtfulness of everything and, second, to *logic*. But, if it is not a business of individual child psychology, how does such a fact become integral to a concept like 'doubt'? Moreover, how does this help to resolve the antinomy of doubting Thomas? How does it give sense to a 'logical' connection between teaching and meaning unreflected in obviously logical truths?

6. A WITTGENSTEINIAN RESOLUTION: POINTS IN PEDAGOGICAL SPACE

We believe that Wittgenstein's answer to these three questions is one and the same: the fact cited lies *in* concepts. If the concept of X is conceived to be all that is required of cognitive apparatus to be able to wield a word for X, then we can rightly say that Wittgenstein sees the fact of learning the certain before the doubtful as an essential part of the concepts of certainty and of doubt. Wittgenstein held that such concepts as 'chair' and 'probable chair' depend for their existence and identities upon a range of pedagogic facts. One way to communicate this dependency would be to say that, in order for concepts to be distinctive, there must be discernible conceptual distances between them. In the case of doubt and certainty, that distance, whether expressed in terms of time or in terms of simplicity, lies in matters educational.

To see Wittgenstein's presumptive connection between teaching and meaning to be a 'logical' one, consider a two-dimensional mathematical coordinate space with distinct abstract points such as <3,4> and <6,4>. These points are 'pure positions': their natures are completely exhausted in their numerical specifications. Until we apply the system to a physical space, there is nothing to the point <3,4> except it's being 3 units to the right of the origin and 4 units up. Should we change either of these distances, should we, say, go from 3 to 6, we have not repositioned the point <3,4> at the place <6,4>. Rather, we are at another point entirely, the point <6,4>. That distance of three units is one of the essential identifying conditions of <3,4> and <6,4> as abstract points. Moreover, that 3 is the first component of <3, 4> is indeed a logical or definitional truth, marking the fact that an abstract distance of three units is an essential feature of <3,4> and one apparent from the notation. This is the case even though, when we apply that notation to an actual space, a physical location named <3,4> may not itself bear any essential relation to three or to four or to whatever appears at location <6,4>. Assume, for instance, that we apply a coordinate mapping to Paris and select the Eiffel Tower as origin and choose measuring units so that the Louvre turns out to be at location <3,4>. It will not follow that it is a necessary or logical truth that the Louvre is three units across and four units up from the Eiffel Tower. The very same building, the Louvre, might have been built somewhere else. We might also have selected different units for our application than we did, ones which put the Louvre at <6,4> instead of <3,4>.

On Wittgenstein's account, the concepts 'doubt' and 'certainty' are akin to abstract points in that they require for their identities facts that one might represent as conceptual distances standing between them. Concepts are certainly abstract entities. In Frege, their structures and identities are insured by mathematical facts independent of spoken language and phenomenal world. In Wittgenstein, however, the being of the concept is bound up with factual conditions, principally ones of, as he would have said, 'human natural history'. A Wittgensteinian concept of X is exhausted in the factual conditions that must be in place for signs or notations for X to be what they are: signs *for* X. To that extent, concepts like 'doubt' and 'certainty' are like points <3,4> or <6,4>: they are distinguished thanks to certain factual matters, which, if altered, amount to a change in the concepts themselves. Indeed, it would not be inapposite to think of Wittgensteinian concepts as simple collections of such facts. Hence, one might say that Wittgenstein is eager to point out that the fact that the certain arises pedagogically prior to the doubt belongs to both the concept (or collection) 'certainty' and the concept 'doubt' and, hence, to what is meant by these words.

Without the temporal and pedagogical distance between certainty and doubt in the space which affords their background, the concepts 'doubt' and 'certainty' cannot be reliably identified and separated. Just as we cannot have that very point <3,4> when 3 is replaced here by 6, so we cannot have doubt when that very concept is imagined to be inculcated prior to certainty. The pedagogical distance along the axis of time is a necessary condition for conceptual identity. Moreover, the analogy between abstract concepts and points in a coordinate space helps to explain how the temporal priority of teaching 'the certain' before the doubtful might intelligibly be described as a matter of logic and yet not give rise to logical truths, how there can be such a logical connection between teaching and meaning without any significant instances of schema A stating necessary truths. It is no necessary truth that *we* can mean doubt by using the word 'doubt' only if *we* have been taught in a particular fashion, in one of the ways doubting Thomas could not have been taught. To insist upon this, on the basis of Wittgenstein's remarks, is akin to insisting that what happens to appear at <3,4> (say, the Eiffel Tower) in one application of a coordinate system is itself necessarily 3 horizontal units distant from what happens to appear at <6,4> (say, the Louvre). What happens to appear in one application of our range of concepts – those acts and goings-on which we call 'doubt' and 'certainty' in that application – bear, in themselves, no essential relation to what happens to appear at the locations of 'teaching' and 'learning'. Yet, in the case of the Louvre, the application is only possible if, as a matter of logic, <3,4> is 3 units away from <6,4>. In the case of teaching and learning, the application of the concepts is only possible if, as a matter of logic – a matter of the internal structure of concepts – both doubt and certainty, as abstract concepts, contain the fact that the certain is learnt prior to the doubtful. The logical connection exists at the level of abstract concepts and not, we might say, at the level of the concrete items to which concepts happen to apply. Just as <3,4> is the point it is in virtue of the fact that 3 lies along a coordinate axis running through the space, we might say that 'certainty' is only the concept it is because it lies in a particular position along a coordinate axis running through the space of concepts, an axis established by facts of education.

Without the metaphor of distance, we might put Wittgenstein's idea this way: for speech and behaviour to be expressive of doubt or of certainty is for the descriptions 'doubtful' or 'certain' to be apposite. In order to apply those descriptions (with their present meanings), certain real, factual conditions have to be in place. Principal among these is the simple fact so often cited: that children acquire the ease of certainty prior in time to the hesitancy of doubt. To summon up the verbal image of a doubting Thomas is not to misdescribe being in doubt or being certain. It is to reject the conditions under which these descriptions describe what we intend; the temporal priority of certainty to doubt is part and parcel of the possibility for correct description. With this fact as background, we make sense of epistemic phenomena; without it, we fall into confusion.

Some confirmation of this reading comes from noting that Wittgenstein adopted a parallel line when he dealt with concepts of colour at RPP, II, # 199.

After asking "How could people learn the use of colour words in a land where everything had only *one* colour?" he wrote,

"This does not interest us: the conditions under which the language-game with colour names is physically impossible or, really, not probable.
Without chessmen one cannot play chess – that is the impossibility that interests us".

Again, it is a truth neither logical nor physical that every chessgame require actual chessmen. Two accomplished players can play each other entirely in their heads, reporting moves verbally but using no men at all. Yet, to describe a game 'in the head' and make sense of the description, we need first to have chessboards and chessmen. How else could we teach someone ignorant of chess what is going on in the game 'in the head'? The concept of 'chessgames in the head' has the contingent existence of ordinary 'outside the head' chess with ordinary chessmen as its logical prerequisite and this marks a pedagogical axis by which the concept of chess is identified as the very concept it is.

7. THE LOGICAL CONNECTION: REMARK # 337 REVISITED

We are now prepared to set out Wittgenstein's reply, from eight passages of RPP, II, to the hypotheticalist. Doubt, he holds, needs to be more than a feeling to be summoned up *ad lib* by engaging intellectual processes of 'imagining' and 'doubting'. There is a great deal more, a great nonintellectual more to the business of doubt, a great more not subject to volition. For there to be this business, there must be a space of concepts surrounding it and, in that space, a distance between doubting and certainty measured along an educational axis. Nonlogically construed, that axis is the simple fact that certainty arises prior to doubt. Logically construed, it is an identity condition on the 'point' which is doubting in the space of all our concepts. The case of doubting Thomas shows us that, without such a factual axis, the intelligible difference between the concepts collapses: we need that distance to ascribe doubt to the child.

Wittgenstein's reply is therefore a radical one: the mechanisms which underpin the workings of language are not transparent to the intellect and not subject to volition. We do not, according to Wittgenstein, express our meanings and communicate our thoughts thanks solely to intellectual or intellectual/emotional processes (plus, perhaps, linguistic conventions). He would have it that we speak and think by being subsumed into a factual colossus, a system of speakings and thinkings that is systemic thanks to a variety of facts. It is as a constitutive feature of that system (if we are careful, we can say, a 'logical feature') that education functions. For Wittgenstein, education not only gives us concepts by inducing us to grasp them, but gives us concepts by making it so that our significant acts express such things as determinate concepts. The system on which we rely, the system in virtue of which a feeling comes to mark a doubt, is not something under conscious or unconscious control. We might express this for Wittgenstein by maintaining that it is not *we* who speak language but a language *system* that speaks us: our certainties and our doubts, as with all our feelings, owe their natures to it.

Now is the time to revisit remark # 337 in our own translation:

> "Am I engaged in child psychology? I am bringing the concept of teaching into association with that of meaning".

Wittgenstein does not offer a determinate, 'yes or no' answer to the question posed. Guardedness is appropriate; chances of misreadings run high. Were he to have answered 'Yes', one would naturally suppose his investigation to be an arrogantly foolhardy attempt at armchair psychology, an effort doomed to failure because 'nonempirical'. On the other hand, were Wittgenstein to have answered 'No', temptation is strong to think that he is in no way contributing to psychology but, instead, to some other recognized subject, e.g., semantics. In either case, we get led badly and sadly astray. Neither is Wittgenstein concerned with cognitive processes in and of themselves, but nor is he wholly unconcerned. The matter is not one of processes themselves but of the ways in which we must describe them, the ways in which they must stand to language if they are to be called as they are.

As we said, Wittgenstein is adverting to conditions that need obtain for people's actions and words to be construed as expressive of doubt or of certainty. These are conditions under which human speech and other behaviours become symbolic of such epistemic states. These are matters of psychology indeed – not of how to do psychology but of what to make of it. If we do not get carried away with historical proprieties, we can speak of Wittgenstein's contribution to psychology here as transcendental, much as his treatment of logic in *Tractatus* was transcendental. Wittgenstein's is a Kantian child psychology, a study of those nonempirical conditions under which we can sensibly ask and answer Kantian questions like 'How is the expression of doubt by a child possible?' In this transcendental sense, Wittgenstein's cogitations are indeed about a psychology, part of a serious study of persons and their bodies but not a study of persons as in law or their behaviours as in choreography. We are to bring persons, bodies and actions under another scheme of comparison, one in which they are compared not as legalities or as figures but as signs for doubt and certainty.

Wittgenstein is not here concerned with the intrinsic natures of individual cognitive processes. Nor is his thought here a roundabout effort to convince us of the truth of claims of individual psychology such as, 'in order for a person to enter into the state of doubt, he or she must already have learned to be certain'. To keep us away from such suppositions, Wittgenstein is careful to write in # 337 not of bringing teaching itself into association with meaning itself but rather of an association between the concepts of these two things. And, for Wittgenstein, the 'concepts' at issue here are not mental mechanisms or physical dispositions or abilities at language games but are rendered as facts which form a rough system and which, in turn, forms the superstructure of our efforts to express thoughts.

8. JUSTIFYING EDUCATION

We read Wittgenstein as insisting, first, that pervasive facts of education, among them that certainty is generally prior in acquisition to doubt, are essential to the concepts 'doubt' and 'certainty'. This essentiality can be laid out in terms of conditions: those under which we succeed in ascribing concepts to people in descriptions. Putting it this way, we can say that Wittgenstein thought no description of the concept 'doubt' specifies it adequately without the aid of certain banal pedagogical regularities. In so far as these regularities contribute to his 'logical' investigations, Wittgenstein maintained a keen interest in them. He would not, however, take as his object the discovery of recherché pedagogical truths in so far as they are of day-to-day interest to the educationalist. Even so, we remain free to ask: if we assume Wittgenstein correct about concepts, are there yet conclusions to be drawn of interest to a (theoretically inclined) pedagogue?

If Wittgenstein is right, it is false that education is fully construable as a set of cognitive processes responsible to conceptual attainments fully given in advance and prior to any discussion of educational details. Wittgenstein's examples – such as that of Thomas – are intended, in part, to expose the nontrivial extent to which our concepts and conceptual attainments are responsible to education. Hence, the setting down of concepts or other conceptual matters as educational goals makes implicit appeal to forms of education and to their mundane details. After all, how is one to call facts of education into question – as philosophers often look to do – when the subsistence of those facts is part of the concepts which I need for any calling into question? Therein lies a circularity for philosophers. Succinctly put, one of Wittgenstein's messages was: education must come first and a philosophy (of cognition) only later.

Wittgenstein's ideas paint for justification-minded philosophers of education a dangerous prospect: that the justifications they attempt to construct for styles or forms of education be viciously circular. To see the difficulty, assume that certain crucial concepts require for their natures salient educational matters. Then think of a philosopher who looks to justify a whole new approach to education, e.g., rational teaching or teaching from a 'knowledge base', one he or she markets as a wholesale revision. The philosopher we imagine maintains that all of education – if conducted in the way he or she recommends – would be rationally justifiable in the desiderated way, if only his or her approach is adopted. His or her goal is to show that an across-the-board alteration in education is reasonable in view of its presumptive efficacy for the inculcation in children of certain desirable concepts. But these concepts may themselves, if Wittgenstein is right, require that a course of education or specific educational details be in place. If pushed, we might have to say that, for Wittgenstein, talk of concepts is a *facon de parler* for educational facts. Now, we must ask, how is all of education to be justified as the philosopher insists if significant parts of that education must already be taken for granted?

To put the potential circularity across most plainly an analogy is apt. Philosophers of the sort under consideration see education as the means for delivering cognitive goods to learners. They think of the goods as conceptual materials: knowledge, belief, attitudes, concepts. It is with respect to these goods and their delivery that they try to see education as reasonable – reasonable to the extent that education as they view it expedites the deliveries desired. By their lights, the best education is simply the best means for transferring those goods. To report the results of Wittgenstein's investigation in these analogical terms is to point out that the 'goods' which education delivers are themselves, at least in part, records of educational deliveries: the goods cannot be specified apart from the means for their own delivery. I cannot even say what goods are to be delivered without relying upon particular ways of delivery and presupposing that they are delivered in these ways. Now, we must ask, 'What does it mean to speak, as philosophers sometimes do, of surveying alternate routes for delivering the same goods and then selecting the best ones for delivery, when the goods to be delivered are themselves, in part, records of delivery routes?' One likely reply is that such speech means very little that is coherent.

NOTE

[1] This idea of spontaneous speakers was inspired by one of Wittgenstein's own imaginations, that of the 'momentary Englishmen' of remark # 34 from Part VI of RFM.

Wittgenstein, Liberal Education, Philosophy

ALVEN NEIMAN

University of Notre Dame, U.S.A.

I

In these remarks I want to discuss liberal education, indicating along the way how my acquaintance and struggle with Wittgenstein have affected both my theory and practice as a liberal educator. In no way, however, do I promise an account of Wittgenstein's view of liberal education (or the view he supposedly would have held or should have held, had he thought about such a thing). For better or for worse he never, either in print or in recorded recollection of friends, discussed the matter (although of course he did have views about the modern university, culture, etc.). This fact makes my job both easier in some ways, and more difficult in others than (for example) that of one writing on Wittgenstein on logic or language or knowledge. It is easier because in many ways there are fewer constraints, and less pressure for accuracy (and of course therefore less worry about trivial debates as to whether there is a theory to be found). But it is more difficult insofar as it is harder to define exactly what one is writing about.

Perhaps a good model for this project can be found in the work of Wittgenstein's student and friend, the psychiatrist Maurice O'C Drury. Drury's *The Danger of Words* was meant to show how his teacher's thought and example had influenced "... the thought of one who was confronted by problems which had both an immediate practical aspect, as well as a deeper, philosophical dimension," how, in effect, it had helped him in his work as a psychiatrist (Drury, 1973, p. viii). As Drury and others have noted, Wittgenstein was fond of insisting that philosophy was of no use if it did not help one live a better life, help one to think better about real life problems and help one do constructive work beyond the realm of purely philosophical speculation. So we can read Drury's book, imagine him engaged in practice, and wonder whether and how Wittgenstein either improved or harmed him. Perhaps the reader of this paper can do the same with me as I reflect in this paper on the theory and practice of liberal education.

As a graduate student in philosophy I fancied myself to be a follower of Wittgenstein. At the time I puzzled much over *The Philosophical Investigations* and *On Certainty*. My major field was epistemology, since my major concern was scepticism. But shortly after I finished my doctoral thesis, I found a way out of 'pure philosophy'. I was asked to participate in the establishment of a 'core course' (hereafter simply referred to as Core or The Core), a general education requirement in Notre Dame's College of Arts and Letters. Mandated in 1979, Core would provide entering students with a year-long, interdisciplinary,

77

Studies in Philosophy and Education **14**: 201–215, 1995.
© 1995 *Kluwer Academic Publishers. Printed in the Netherlands.*

seminar-style introduction to a College composed of departments in the fine arts, social sciences and humanities. From a rather abstract proposal voted on by our College Council a group of faculty, of which I was a part, was both to develop the theory of such a course, and put it into practice. This work, I am happy to say, lifted me out of my previous, rather addled world of Cartesian doubts, Moorean claims to know, better Gettier counter-examples, et al. It gave me a kind of peace that comes from doing more honest and practical work than epistemology.

I have worked on Core, first as an assistant director, and now as director, since 1979. Since then I have done little work on Wittgenstein *per se*. And I often wonder whether my time 'with him' changed me, and if it did, whether for better or worse. I know some of my colleagues believe that too much of Wittgenstein can only cripple that lovely quasi-Platonic faculty that produces the necessary and sufficient conditions that our analysts still love so much. Yet I like to imagine that my time reading him improved me, made me better able to engage in the theory and practice of liberal education than I would otherwise have been. My desire in this paper is to begin something of a test case for this hope.

I shall proceed by examining three uses of the metaphor of liberal education as philosophy. I do not, however, wish to define liberal education; rather, I want to imagine what sorts of things can be mined from an idea that has been popular with philosophers from Plato to Dewey. My goal is to develop some of the possibilities of a popular figure of speech for the practitioner/theorist operating in a particular historical and social context.

This strategy will allow us to imagine what philosophy is and might be in itself, as well as in liberal education. Wittgenstein's habit of continuous reflection upon the nature of philosophy and its relationship to culture is well known; my rather constant references to aspects of that reflection is meant to mark my thinking as recognizably Wittgensteinian in inspiration. But, once again, I insist that the reader recognize that this work is meant to extend Wittgenstein's own work in ways he quite clearly would not have recognized as his own. It is important to recognize from the outset the difficulty involved in this appropriation.

For example: these remarks and the ongoing inquiry they represent deal with a topic, liberal education, that Wittgenstein does not directly address. They focus on a problem, the current crisis of liberal education in the university, that was unknown to him. The inquirer in question has a commitment to *Catholic* liberal education in a *democratic* context that will affect his orientation and arguments. They mark a perspective that, it must be admitted, makes any extended use of Wittgenstein's thinking *verbatim* problematic. What will be offered here is extension and rational reconstruction, not mere copying.

What is the problem? It can be defined as a dispute over the nature and purpose of liberal education. Most generally, it involves consideration of and disagreement about the role of unity and diversity both in educational method and content. So, for example, an author such as Allan Bloom, in his book *The Closing of The American Mind* champions the cause of 'the great books' and 'Western civilization' in the elite universities (Bloom, 1987). Those who disagree with him and instead champion diversity, difference, Bloom labels nihilists. In response the latter call Bloom reactionary, fascist, etc. Middle ground seems hard to find, but must be found. In short I want to begin to suggest ways in which Wittgenstein's inspirations have been useful to one educator who is attempting to find such a way.

II

As Alasdair MacIntyre notes, every agent engaged in a practice must (implicitly if not explicitly) appeal to some narrative in which self-understanding is possible (MacIntyre, 1981). The possibility of producing such a narrative is necessary for such self-understanding to exist. In short, this narrative will inevitably suggest to the practitioner some idea of his *telos*, i.e. the point of what one is doing. Whether or not some telos *naturally* resides in a true understanding of each practice, every practitioner, in order to arrive at a coherent, an integrated, sense of who s/he is, must integrate some such ideal into his or her self-understanding of practice.

What *telos* governs the practice of liberal education? Whether or not the Aristotelian is right about what is or isn't natural to human beings as such, each liberal educator, to the extent that he reflects upon his practice, must ponder his intent in teaching. I believe that part of what must be involved in such reflection is a concern with philosophy.

Most commentators will, I think, agree rather easily with the idea that Wittgenstein's work at least contains a negative, destructive vision. There is much in that work that is critical not only of the practice of philosophy but also of the culture and society in which it is practised. There is, however, much less agreement over the possibility that a more constructive vision can be found in his work. Here, however, I shall presuppose the existence of both a negative and positive critique of philosophy and in the end try to expand and utilize the latter in the context of my educational concerns. Moreover, I shall in later sections of the paper presuppose that among recent commentators James Edwards has done the best job of understanding and portraying Wittgenstein's larger vision. In the rest of this section I shall discuss the conclusions of Edwards' *Ethics Without Philosophy* in some detail (Edwards, 1982). I agree in general both with Edwards' portrayal of that positive vision as central to Wittgenstein's philosophizing and his sense of how Wittgenstein saw our age as lacking in this regard. Moreover, I believe that such a vision, suitably understood and rationally reconstructed, can help inform a viable practice of liberal education. It can help provide for the liberal educator something of what Aristotle's *telos* provided for his followers, i.e. the beginnings of sustaining narrative for his conscious and conscientious practice.

What, for Edwards, is that vision? First of all, it can be characterized as having three major aspects. Edwards refers to the first as Wittgenstein's non-literalizing sensibility. According to Edwards, this sensibility allows one to always remain aware that our knowledge is a product and invention of human practice. It prevents our taking literally any human image as a picture of the world.

In an earlier paper I have tried to capture and promote this sensibility in terms of the notion of irony (Neiman, 1991). However, I now think Edwards is right to point out the dangers of this designation. If the non-literalizing sensibility is ironic, it certainly is ironic in a way in which humility rather than self-enchantment is promoted. On Edwards' account, Wittgenstein shares with the later Heidegger a feeling that traditional philosophy and science resists humility; rather it aims, in a colossal display of the will to power, to reduce the mystery of existence to a set of riddles to be solved or dissolved. It aims, most of all, at the mastery of the use of reality to fulfil instrumental human needs.

Thus, on Edwards' account a second aspect of Wittgenstein's vision of sound human understanding is its resistance to philosophy both as a practice and a way of facing the world. While philosophy and science place us in a position of technological mastery of the world, they paradoxically alienate us from the means of solving our larger, most human problems of community and meaning. Thus, according to Edwards, the third aspect of Wittgenstein's vision involves a means by which direct action (might I add, in terms *of our nature*) is facilitated. Here of course figures such as Tolstoy come to mind as exemplars of those who have tried to face down the sensibility of power in order to achieve meaning in life, i.e. honest work within the community of human beings.

Behind these aspects of Wittgenstein's vision Edwards finds a critique of what he calls the idea and practice of 'rationality as representation', the hubris of thinking that human thought is somehow meant to, and in some ideal setting can, comprehend reality *sub specie aeternitatis*. For Edwards' Wittgenstein such a praxis lurks behind what I'll refer to as *scientism*, the idea that in modern times we have arrived at a method that can, in principle, provide *complete* intelligibility. It functions in the rendering of philosophy as the most general science of all, a 'physics of the abstract'.

In *Ethics without Philosophy* Edwards does a good job of showing the manner in which most of Wittgenstein's explicit philosophizing functions as a critique of the praxis of 'reality as representation'. Again, I think it is fairly common to recognize this destructive movement in Wittgenstein's thought. However, what is less well understood is that we can there find a correlative, positive movement. Edwards is useful in recognizing this movement as involving the implicit advocacy of a positive vision of human well being, of philosophy as a valid form of life.

I think Wittgenstein's friend Maurice Drury does a good job of locating most precisely the positive ethical dimension that Edwards finds in Wittgenstein's thought. Thus Drury, in his recollections of his friend, suggests that this demand functions as a demand in philosophers for depth rather than cleverness. So Wittgenstein, in speaking of Hume, is quoted by Drury as saying "...the distinction between a philosopher and a very clever man is a real one and of great importance" (Drury, 1984, p. 82). The clever thinker may have something clear to say, while the shallow thinker inevitably speaks without clarity. But the deep thinker, on Drury's gloss, speaks so as to make us see that there is something that cannot be said. For Drury, Wittgenstein's intent in philosophizing is to point us to this something. What is this something? Drury points towards an explanation here by quoting from Simone Weil:

"There is a reality outside the world, that is to say outside space and time, outside man's mental universe, outside any sphere whatsoever that is accessible to human faculty" (ibid., p. 83).

Weil goes on to say that we can each discover in ourselves a longing that corresponds to this something, "... a longing for an absolute good, a longing which is always there and never appeased by an object in this world" (op cit., p. 84).

Drury does well to recognize, along with Edwards, that this ethical dimension in Wittgenstein's thought is a religious dimension as well. If, with William James, we think of the religious impulse as characteristically one that insists on the limitations of the 'merely' natural world to truly satisfy our real needs, of the need to reside in something 'beyond' what can only be shown, surely Wittgenstein is a religious thinker (James, 1982).

This discussion of the positive elements in Wittgenstein is, once again, meant to respond, at least initially, to the idea of Wittgenstein's works as a possible source of ideas of liberal education. In what follows I will bring this vision to bear on my account of liberal education as philosophy. Already it is apparent that any such account, if it is to be truly Wittgensteinian in inspiration, must include a religious element in liberal education. In fact, on my own reading of Wittgenstein's message one must, in order to be the sort of liberal educator Wittgenstein was, see one's own life as an educator in profoundly religious terms.

This religious element will become apparent in my discussion of the three metaphors of liberal education as philosophy that I referred to earlier. The second, Socratic philosophy, builds, I shall argue, upon a more basic kind of philosophy, in which one is socialized into a human world. Building upon socialization, Socratic philosophy individualizes, calls for autonomy, self-creation and justification. Yet as a moment within the process of liberal education it is, I believe, radically incomplete. Competing answers to the question of how Socratic questioning is to be completed yield radically different visions of the nature and task of liberal education, as well as the nature and function of the university as a whole. In discussing these competing visions I shall return to further discussions of the positive dimension of Wittgenstein's thought. In that discussion I shall ask whether and how even the perspectives of Drury and Edwards might need, at least from the perspective of one liberal educator, operating from his own unique perspective, to be refined and redirected. In this way my discussion of Wittgenstein and liberal education will culminate in a discussion of what the *telos* of Socratic questioning might properly amount to in a context such as mine.

III

The start of the most recent round of debate over the crisis of liberal education can usefully be linked to the polemic of a number of writers on the political,

conservative right. Thus, it may be useful to begin discussion of our first metaphor with a somewhat detailed discussion of aspects of Wittgenstein's own
conservative bias. As J.C. Nyíri has so well argued, there is something inherently
conservative in Wittgenstein's point of view (Nyíri, 1982). It is clear, for example,
that the idea of tradition is fundamental to his thought. His discussions of following a rule and private language in *The Philosophical Investigations* and of
scepticism in *On Certainty* highlight the ways in which, for him, historically and
materially grounded practices, the doing of deeds, must always be fundamental
to those activities so often praised by philosophers, i.e. the search for rationality,
knowledge. That such a viewpoint has wide-ranging implication for our thinking
about education, in general, should be obvious.

So, for example: before we can even begin to talk of *liberal* education we
must refer to a process akin to what social scientists call socialization. Here
infants are initiated into the human community. In spite of what some Sartreans
and Cartesians might say, we are social animals. *Human* life, as opposed to a life
of imagined Hobbesian isolation, requires a shared context of disposition,
meaning and belief. And there is a sense in which learning or entering into such
a context already involves *something like* an initiation into a substantive metaphysics.

Take, for example, the concept 'tree'. Our way of picking out trees implies a
deeply grounded predilection for viewing the world as made up of something
like Aristotelian substances, entities that persist through time in spite of qualita-
tive and quantitative change. (I suppose that, theoretically, we could have come
to speak of what we now view as glances at one tree as glances at different trees,
or time slices of trees, or tree parts of 'TREE', but *our* learning rules out these
possibilities.)

Fate plays a role in our lives. Our material, institutional context provides con-
tours, parameters, for what can possibly and legitimately be thought. For
example, the use of terms like 'dollar' presupposes not only a common way of
following linguistic rules but an institutional context of banks, monetary reserve
boards, the worth of gold, etc. that make possible those responses. In learning to
speak, we learn to share a culture. To share a culture involves a shared understanding of meanings, proto-beliefs, etc. that, in turn, make sense in light of
material circumstances.

Many philosophers, less mindful of tradition than Wittgenstein, have tried to
call this socialization process into question with Enlightenment hope and
Cartesian inquiry as their inspiration. They have suggested that the sort of learning (or training, as I imagine Wittgenstein would put it) is somehow illegitimate,
akin to indoctrination. Surely this suggestion is misleading insofar as it has a
tendency to lump an inevitable preliminary to human life with the excesses of,
say, Huxley's *Brave New World* or Orwell's *1984*. There is nothing evil *per se*
about this process, nor even anything that requires a moderate amount of regret.
This is a given in human life, a given both logically and substantively. As such it
is a process deserving of respect and awe rather than scientistic ridicule.

Even granted this, another philosophical mistake is possible. Might it not be the case that even though this acting in common, this culture, comes first in time, it need not remain primary? Even though a project of *pure* rationality is impossible for the young human animal, might it not be legitimately sought by the more mature, already encultured philosophy? On this view liberal education becomes a process of radical questioning that follows an earlier stage of social-ization.

There is *something* to this idea, and I shall discuss it in the next section. But here, I want to indicate a false way of specifying what this radical questioning is about. If Wittgenstein's remarks in *On Certainty* are correct, even inquiry at these higher levels requires a shared context of action, meaning and belief. In my own thinking I have found useful (because more fully developed) resonances to these ideas in the work of one of Wittgenstein's philosophical heroes, St. Augustine. Elsewhere I have argued that these Augustinian ideas on teaching and learning mark a sensibility that is central to Wittgenstein's reaction against our modern age. (Neiman, 1984).

In a famous passage in his *Confessions* Augustine criticizes the Manichaean claim to rely on reason alone in inquiring into the existence and nature of God, of the soul, etc. He says:

"...for I began to realize that I believed countless things which I had never seen or which had taken place when I was not there to see – so many events in the history of the world, so many facts about places and towns which I had never seen, and so much that I believed on the word of friends or doctors or various other people. Unless we took these things on trust, we should accomplish absolutely nothing in this life. Most of all it came home to me how firm and unshakable was the faith which told me who my parents were, because I could never have known this unless I believed what I was told.... I thought that the Church was entirely honest in this and far less pre-tentious than the Manichees, who laughed at people who took things on faith, made rash promises, of scientific knowledge, and then put forward a whole system of preposterous inventions which they expected their followers to believe on trust because they could not be proved" (Augustine, 1961).

The claim here is not simply that we *begin* human life by being initiated into a tradition, a form of life. Rather the claim is more basic. All inquiry, at whatever age, requires a grounding not in indubitable truth but in a form of life, or a web of practices. This, Augustine suggests, is as true of becoming a scientist or doing science as it is of learning to multiply, to speak French or to properly worship God. All inquiry from beginning to end is codifiable in Augustine's terms as 'Faith seeking understanding'.

In a treatise entitled *De Utilitate Credendi* Augustine spells this out in more detail. There, he raises, as he does in the very beginning of *The Confessions*, questions of the kind raised by Plato in *The Meno*. In that dialogue, Plato sug-gests that in order to account for learning we must postulate the idea of knowl-edge as recollection. Augustine, without recourse to a hypothesis that presumes the soul's pre-existence, says instead that learning is possible only by trusting authority. And some reflections, inspired in part by Augustine and in part by Wittgenstein, seem to validate his point.

Consider some elementary cases of teaching and learning. A teacher is to teach and a student is to learn the pattern for first conjugation verbs in Latin; porto, portas, etc. In such a case teaching begins in faith. The student does not know Latin, so he does not know that the teacher is conjugating correctly. He *trusts* the teacher, even though he is not usually aware of this. Similar things can be said about students learning multiplication tables, or elementary physics or any such subject. Moreover, it does not seem to be an accident, a contingent fact, that such trust is involved, at least at the beginning of teaching. To see this, imagine a student who becomes conscious that he has trusted, and now asks for reasons; "How do I know", he asks the teacher, "that you are a legitimate authority?" Many legitimate answers are possible here. The teacher might tell the student to check the Latin book or ask the department chair. To do such things, of course, would be to check the veracity of one authority by referring to others. But isn't it possible for our hypothetical student to ask questions concerning *these* authorities? Unless *some* authority is accepted as if self-evidently legitimate, teaching cannot even begin. As Augustine puts it, we can learn only by being docile at first.

One ramification of this is that faith is necessary not only in the teaching of religion, but in any teaching at all. In saying that we must take many beliefs on trust if anything is to be accomplished in this life, Augustine is making a general point about teaching and learning as well as reason and faith. Unless I trust my teachers, learning is impossible. Unless I trust the authority of my senses, action is impossible. Unless I trust my faculty of self-evidence (i.e. that judges the truth of, say, *modus ponens*), reasoning itself is impossible. All human activity, including teaching and learning must begin in faith. This medieval sentiment is, I would argue, central to Wittgenstein's *modus operandi*.

I want also to suggest that we can read a work like Thomas Kuhn's *The Structure of Scientific Revolution* as a Wittgensteinian-Augustinean meditation on science as rational inquiry (Kuhn, 1962). Kuhn can be taken as showing that even the supposedly most rational of human endeavors, science, begins in the acceptance of paradigms and continues to rest upon platforms of faith that make research possible. If Kuhn is right, a large part of scientific education involves transmission of such paradigms from master to student. Progress involves not doing away with paradigms *per se*, but rather their instantiation, modification, development (and in extreme cases replacement by other paradigms.) Kuhn, like Wittgenstein, '*progresses*' by *returning* to the understanding of inquiry codified in Augustine's 'credo ut intelligum'.

In this context it seems possible to *imagine* that a Wittgensteinian would be sympathetic to the remarks of former U.S. Secretary of the Department of Education William Bennett, concerning liberal education. For Bennett a liberal education, at the very least ought, to "... transmit to students a common culture rooted in civilization's leading visions, its highest shared ideals and aspirations and its heritage (Bennett, 1984). Is one who is committed to the Wittgensteinian/ Augustinian ideas discussed in this section necessarily committed to Bennett's conservativa agenda? What are the limits, from a Wittgensteinian perspective, of Bennett's use of the socialization metaphor?

IV

One worry shared by critics of Bennett has to do with his use of evaluative terms like 'highest'. For some the very idea of one culture being better or truer than another is misguided. We can share something of the concern of these critics without sharing their implicit relativism.

At times writers like Bennett sound as if their education involves the transmission of a world picture to be accepted blindly, once and for all, without question. It is as if the common culture Bennett speaks of is a *seamless web*, a form of life into which one is blindly socialized, into which one is indoctrinated. It is important in this regard to distinguish between philosophy as a set of truths, perhaps taken as including a Cartesian or Baconian incorrigible foundation of knowledge and philosophy, and what Wittgenstein in *On Certainty* thinks of as a sort of 'vor-wissen', a context for living and a paradigm for further inquiry (Von Wright, 1972).

Initiation into such a paradigm is not necessarily indoctrination. Rational inquiry must start somewhere and, given our limitations it will inevitably start from where we are, ethnocentrically. Moreover, it can be argued, (from a Deweyan rather than a Wittgensteinian point of view but nonetheless validly) that perhaps our liberal democratic starting place is better than most (Neiman, 1991).

There are, I am suggesting, reasons (beyond the purely contingent fact that it is ours) for preferring an initiation into something like the common culture Bennett advocates as long as it is seen not as an incorrigible foundation but, rather, as a 'vor-wissen'. For the culture Bennett refers to, understood properly, presupposes a Socratic life of examination. First of all, this heritage consists of books and ideas (e.g. Plato and Nietzsche, Descartes and Montaigne, Marx and Jefferson, Aquinas and Tom Paine) that conflict in ways that inevitably stimulate critical thinking. The traditions involved here are often *literally* revolutionary ones (e.g., works of the American revolution, French revolution, etc.), or ones that at the very least insist on the possibility of ongoing self-correction (e.g., works derived from or written in homage to science, Nietzsche, works of the pragmatist tradition, etc.). Finally, it can be insisted that any sort of initiation into *this* culture will concentrate most centrally on the figure of Socrates, who presents us with a second specification of liberal education as philosophy, a specification complementary to and in some ways corrective of our first. Here, in liberal education as in Socratic philosophy, it is philosophy *as an activity* that is key. Here liberal education consists of a sort of radical questioning, an awareness of the contingency of our own 'vor-wissen' as contingent, as subject at least to some extent, to critique. In this section I want to discuss this second idea of liberal education as philosophy in more detail.

In his introduction to his *The Closing of the American Mind* Allan Bloom describes this *activity* of liberal education. For Bloom such an education concentrates on the question of human identity. A liberal education "... means precisely helping students to pose this question (Who am I?) to themselves, to become aware that the answer is neither obvious nor simply unavailable, and that there is no serious life in which this question is not a continuous concern" (Bloom, 1987, p. 21). For Bloom there is something *natural* about this question. Every student is, like Socrates, addressed by the delphic oracle, called to 'know thyself'. To be liberally educated is, then, for Bloom, to know the alternative answers to this question and to make thinking about them the centre of one's life. The polemic of Bloom's book is aimed in the direction of forces in our Western culture that he believes call this aspect of liberal education into question, that make its enactment, at even our best universities, either difficult or impossible.

Bloom's position is an improvement over Bennett's view because he seems, unlike Bennett, to be aware of the diversity of substance found in 'the great books and ideas' of the West. Bloom seems aware that liberal education can't simply endorse as true the ideas found in these great books, for the ideas often conflict or call their own authority into question. In Bloom's better moments he seems aware that it is possible to understand liberal education as a tradition of which Socratic discussion or conversation is paradigmatic. The natural result of socialisation into the West's pluralistic heritage is such radical questioning and in fact includes it. Liberal education, thus imagined, conserves and passes on not simply particular truth claims but that very open mindedness that characterizes the conversation of Socrates and Plato, Plato and Aristotle and on down through the tradition of philosophy. It is therefore, for Bloom, into this tradition of philosophizing that liberal education is meant to initiate students. What Bloom fears is the current conditions in the university that make that initiating practice less and less likely to occur.

What are these conditions? A large portion of Bloom's *Closing* is devoted to his argument that it is the introduction of a German philosophical ideology of value and truth relativism into our academic and general cultural milieu that is to blame. With Nietzsche, the Socratic endeavour of distinguishing appearance from reality, the true from the false, good from evil is called into question. According to Bloom it is through the thought of Nietzsche, by way of 'descendants' such as Freud, Weber and Heidegger that this value relativism conquered academia. In the context of such relativism, the Socratic inquiry into Truth, Beauty, or Goodness etc. makes no sense. Much of the last part of Bloom's book is devoted to attacking what he imagines to be a proto – Nietzschean class in the academy, a class that supposedly equates knowledge with power and, thus, reduces education to left-wing political indoctrination.

I have already suggested how Wittgenstein's philosophy might be enlisted in at least one conservative cause. Here I want to mention one way that someone sympathetic to Bloom might see Wittgenstein as a villain of the left. I have in mind here an aspect of Wittgenstein's thought that commentators have referred to as his anthropomorphism, his anti-realism. For many who, like Bloom, espouse a Socratic liberal education, it is Wittgenstein as much as Nietzsche who functions as a villain. Yet it is easy enough to distance Wittgenstein's views here from the proto-Nietzscheans attacked by Bloom. Wittgenstein, like Kuhn, is not trying to show us that there is no knowledge, no rationality, etc. Instead, he wants us to understand what knowledge and rational inquiry amount to. Just as Wittgenstein is neither a Cartesian nor Behaviourist in the philosophy of mind, nor is he a foundationalist/metaphysician, nihilist/sceptic, or realist/anti-realist in epistemology. (Furthermore *all* of these dichotomies follow from a modernist, Cartesian/Enlightenment philosophical agenda which Wittgenstein repudiates.) When a Foucault or Derrida speak of knowledge as power, or meaning as indeterminate, they risk being taken as the sort of metaphysicians they detest, bringing us new quasi-scientific theories about meaning or knowledge. They appear, in other words, to resort to the 'rationality as representation' mode they pretend to reject. Bloom may be right that such writers, taken in this way, have done some harm. But he is surely wrong that such thinking is solely responsible for the current ills of the university.

Stanley Aronowitz offers an equally plausible explanation of the crisis. Aronowitz, in a paper entitled *The New Conservative Discourse* points out that thinkers on the left have tended to diagnose and object to the same moral chaos and decay perceived by Bloom and Bennett (Aronowitz, 1989). According to Aronowitz, the programmes Bloom attacks, such as gender and ethnic studies, etc. are responses to, rather than causes of, that chaos and decay. The true enemy, the cause of the professionalism, specialization and vocationalism that makes liberal Socratic education impossible or difficult in today's academy is, according to Aronowitz (in the words of Nancy Warehime), "... the ideological hegemony of technology, the overwhelming drive to dominate all of nature including humans – through the application of scientific techniques". According to Warehime's gloss of Aronowitz it is "... this enemy, particularly when united with postindustrial capitalism and a form of nationalism that Bloom's philosophy appears to support, that obstructs the search for and dedication to wisdom in higher education" (Warehime, 1993, p. 62).

I think Wittgenstein, whom I imagine could be described as at least a cultural conservative, would, in principle, appreciate *this* sort of explanation. Certainly it fits well into his zealous anti-scientism which I described in part II. That Wittgenstein's own mode of philosophizing, that his own practice as an educator, was Socratic in mode, involved radical questioning of some ingrained practices (e.g. academic philosophy and some aspects of culture including scientism) is certain. Thus from a Wittgensteinian perspective there is something to Bloom's idea of liberal education if it is linked to the sort of philosophical conversation initiated by Socrates, just as there is something to Bennett's idea of liberal education as transmission of substantive paradigms understood as vehicles of continuing inquiry. But I have come to believe that neither Bloom nor Bennett alone, nor the two taken together, offer us a wide enough view of liberal education as it stands, at its best, before us. Thus, to conclude our discussion we need to begin, at least, to examine yet a third idea of liberal education as philosophy, and see how it might relate to the other two.

V

Here we can start with John Henry Newman's idea of philosophy as the culmination of higher learning. In his famous *The Idea of the University* Newman

expresses his concern for the fragmentation of his times as it expressed itself in
the confusion and fragmentation of studies in the university (Newman, 1982).
He believed knowledge was one, all of a piece, connected. Yet the various disciplines of the university seemed to him to present, when taken together, only a
chaotic, unrelated (or even inconsistent) mass. In response to this state of affairs,
Newman offered a science or discipline that he called philosophy.

To get a better sense of what Newman is worried about we can adopt one of
his own examples. Take, for instance, the study of a human being. How can we
reconcile what, for instance, Biology and Theology say about the person?
Sociology and Chemistry? How can value and freedom exist in a world of
natural selection or quarks? Where does the social exist in a world of energy
transfers? Newman responds by speaking about the abstract, limiting character
of each of these perspectives, and the confusion the mind initially faces in trying
to get a vision of the whole. What is needed in light of all of this is something of
a science of sciences, a means to reconciling the partial looks provided by lesser
methodologies. This science Newman calls philosophy:

> "... the comprehension of the bearings of one science on another, and the use of each to each, and
> the location and limitations and adjustment and due appreciation of them all, one with another,
> thus belongs, I conceive, to a sort of science of sciences, which is my conception of what is meant
> by philosophy, in the true sense of the word..." (Newman, 1982, p. 38).

Corresponding to this science is a habit of mind Newman calls philosophical.
This is a habit "... of order and system, a habit of referring every accession of
knowledge to what we already know, of adjusting the one with the other" (ibid.,
p. 38). The job of liberal education, according to Newman, is to a large extent,
that of stimulating the development of this habit of mind in students. According
to Newman, it is crucial that a university be set up so as to make this job possible. Without this moment in liberal education the process yields only confusion
rather than integration, only a series of seemingly incoherent pieces of knowledge rather than what Newman might call wisdom.

How does Newman's idea of liberal education as philosophy relate to our
earlier discussions? In this regard, first of all, we can think of Newman's philosophy as a sort of culmination of a process that begins with Bennett's socialization and Bloom's Socratic questioning. Newman's remarks in this context return
us to earlier remarks, from section II, concerning the *telos* of this Socratic questioning, and liberal education as a whole. They suggest that the liberal educator,
most of all, seeks a view of how things are in the most inclusive sense possible.

But what can this have to do with Wittgenstein? Doesn't *this* vision of the
liberal educator imply adherence to the 'rationality as representation' mode discussed earlier? In this context I can only conclude with some brief remarks indicating why I think that it need *not* do so. In fact I will suggest that Newman's
philosophy is plausibly thought of as *essential* to Wittgenstein's vision.

In *Ethics Without Philosophy* Edwards suggests that there are two possible
'philosophical' positions left for the sincere and consistent Wittgensteinian. One
is Pragmatism, the other (to use my own terminology) is Poetic Mysticism.
Pragmatism replaces the search for 'rationality as representation' with a search

for instrumental solutions to various problems organisms like us face at one particular time or another. Poetic Mysticism, perhaps more consistent with the Wittgensteinian religious ethos than Pragmatism, sees the end result of philosophizing as a kind of Heideggerian 'breakthrough' to poetic inspiration. One can easily imagine telic visions of liberal education based on either of these positions. But, there is, I want to suggest, a third alternative.

The alternative I have in mind is a perennial one, but it has recently been highlighted by the work of Alasdair MacIntyre. For convenience, this alternative might be labelled Classical-Medieval Philosophy. If MacIntyre is right, the kinds of errors Wittgenstein (as well as Heidegger) claimed to find within the entire Western tradition of philosophy are actually avoided in the works of Plato and Aristotle, Augustine and Aquinas. While these pre-Cartesian philosophers resorted to a study we can refer to as metaphysics, this metaphysics avoids the 'rationality as representation' mode. They found a way to theorize philosophically without thinking of the mind as mirror or person as abstracted knower (MacIntyre 1990a, 1990b; Caputo, 1982). Moreover, over forty years ago Josef Pieper, in his masterful *Leisure: The Basis of Culture* (Pieper, 1952) made use of the idea of such a tradition to arrive at a profoundly contemplative ideal of liberal education.

What does Pieper's model of liberal education offer us that is not found in Pragmatism or Poetic Mysticism? The problem with *those* ideals is that they fail to properly honour Newman's imperative. Newman is right in noting that students (and their teachers) inevitably philosophise; they make use of what can only be seen as extra-scientific, i.e. metaphysical remarks, in order to imagine comprehensive visions of the whole. But without the explicit and disciplined reflection upon the philosophical or metaphysical ideas governing their inquiries, students of Pragmatist and Heideggerian liberal educators may be prone to *bad* philosophy. In the case of the Pragmatist, this often amounts to crude nominalism, materialism, and Darwinianism. In the case of the Heideggerian, the danger most often is espousal of some sort of Nietzschean relativism or nihilism (as Bloom points out this, in the American context, often arises as 'cheerful nihilism'). One value of Pieper's contemplative ideal is that it remains true to so much of the Wittgensteinian ethos while avoiding these dangers. It manages to honour the need for metaphysics without making it into an idol. As in Pieper's Thomism, such a metaphysics succeeds in providing a sense of 'what is' by, primarily, ruling out what is not (Pieper, 1957).[1]

In the recent work of MacIntyre Classical-Medieval Philosophy is meant to help us reconstruct ideas such as 'the *telos* of human beings', 'objectivity', 'the human person', and (even) 'the soul' while avoiding *both* 'rationality as representation' *and* the incipient relativism-nihilism of Pragmatic and Heideggerian thought (MacIntyre, 1990b). In terms of 'our' mission as Wittgensteinian liberal educators nothing is more important, in the midst of this crisis of the humanities, than avoiding *these* dangers, than finding some middle ground between them.

Today we find ourselves immersed in what Pieper so well characterized as a world of 'total work'. The university, rather than functioning as a place of contemplation (in contrast to the world around it), today operates more and more as yet another producer of goods. Given our current understanding of 'inquiry' in the humanities, the fact that universities produce "knowledge", rather than (say) chairs, or chemicals or cars makes little difference. Liberal education, again in the words of Pieper, is 'a process between living persons, rather than a report on the results of research' (Pieper, 1957, p. 23).

What would a Core Course inspired by Pieper's, by MacIntyre's telic vision, look like? How exactly would it differ from one constructed by a Wittgenstein-inspired Pragmatist or Poet? How would each work not only as theory but as *praxis* in real contexts? (Here surely Wittgenstein agreed with those Pragmatists, like James, who insisted that such testing in *practice* is essential in evaluating philosophical visions.) These remarks have been meant to lay the ground work for more explicit experimentation in this regard by Wittgensteinian-oriented liberal educators. They aim to provide a rationale for those who would move liberal education away from its current preoccupation with productiveness, and toward a more contemplative idea.

Any suggestion that Wittgenstein's sensibility is in important respects Classical-Medieval will require a good deal of support. First of all, it must be shown that work that portrays Plato or Aristotle, Augustine or Aquinas, etc. as quasi-Cartesians, as writers in the 'rationality as representation' mode are radically misguided. Secondly, more explicit comparison between Wittgenstein and medieval thinkers, of the sort I presented in section III, will be necessary. In this paper I mean to provide a rationale for such ongoing work, along with work by pragmatic and poetic Wittgensteinians, to proceed.[2]

In such enterprises we may find ourselves not only in opposition to cultural practices and attitudes outside the academy, but perhaps even the major imperatives of the university as it now operates in a world devoted more and more to production, to progress, to the happiness of our stomachs and brains, rather than our minds and souls. Surely in this regard Wittgenstein's own counter-hegemonic practice within the university is not only valuable but awe-inspiring.[3]

NOTES

[1] Pieper's suggestion here can be phrased as follows: Aquinas' work on analogy, understood as a doctrine about Being and predication, allows us to speak with care and humility about the subject matter of metaphysics, i.e. God and the soul. The suggestion, which of course must be substantiated, is that Wittgenstein was right to see the need to avoid "Transcendental Twaddle" but wrong to see the only alternatives to irresponsible philosophy as poetry or silence. For an example of one of the best recent works on the Thomistic doctrine in this regard see Burrell, 1986.

[2] Examples of such work already done include recent books by distinguished analytic philosophers John McDowell and Hilary Putnam. Both of these philosophers suggest explicit parallels between Aristotle's and Wittgenstein's views of mind and world (see McDowell, 1994, Putnam, 1994). David Braine, in his compelling *The Human Person: Animal and Spirit*, expands on this sort of comparison by explicitly including Aquinas (Braine, 1993). See also Anscombe and Geach, 1961 as well as Kenny, 1980 for earlier attempts to compare Aquinas and Wittgenstein in related ways. My own

work in this regard has concentrated, as indicated earlier, on comparing Wittgenstein and Augustine on issues of faith and reason. Besides Neiman, 1984 see Neiman 1982.

[3] I wish to thank David Burrell for his comments on an earlier draft of this paper.

The Unjustifiability of Education

EDWIN P. BRANDON

The University of the West Indies, Barbados

I

It is a characteristic Wittgensteinian thought that justifications or explanations pretty quickly come to an end; they give out some way before they have achieved the typical philosopher's goal of demonstrating a correspondence with immutable external reality of some sort or other. So, for instance, Wittgenstein himself remarked of mathematical calculations: "The danger here, I believe, is one of giving a justification of our procedure where there is no such thing as a justification and we ought simply to have said: *that's how we do it*" (RFM, II, # 74). Urging us not to continue these necessarily fruitless efforts, the Wittgensteinian tells us to pay exclusive attention to the actual place in our kind of life of whatever it was we wanted explaining or justifying. Given what we are like and what the world we live in is like, isn't that enough? That is how we do it, what more can you want? Nevertheless, as Pears remarks, it can produce "a sort of intellectual vertigo" (1971, p. 134) to be told that the rules we follow for arithmetic are as ungrounded as dogs' barking (cf. Malcolm's remark quoted by the editors).

There is in any case an undecided question of scope here (cf. P. Smith, 1993). In our ordinary lives, we do explain and justify some things to each other; and that is presumably to be left undisturbed by philosophical reflection. At some rather indeterminate point, our quotidian justifications try for too much, and the philosopher in us (cf. Kenny, 1975, p. 13) has been trapped by the snares of ordinary language philosophically misunderstood. We can say why a television broadcast of a speech should be believed, but we cannot say why one must adjust beliefs by reference to experience of the world. We can say why a book borrowed from the library should be returned; but we must draw the line at trying to say why one should be moral.

When we are told that we have illegitimately extended everyday activities to an impossibly wider issue, we are not often shown precisely where we have gone off the rails. Commentators sometimes suggest a comparatively banal explication: thus Luckhardt (1980) fills in the argument for the meaninglessness of ethical relativism by saying that the original home of morally evaluative language is the appraisal of behaviour, traits, motives and so on; this appraisal is not arbitrary but embodies moral standards; but the standards cannot be appraised in their turn. Why appraisal or moral justification should not be a motley of somewhat different activities – language games as diverse as Wittgenstein thought games themselves (but see Suits, 1978) – among which there would be

93

Studies in Philosophy and Education **14**: 217–227, 1995.
© 1995 *Kluwer Academic Publishers. Printed in the Netherlands.*

provision for the rational evaluation of the standards employed in everyday comparatively unreflective moralizing, is a question Luckhardt fails to answer. But at least his story shows how the logical structure of our everyday starting point may constrain possible answers to our philosophical worries.

In other cases the account offered remains at the level of metaphor: frameworks and what lies inside them, or rivers and river-beds. The point of this paper is not primarily to argue that these metaphors are misleading, at least in the particular case of the justifiability of education which will be in focus, but rather to motivate the choice of a different style of philosophizing. When one believes, as Wittgenstein did at least in his earlier work, that many important insights cannot be enunciated, but only 'shown', it is natural merely to gesture at the limits of our capacities for explanation or justification. For those of us less taken with Zen riddles, one of the tasks of philosophy is to make clear and distinct the structures of our thinking, or of the world as thought about, in the hope that we can spell out the possibilities and impossibilities they leave us with.

It may be that the philosophy of education ought to grapple with the metaphysical issues that the Wittgensteinian is warning us to avoid (cf. Allen, 1989, and other of his writings). But, whether or not that is so, it usually starts, at least, at a less ambitious level, with questions related to the life of children in schools. A prime candidate is one Marshall used for a book title: *Why go to School?* (1988a). I shall try to show that here the Wittgensteinian suggestion, while its content might be correct, fails to reveal the instructive detail of the case. We can say, we like to think, why a pupil should learn elementary algebra in mathematics or read *Macbeth* as part of an English literature course;[1] but we cannot try to say why he or she should get an education.

Before embarking on the main argument, it may be useful to forestall a misunderstanding and to place my project more fully in a Wittgensteinian context. A common reaction of trainee teachers, when first presented with the question of justifying education, is to acknowledge that they had never thought of the matter. It is a taken-for-granted of their lives, and of course of many other people's. If the question is seen as deserving an answer, it is then usually answered in what has traditionally been called 'extrinsic' terms: education, or more precisely educational certification, gives people access to better paying jobs, or a middle-class, 'white collar' life-style. Without getting embroiled in the sociological work in this area, we can admit that these are important factors, perhaps especially so for typical teachers. But clearly, this is not the sort of justification being sought. What we are looking for is an account of why anyone should seek an education, whether or not it happens to give them greater power or riches. The story of the ring of Gyges forces Plato's Socrates to face the full difficulty of the question "Why be just?" In a similar way, we might ask our trainees why a prince of the blood, or the daughter of a drug baron, or a slum child destined to cycles of unemployment and deprivation should still prefer to be educated rather than uneducated people.

So much for the kind of issue at stake. Wittgenstein himself seems not to have dealt with this kind of question. Indeed a general problem for his interpreters in education is the fact that his own work, whatever its eschewal of general answers, remained focused on the highly general problems other philosophers had marked out for their disputations. Again, we have very little, and that as always aphoristic and disdaining explicitness, on philosophical aspects of ethics. Philosophy of education is usually regarded as one of the applied branches of the subject, applied in this case to topics of some specialisation or particularity. This intermediate level of generality, to use our own metaphor, seems to me to preclude the straightforward extrapolation of Wittgensteinian ideas from his context of their use to that of the philosopher of education's. Thus I do not agree with our editors that "the notion of 'form of life' is ... pre-eminently the pedagogical notion", unless, at least, they concede that their notion of pedagogy applies as much to the street children of Rio as to the inmates of Eton or Timber Top. It does not seem helpful to me to run together questions that relate to the universal upbringing of members of our species with questions that concern very specific choices among ways of bringing up people. It is no good telling a teacher who wants to know whether he can properly insist that his pupils try to learn elementary algebra that humans must provide something somehow to their young, else they would not survive.

Of course, as the last but one paragraph suggests, people who read books or become teachers do concern themselves that their children go to school and do well at it. Its justification hardly arises, unlike whether to send a child to Saturday morning ballet or swimming lessons. One may choose among schools, but for most it is unthinkable that children do not go to school. Even if people think it and act on the thought, they will still endeavour to educate their children; they do it at home in the hope of doing a better job than the schools can achieve. It might appear that here we have a 'form of life' of sufficient extent; but to suppose so would be to suppose that the world of people who read simply is the world. Historians of medieval Europe often warn us not to make this mistake; my point is merely that it is still a mistake, and one that must not be tolerated in philosophy of education for practising teachers.

II

Philosophy has been embarrassed by certain values. Philosophers have not in general had problems with the avoidance of pain, with health, or – if they think of them – with wealth or power. These are things that everyone wants – "a perpetual and restless desire of Power after power" (Hobbes, 1929, p. 75). Moral philosophers have centrally focused their energies on truth-telling, justice, duties and obligations. Not everyone wants these, but at least it is generally agreed that these things make up a morally praiseworthy life; few have seriously argued for the virtues of a Thrasymachus, at least within the pages of *Mind*. The values I am alluding to are distinct from this second set in being morally neutral – a man is not vicious if he fails to subscribe to them – but they are certainly not socially neutral and the philosophical consensus is unanimously in favour of them.

It will hardly be a surprise to learn that education, or the state of being educated, is one such value. The embarrassment I have alluded to arises from the
appalling arguments that have been offered on those rare occasions when a
philosopher has ventured to justify the taken-for-granted positive consensus.
Mill told us it was better to be Socrates unsatisfied, because competent judges
judge so; and how do we know a competent judge? Because he judges it is better
to be Socrates unsatisfied. Peters has struggled at length with our question (for
instance in his 1973b), and it might still be worth devoting some attention to his
work at this late date – it remains one of the few attempts in the philosophy of
education to answer Marshall's question. But one part of Peters' answer amounts
to little more than supposing that if asking a question presupposes a genuine
desire for getting its answer by rational means this can be taken to be a commitment to rational means of answering any and every question that might occur to
you. It is not, however, that easy to get from at least one to all (cf. my detailed
analysis, 1982c, of a similar argument offered by Finnis, 1977).

As noted above, we do in everyday life offer successful justifications. I am
thirsty; I have cold water and a cold beer in the fridge. Can I not justify choosing
the water? Perhaps by reference to comparative contributions to my health.
Could I not justify the beer, by reference to taste, perhaps? These are deliberately unimpressive examples; they are somewhat less involved than Wittgenstein's own engineering example of an unexceptionable justification – justifying the size and shape of a bridge by performing loading tests on its materials
(PI, I, # 267). But they allow us to see the structure of one standard model of
justification.

In this standard model, the context for a question of justifying X involves a
person faced with a choice of X or not-X, where the latter might be made up of
several definite alternatives or be left unspecified. A successful justification can
be viewed as an argument to show that overall X is preferable to not-X for that
person. (I am ignoring as secondary or parasitic the imperialistic cases, common
enough in educational thought, where we regard a justification of X for A as
successful when we have shown that X is preferable for some other person.)

Once we note explicitly that this sort of justification involves justifying something for a particular person, it is clear that a question of identity or self-
identification or self-definition is presupposed. Any normal argument for John,
say, to prefer X to Y will assume that John with X is identical with John with Y:
the same person in different circumstances but with the same values, wants, and
preferences. Suppose in choosing between a car and a motor-bike, we are given
that John wants to be able to transport bulky shopping purchases; then it would
seem that there is a reason for him to buy a car. That consideration only works if
we can assume that John with a bike will still want to transport bulky purchases;
if he didn't its force would be annulled. Or rather, if John with a car would still
have that want and John without wouldn't, it cannot be used to make the choice;
the prior decision is whether John wants to keep that want or not. To model my
choice between beer and water we assume that it is the same me faced with the
alternatives, and that it will be the same me afterwards.

Similarly in another major type of justification – an appeal to moral consider-ations – we assume identity of person between the good and the bad action. We assume that moral considerations continue to weigh with the person, whichever way he chooses. The horror of the psychopath is that for him or her moral con-siderations simply don't count; his or her behaviour is as indifferent as Mother Nature's. One danger of persistent vice is that it erases the force of these consid-erations; following Aristotle on becoming good or bad by performing good or bad actions, we should not simply assume that what works for an individual choice works for a long series of such choices. But we do assume that moral considerations cannot be totally erased; they may not be noticed but when pointed out they may, and should, regain their force – hardened criminals can still be brought to a just realization of their guilt. We should note that we assume these things; but they are actually empirical claims of a somewhat involved sort. One expression of the kind of assumption I am talking about can be found in this remark by Sutton on Kant's views: "in *Religion within the Bounds of Reason Alone* life can be a vicious spiral of increasing degeneration, but a man can never completely shake off the feeling of a duty to rehabilitate himself" (1974, p. 27).

The point I am focusing on is that everyday justification assumes identity of persons, or what might be better called 'self-concepts', had not the social psy-chologists got there first. The linguistic quibble arises because it would be good to avoid a term that carries the usual connotations of 'personal identity' for philosophers – continuities of bare memory such as united the cockroach and the human in Kafka's famous story, and which Locke used in his account of per-sonal identify, or sheer spatio-temporal continuity of body such as suits recent philosophers inspired by Aristotle; in neither case attending to the detail of our being-in-the-world that matters to us (cf. Hollis, 1977, ch. 5). However, one con-tributor to the current philosophical debate about personal identity gave in his earliest paper (Parfit, 1971) an account of being a person which stressed an element of choice with respect to one's boundaries, a choice to be based on the more substantive elements of one's make-up: character traits, memories, inten-tions, hopes, etc. For my purposes, he may be seen as shifting the question from "Would that still be me?" to "Would I want to count that as my survival?" By way of acknowledgement, I shall speak here of a 'parfitson' when I wish to con-trast a meatier, more substantive identity of character with the bare bones of Lockean or Aristotelian analyses, or to focus on the idea of a self-defining person.[2]

In the standard models of justification, the identity of person involved is much more than minimal personal identity, or Parfit's survival. What matters in these assumptions are the circumstances, preferences, wants, interests, etc., upon which a parfitson would normally base decisions about whether some possible person should count as him or her. As we noted, it matters that John would still want to transport bulky goods, whether he buys a car or a bike, not just that he preserves the same body or consciousness. We might note here also that Peters' example of ordinary justification (choosing between business or medicine, 1973b, p. 252) is itself somewhat problematic, at least to the extent that these careers are likely to lead to comparatively profound changes in a parfitson's outlook and values.

My suggestion is that one source of the awkwardness of the kinds of values I have focused on is that they cannot be fitted into the standard model since they are precisely matters which give a parfitson reason to declare himself different. When education results in a transformation of the ways things are conceived, when it opens up ranges of experience "beyond the ken of the uneducated" (Peters, 1973b, p. 248), educated John is not the same parfitson as uneducated John; going to college rather than getting a job might not be the same sort of choice as buying a Ford rather than a Harley Davidson. To the extent that this is so, the justification of education would therefore involve giving a reason for preferring to be this sort of person rather than that. And this changes the game; the standard moves cannot find a toe-hold here.

But since the standard models are standard, we commonly find attempts to skirt the problem either by offering reasons everyone is supposed to accept (thus assimilating education to one of the comparatively unproblematic values like health or power I mentioned at the beginning) or by assimilating it to a moral virtue, as Peters seems to have done. In the first kind of case (e.g., knowledge is power; education as self-liberation à la Freire) all persons, so a fortiori all parfitsons, want these goods, so the substantive change of parfitson involved in becoming educated would not matter. But unfortunately, as Anderson (1962) for one clearly stressed, education in Peters' distinctive sense is certainly not something everyone wants, so this sort of argument goes off the rails somewhere. If we adopt the second sort of solution, we can risk our faith in the assumption of identity in moral judgement, but only by grossly distorting our perception of the kind of value this education has.

The two kinds of response come together in Peters' argument. In briefly characterizing his paper, Peters says "various considerations are discussed that support the claim that the possession and pursuit of knowledge make life less boring, and a rationale is finally attempted for Socrates' contention that the unexamined life is not worth living" (1973a, p. 7). He also notes that his approach is "more from the standpoint of ethics". This may suggest that Peters would not accept my claim that education is a morally neutral value, for the flavour of some of his discussion is certainly of the morally praiseworthy educated man[3] and his brutish uneducated counterpart who will think of a glass of wine as simply a way of satisfying thirst, who will "regard a woman as a necessary object for satisfying his lust; ... [and] be indifferent to her idiosyncrasies and point of view as a person" (1973b, p. 263). I think it is true that while Peters recognizes other values and their possible greater importance he does nonetheless regard the uneducated as evaluatively deficient, if one may so phrase it, if not morally deficient. The beliefs and cognitive procedures of ordinary people, not now conceived as brutish but simply unreflective, are "ultimately... inappropriate to the demand that they are meant to serve" (1973b, p. 255).

But here we find once again that indulgence in the naturalistic fallacy that is pervasive in educational thought and which Peters explicitly says he is avoiding:

while ordinary human existence bears witness to "the demands of reason" to a certain extent, all that an appeal to "man as a rational animal" can extract is precisely that amount of reasoning and reflecting, not a jot more. But the conclusion Peters wants is that to say "that men ought to rely more on their reason, that they ought to be more concerned with first-hand justification, is to claim that they are systematically falling down on a job on which they are already engaged" (1973b, p. 255). Either Peters is appealing to the human facts, in which case he cannot extract more reflection than we actually find, or he is invoking an evaluatively coloured picture of human life, in which case he begs the question at issue – as Kleinig for one claims, "What Peters speaks of baldly as 'human life' trades on an implicitly normative understanding of 'human'. It is a life in which the activities for which reason is a prerequisite are held to be not simply necessary, but valuable" (Kleinig, 1982, p. 87).

To put it in terms of one of Peters' examples, if an ordinary person who enjoys a glass of wine, but without the sophistication of an educated taste, counts as evaluatively deficient, Peters surely owes us a reason for agreeing with him; whereas if such a person passes the evaluative test, what has become of the educatedness Peters is trying to justify? An educated palate may be a nice thing to have, but to lack one does not of itself make one deficient – in that sense it is morally neutral. There is swinish swilling at the trough; there is ordinary unsophisticated enjoyment of food; and there is the special approach of the gourmet. Peters, like Mill before him, oversimplifies his problem by ignoring the middle ground. At times, the force of Peters' argument comes close to a case for preferring the middle ground to pre-human savagery (when he says that "civilization begins when conventions develop which protect others from the starkness of such 'natural' behaviour" (1973b, p. 248)) but all human societies display such conventions – "People who live in a state of complete nudity are not unaware of what we call modesty: they define it differently" (Lévi-Strauss, 1976, p. 374) – and Peters has already alerted us to the distinctive sense of 'education', much narrower than socialization, which is his target.

We can see the traces of the same fallacy if we note the irrelevance of Marshall's appeal from Wittgensteinian thoughts about rule-governed social life (similar to those offered by the editors) to any programme for the philosophy of education he might wish to advocate (1988, p. 93 et seq.). The rules embodied in our social life at its most basic level (our language, say) may be malleable and derive their power from shared practices rather than authoritarian *diktat*, but the fact that we speak a common language does not make the police or the military disappear. If education takes place in a community, it does; all of it, the repressive, 'contradictory' schooling Marshall deplores just as much as the liberating dialogue he endorses. Certainly Wittgenstein's rules are not restricted to the type of rules issued to pupils and their parents by traditional schools; one might enlighten someone who thought that the latter were the only conceivable kind of rule; but traditional repressive unimaginative schooling is just as much part of a form of life, a social interaction (*pace* Dewey, 1966), as any other. There is nothing in the Wittgensteinian insight to tell us that what goes for learning your mother tongue (cf. Marshall, 1983) should be extended to what goes on in school.

To return to our diagnosis of the problem with justifying education, let me conclude this section with an acknowledgement of work which has uncovered and explicitly presented a different problem for the standard models of justification. Schelling and Elster have recently focused attention on a range of cases in which we might be tempted to think of two (or more) characters competing for present command of a person: Odysseus having himself tied to the mast to frustrate what he would soon want on hearing the sirens' song. As Schelling puts it, "people behave sometimes as if they had two selves, one who wants clean lungs and long life and another who adores tobacco.... The two are in continual contest for control" (1984, p. 58). After reviewing a range of cases, in some of which we tend to find a basis for preferring one of the competing characters, Schelling claims that for other cases we must simply take sides – there is no rational basis for preferring one to the others. With the kind of more settled but equally diverse characters we have unearthed in trying to justify becoming educated, I suspect the situation is the same. At least, Elster has written, concerning this possibility, "I would say that the mark of a successful education is that the child comes to see that no such justification is possible, but that the parents nevertheless had to make some (unjustified) choice" (1979, p. 47).

III

The argument has been that we cannot use the standard models of justification in the case of education because education is a matter of changing one of the parameters whose stability is taken for granted by these models. This, if correct, seems somewhat more illuminating than simply being told that here justification breaks down and all we have is initiation into a form of life.

Appeal to our form of life may be persuasive when that form of life is universally shared, or even better when an alternative is, for all practical purposes, inconceivable. But of course, the challenge Marshall uses as his title is not pitched at such an exalted (or such a basic) level. Our societies offer a whole range of possible futures for growing parfitsons. The fact that they are growing up as humans and not mosquitoes or bats does not provide enough constraints to answer the teenager who genuinely wants to know why he or she should keep going to school. The career of a Homeric warrior or a Shinto priest may not be practically accessible for a pupil in Barbados in 1993, but still an amazing variety of options do remain open. The different ways of life bring with them changes sufficient for a parfitson to deny trans-way of life identity. In such circumstances, it is clear that simply being told to do your way of life's thing is to be told nothing. By the earlier argument, we cannot try to impute a moral flavour to the question; and simple observation tells us that we cannot assume that everyone does want to be educated.

Providing greater opportunity to make what (the dominant group in) the society reckons a success of your life may not seem sufficiently intrinsic a reason for pursuing education, or simply for staying on and 'doing well' at school; but can we honestly find a better reason to offer the disenchanted young? Nor should we be surprised if they don't bother when the resulting opportunity remains pretty minimal.

Before concluding, it might be worth stressing that the failure of uniqueness applies not only, as is patently obvious, to the normal results of schooling but also to whatever people are talking about under the heading of 'moral education'. A recent article by Kazepides (1991a) supports my earlier contention that appeal to our form of life needs uniqueness, since he draws a parallel between the 'river-bed' propositions Wittgenstein characterised in *On Certainty* and some of our moral beliefs. He claims that "the fundamental principles of morality occupy a position akin to the river-bed propositions with regard to our moral development" (p. 267) and goes on to make the startling claim that "no-one ever chooses his or her own moral code" (p. 268). He borrows from Wittgenstein a contrast between 'our' attitudes to a mediocre tennis player and to someone who behaves like a beast. 'We' are not inclined to say, "oh well, it's OK to be a beast". The problem is that while it is only in the odd asylum that we will find people who do not believe the earth existed before their birth, we find people behaving in an atrocious fashion every day, and we find other people condoning them. It is perhaps high time to complain about the insularity of the professional philosopher. At least Plato brought Thrasymachus on stage. His well-educated, reasonably decent intellectual descendants writing from such a position to others within it have usually taken its values for granted (the 'naturalness' of the distinctly unnatural[4]) and have not seen any need to argue in their favour – so much for the unexamined life![5]

I have been stressing the obvious diversity of the ways of life open to our young. Some, but not all of them, involve the kind of cognitive transformation that Peters focused on in his early accounts of education. All I have needed for the argument is the fact of a transformation profound enough for a parfitson to deny 'identity'. But it is perhaps worth digging a little deeper into the cognitive transformation account of education to reveal a further clash with the world in which we live. Gellner, who has insisted on the diversity already mentioned, has also noted that the cognitive perspective demanded by the modern world undercuts its own social existence: it denies special status to anything, but yet a group of people cannot live without investing something with special status. "We must needs live in and with the help of *some* culture" (1989, p. 207). Part of the trick, he suggests, is not to take the culture too seriously. The conjectural, critical cognitive stance he envisages here demands coherence and consistency; its cognitive ethic requires commitment to track reliability. Such is not the typical product of school systems that mandate religious instruction, that glorify national achievements and call it history, or that avoid political or social discussions.

If we look, then, beyond what is conventionally regarded as educational success to seek an embodiment of the cognitive ideals ostensibly espoused by many educators, what we find is something profoundly alienated, *déraciné*. If we do not move beyond the conventional, should we continue to try to tie the acquisition of socially useful certification with truth, beauty, and goodness? Are these tattered ideals necessary for the all-but universal misrecognition of its activity that Bourdieu attributes to the educational system?

IV

We have got some way from Wittgenstein on arithmetic. The thrust of the preceding reflections is to recommend educators to become more aware of the distinctive, partisan nature of education as it is commonly explicated. Just as no political party ever really gets unanimous support, so education – as commonly conceived – will not get everyone's commitment. I have tried to show in some detail why the case of education is different from less ambitious examples of attempted justification. It is unjustifiable in terms of the two main models of justification. One challenge is whether there is some other kind of justification that can get a grip on the issue. The failure of the standard models allows us also to see why attempts to justify education tend to move to some features shared by educated and uneducated John, and thus to arguments that assume universally shared aims. But for these to get a grip on the distinctive, often minority and élitist conceptions involved, it must seem perverse for any man or woman, as such, to reject them, and so we veer towards the moral tone of the other type of argument. But just to want to move about is not a reason that will serve to decide a person's transportation question, and it is nearer that level of lack of specificity that we have to justify education if we can. It is after all fairly easy to 'justify' it for the élites who typically succeed.

NOTES

[1] As a glance at many attempted justifications for curricular contents will reveal, it may not be so easy as people would like to think. As I hope to show elsewhere, part of the difficulty arises from the pervasiveness of the *inus*-conditional structure in these questions, to use Mackie's, 1965, neologism: an insufficient but necessary part of an unnecessary but sufficient condition.

[2] To be accurate, I have pushed Parfit further than in fact he went. For Parfit, survival is linked directly to one's actual memories. Kafka's character should certainly have reckoned that he survived as a cockroach; the point I want to stress is that he could still have said it would be so different a mode of survival as to be worth the same as death. 'That won't be me' would have been an understandable reaction, if anyone had asked him to consider possibilities in his future cockroach state.

[3] We may add this essay to the one case noted by Jane Martin (1982) where Peters seems to be thinking of his (un)educated man as specifically male.

[4] Compare Bourdieu and Passeron's gloss: 'It is clear why the social definition of excellence always tends to make reference to 'naturalness', i.e. to a modality of practice entailing a degree of accomplishment of PW [pedagogic work] capable of effacing awareness not only of the twofold arbitrari-

ness of the PA [pedagogic action] of which it is the product, but also of all that accomplished practice owes to PW' (1977, p. 39).

[5] I have adverted elsewhere to the way in which people, including professional philosophers most of the time, operate within frameworks of ideas and how this can undermine the pretensions of their philosophical arguments: 1982a; 1982b. See also my 1987, ch. 4, for some further remarks about the optional nature of moral thinking.

Initiation and Newness in Education and Child-rearing

PAUL SMEYERS

University of Leuven, Belgium

The general introduction to this volume stressed Wittgenstein's insistence on initiation into the 'language-game'. After all, in order to understand the meaning of a concept one has to take into account the particular circumstances of its use and in a case of difficulty, Wittgenstein suggests, to ask oneself how we learned the meaning of this word. Together with the social determination of 'action', it brings out one of the basic themes of this philosophy: the third-person perspective. Section 298 of *On Certainty* reads:

> "'We are quite sure of it' does not mean just that every single person is certain of it, but that we belong to a community which is bound together by science and education" and somewhat further he writes: "You must bear in mind that the language-game is so to say something unpredictable. I mean: it is not based on grounds. It is not reasonable (or unreasonable). It is there – like our life" (C, # 559).

It was argued that the 'form of life', the 'certainty' in which our action is embedded, is of crucial importance for thinking about education. To this 'bedrock', to the most fundamental propositions on the ethical, epistemological, metaphysical and religious level, the child is 'embedded' within initiation. Furthermore, a process of education was generally characterized as a dynamical initiation, a motivational aspect. Children mean a lot indeed to their parents – what they are, and what they achieve, doesn't leave them unmoved. The 'first educators' offer the child the truth by which they live, and their idea of 'human being', which they offer the child hoping for participation. The initiation into what is self evident (for them) makes present a horizon of meaning, which is at the same time a taken or accepted responsibility, thus forming also the intentional aspect of the process of child-rearing. 'Aims' of this process can be conceived as summarized formulations, as elucidations of the idea of humankind, and as anticipations from the point of view of the parent, embedded in the 'form of life'.

The educational importance of these aspects of his philosophy are only hinted at by Wittgenstein. In one of the sections of *Zettel* he writes for instance: "Any explanation has its foundation in training. (Educators ought to remember this)" (# 419). Something more needs first of all to be said on the way an educational situation can be conceived from a Wittgensteinian perspective. After the elaboration of education and child-rearing in terms of an initiation into what one cares for, the ways in which this weaker type of justification of educational practices can be attacked, as just conserving traditions for their own sake, are indicated. Particular attention will be paid to child-centred pedagogy, which has criticized such 'traditional' positions through the concept of 'experience'. Referring to

105

Studies in Philosophy and Education **14**: 229–249, 1995.
© 1995 *Kluwer Academic Publishers. Printed in the Netherlands.*

Wittgenstein's 'private language argument', a new place for 'experience', together with the possibility of criticizing a particular interpretation of it, is outlined. It will be argued that though initiation into a 'form of life' necessarily proceeds through the use of elements 'of the past', this does not preclude the possibility of newness. On the contrary only in this way can it integrate what 'is different' into 'what is'. In this sense the human condition reveals itself by being bound together with other human beings and by a givenness in two senses: of 'what is there' and of 'what is there for us'. At the same time it comes forward as bearing the seeds for 'new ways of looking at things' which will or will not be taken up.

EDUCATION AS INITIATION INTO 'WHAT ONE CARES FOR'

That the educational situation has to be conceived in ethical terms, is probably one of its most essential characteristics. Besides this, whether it is within the context of the school or within that of the family, one of its aspects can be indicated as 'caring for'. Because, in general, parents love their children they want the best for them, and what else could that be than what they regard as the best? Also, the fact that parents and children to a large extent share the same 'destiny', not having chosen each other, will influence the educational situation. Children get in the way, make a mess, spill lemonade on themselves and significant others and so forth and so on, and want, regrettably very often, something other than what their parents would like. They cost a lot of money and effort, and demand a lot of time. On the other hand, lots of decisions parents make are perceived by children as completely arbitrary, and a large number of them (at least in my opinion) are exactly that. This is true on both the level of material goods and of the way parents and children live their lives. It is also true, that parents sometimes deny themselves a lot for the benefit of their children. This, among other things, makes their lives to be determined to a large extent by those of their children, and their happiness and sorrow. Evidently, here, as elsewhere, there will exist relationships of power.

However the way that parents deal with their children doesn't arise from nowhere, even when it appears to be arbitrary. In a general way they 'know' how to proceed, and it goes without saying that what they do will precipitate future actions. Wittgenstein asked himself what the time was on the sun and showed that the criteria themselves, at the same time, cannot be under scrutiny. Our freedom to question certain values is not possible without a constraint on other values. We find ourselves in certain ties and require others to undo them. The infinity of human desire makes this, as Lacan has argued, a lifelong task. It creates the tragic character of human life. What I do has its foundations within the form of life. It is not the same whatever I say if I want to be understood. It is not the same whatever I do if I want my actions to be understood by others, even more if I want them to be accepted by others. However, the conditions and impact of my activities are not at my disposal beforehand. No deduction of general principles will be of any help towards knowing exactly how to act in a certain situation. The definition itself of this situation is at stake. Of course, we go on in a certain way, which can be understood and evaluated by others. However, that does not mean that only one possibility is open to us. The banks of the river change precisely because of this (cf. C, # 99).

The way I act is not indifferent to me because it makes explicit what I stand for. If it matters one is tempted to say "I can't but". The tension between what could be the case and what I until now have held to be true is ultimately insoluble. Of course, what is considered to be important is liable to change, also it could have been different, but it is so and so now. Precisely because of the particularity of the context I am answerable for what I do. The lack of an ultimate foundation makes me long for a universality which would free me from this burden and give me certainty. But the kind of absolute certainty that is longed for will reveal itself as a fraud. It haunts my existence and asks for an answer that cannot be given because we cannot live but in the particular. This position is threatening to the individual, as it confronts her or him with the fact that not *the* but only *a* solution is possible; that things are very complicated, that no simple answer will do and that all solutions are conditional; it leaves her or him very literally alone and ascribes responsibility for one's choice. The only way to deal with this un-groundability consists, according to Wittgenstein, in the acceptance of this unavoidability and with that its correlative: one's engagement. That we cannot but act out of what appeals to us and that we cannot answer questions of ultimate justification is the essence of our tragic human existence. It is difficult but not impossible to live with this kind of uncertainty, in the midst, moreover, of the irreconcilable desires of others and what appeals to them.

To act morally in an educational context concerning child-rearing presupposes being prepared to question one's own position in relation to the input of the educandus; to think it over again, given his or her 'contribution'. Precisely because of this it is for more than one reason not evidently clear how one should act. The rightness or wrongness of my actions is not to be decided by an individual in the privacy of what she or he thinks. In the end our fellow human beings will mainly help to determine this. As there is no private language, there may be no private ethical rules either. However, this does not mean that one cannot try to convince others by what one considers to be good arguments and make explicit one's reasons. This could mean that we will look to discussion to reveal what we do share and what we do agree upon. It can also mean that we will try to convince the other person, to 'convert' him, as Wittgenstein puts it, so that she or he sees what I see and is prepared to look at the problem in a 'new' way. This doesn't mean of course that I can only repeat what has been done before; on the contrary even such a repetition would itself be a 'new' application. However, it means that the educator has to live with the fact that she or he will not be able to give an ultimate justification. It also means that given several options are possible, there is not necessarily only one that is so certain, so vital for the happiness of the educandus that it urges the educator to choose it necessarily. Things are rarely that clear-cut.

A similar position can be argued for concerning the justification of the education that goes on in schools. Here as elsewhere it is claimed that if education ought to provoke new ideas, ideas which are different from the existing ideas of 'human society' and 'human dealings', it nevertheless has to start from somewhere. To argue this one could recall section 115 of *On Certainty*:

"If you tried to doubt everything you would not get as far as doubting anything. The game of doubting itself presupposes certainty".

Within the context of education, Oakeshott may be regarded as an author who particularly adopts this stance. He indicates the aim of education as being to enter a relationship of 'conversation' informed by familiarity with the traditional literary, philosophical, artistic and scientific expressions of European civilisation. Such conversation is characterised by having strong resemblances with gambling, its significance to be found neither in winning nor in losing, but in wagering. Learning itself is described by Oakeshott as the comprehensive engagement in which we come to know ourselves and the world around us, and the paradoxical activity of doing and submitting at the same time. Teaching is outlined as the activity in which a 'learned' person 'learns' his pupils. Education in its most general sense becomes a specific transmission which may go on between the generations of human beings, in which newcomers to the scene are initiated into the world they are to inhabit. Being human, Oakeshott writes

". . . is recognising oneself to be related to others . . . in virtue of participation in multiple understood relationships and in the enjoyment of understood, historic languages of feelings, sentiments, imaginings, fancies, desires, recognitions, moral and religious beliefs, intellectual and practical enterprises, customs, conventions, procedures and practices, canons, maxims and principles of conduct, rules which denote obligations and offices which specify duties" (Oakeshott in Fuller, 1989, p. 65). And he continues: "These languages are continuously invented by those who share them; using them is adding to their resources" (ibid., p. 65).

Oakeshott also stresses that a teacher is someone in whom some part or aspect or passage of this inheritance is alive. He or she has something of which one is a master to impart, one has deliberated upon its worth, and furthermore one knows the learner. The transaction between generations has no extrinsic end or purpose, education being acquiring in some measure an understanding of the human condition in which the 'fact of life' continuously is illuminated by a 'quality of life'.

More recently Rorty (1982b) argued similarly for an encounter with great thinkers, who solved the problems of their time by creating new languages, new disciplines and new societies. He wants to encourage students to fall in love with their intellectual tradition and emulate the achievements of their heroes by solving new problems of their own. General study, he says, is basically 'erotic' and should be more like 'seduction' than instruction. And for that matter it is not important who the students' heroes are, as long as everybody has more than one and is able to appreciate and respect those who have different ones. He continues by arguing that one should make sure there is some overlap in the courses so that interesting conversations can take place. Finally he states that the best way of fixing the content of the core curriculum is the way it always has been done, that is by the most influential faculty members' choice of books that have given them pleasure, and university libraries are the place in which students can find practically any book and then find somebody 'around there' to talk with about it.

Notwithstanding a number of difficulties which both of these positions, in my opinion, generate, they offer – as is argued more extensively elsewhere (cf. Smeyers, 1995a, 1995b) – an interesting perspective. Combined with Frankfurt's stance (1988) 'on what we care about', they may offer us within the context of education exactly what we need. Frankfurt argued that the notion of what a person cares about, coincides in part with the notion of something with reference to which the person guides her or himself in what she or he does with his life and his conduct. It presupposes both agency and self-consciousness and further-more that one cares about 'caring for certain things'. According to Frankfurt there are some things, for which he uses the concept of 'volitional necessity', that a person cares for in a way that it is impossible for her or him to forbear from, and that she or he is unwilling to oppose. At a different level something analogously can be indicated for the culture, the 'form of life' one is living and into which the child is initiated. Instead of thinking of education as a form of lib-eration, of emancipation, and in this way an initiation into the human, it can be thought of as an initiation into what is 'worthwhile for us'. It is not the case that one becomes human by being educated, but it is the case that education tries to convey what is regarded at least by a certain number of human beings as worth-while to them. To accept this historisation and at the same time de-centralisation of what one is engaged in, makes the justification of the content of education a risky business. What proves and is important to those who share a particular culture, is guarded and bestowed upon the persons being educated for whom they care. There should not only be a place where new ideas can grow, there should also be a place where what is worthwhile can be kept. It is beyond doubt that to take a stance on whatever topic, necessitates not only to take notice of what has been said and written, but in a logical sense is not possible at all without being initiated into the existing frameworks, as Wittgenstein has over-whelmingly demonstrated.

Therefore, the aim of education should be a personal way of dealing with 'what matters': how people have struggled in the past with what troubled them most and how they dealt with it. In this process one gets acquainted foremost with questions rather than with answers, and to be initiated, to be touched by the questions, seems what it is all about. It is not clear how such initiation will be different from what Rorty (1982b) proposed. Of course education will be initia-tion into the Great Books, not for the sake of the Great Books, but because their content contains what generations before us considered to be worthwhile. This is not to say that the content can't be changed, nor that it is justified only because it has been on the curriculum for so long already, but 'only', that it is valued by a number of people for its own sake, because it has made such an impression on us that it continued to be cherished for the next generation. Because it is some-thing that is important for a number of us, it is something we care about. This way of thinking of education also has a message for those who are concerned with it in the first place, the teachers, and the place where they work, the school. The place of learning should offer an educational project and has to make it its business to provide opportunities to all those involved, for the ongoing discussion of what it offers.

The concept of discussion suggests here that starting from what is given is not enough (though necessary), that it is the first step followed by the shaping to the particular situation that is at issue (through which the general will become clear), and to end with the contribution of the newly involved partners, i.e., the way they are struck by what is at issue in a particular situation. In its more elaborated forms, this discussion can be thought of in a full dialogical sense.

Though the justification of the content might be differently conceived, in a way there is no real difference between the present break between the culture of the school and that of society. Schools and universities have always had to battle against 'what can be used' in day to day life. To avoid instrumentalism, both in the sense of preparing for one's career and promoting social mobility within society, education has to be thought of in its own terms. Instead of being technicians, teachers pre-eminently 'have to' care about what they convey. Only in such a way can the content be transmitted in an educationally acceptable manner. They, more than anyone else, have to be representatives of what they believe in. Therefore they, first of all, have to be those who love what they teach, and be the principal advocates of the curriculum. In this sense they ought to be the representatives of the educational project on which they and others reflect as an ongoing conversation of mankind. Their hopes nourished by the 'certainty' that what appeals to them, cannot be indifferent to everyone.

It is important to realise that in our dealings with children, be it at home or at school, 'the empty place of values' is filled in, in a particular way. The way this is done will be in continuance with the past, with what I cared for yesterday, with what I valued 'yesterday'. 'Good reasons' for this acting have their place within a frame-work of 'good reasons for us'. Though not unchangeable, there are still good reasons for now, yesterday and tomorrow. And every reconstruction of these reasons entails in some sense a prescription for future behaviour. This idea of education as dynamic initiation, be it child-rearing or 'education' (schooling), seems to surpass any instrumental justification at both the level of social mobility (one of the traditional functions of education) and preparation for jobs. It is not so much that we need a project of human being (a definitive outlining of what we are, what we have to value, how we have to live and so forth) in order to be able to act, nor that by such a project everything will be already decided upon including all practical decisions within the context of education. But it seems to be the case that such a project (in a less stronger and definitive form) is implicitly present in what we do, whether we like that or not. Such a project of human being and thus of education will necessarily always also be something that is 'ongoing'. This conception is different from the postmodernist one, in so far as it, for instance, explicitly states that though not everything can be determined from the beginning concerning education and humanhood, it does not follow from this that nothing can be nor that one can start ex nihilo.

LEAVING EVERYTHING AS IT IS?

The implications of the fore-going, some noticed as early as the publication of the *Philosophical Investigations*, and intensified by sections such as 124, in which philosophy is indicated as 'leaving everything as it is', have given fuel to the reproach of conservatism in the Wittgensteinian position. This is analogous to the debate within philosophy of education, particularly in the context of the child-centred movement, where the possibility to change society through the individual was discussed.

Within the German educational tradition – in itself particularly developed during the Enlightenment – education was the 'means' to become human, i.e. rational. Rationality as the proper end of what being a human being is, does not involve a means-end reasoning. In becoming free from one's inclinations and passions, one realises one's true nature: one puts oneself under the guidance of reason, which is never alienating, given the fact that to be rational is the same for everyone. Given a 'mathematical ideal of rationality' exemplified for instance in the way the first categorical imperative in the ethical domain is deduced (the demand for universalisability), but present in the general manner, Kant is dealing with epistemological problems – what do we have to presuppose on behalf of the subject to understand the way we think – it is clear that there is for Kant only one way to think properly i.e. rationally, which as a consequence has to be acquired by everyone.

Herbart, successor to Kant's chair of philosophy, argues that the child is born with lack of will, that his impetuosity has to be subdued and that such requires some form of 'violence'. This force he says has to be strong enough (or to be repeated frequently enough) in order that the child will develop a real will. The art to disturb the peace of a child's mind, to bind it to trust and love, in order to push and provoke it arbitrarily, and to turn it around for a while in the restless-ness of later years, would be the most hateful of all the bad arts. It would not serve to reach an aim that will apologize using such means from the eyes of the child itself, from whom such a reproach is feared for, Herbart argues: "You will thank me for this", says the educator to the weeping child, and only this hope can serve as an excuse for the tears he drew with him (cf. Herbart, 1965, p. 38–39).

Kerschensteiner on the other hand, taught us that the educator sees the child as the future bearer of values. And when the educator, so he says, loves the values and realizes more and more his own imperfection, so he loves his work i.e. the educandus, whose soul he or she sympathizes with, faithfully hopes with, loves and respects (cf. 1949, p. 50). The educator's love goes back to the edu-candus' possibility of realizing in himself humanhood, which means in the Enlightenment tradition to become rational. In such a way the educator is of service to the community. The educator will influence the becoming person, the future bearer of eternal values, and will find in this his highest reward. Kerschensteiner refers to the Bible: "God chastises whom he loves'. The power of the true educator is the power of love, the power of the moral values so that the child can become human. In a paper published after the Second World war (1952) Flitner – a representative of the Geisteswissenschaftliche Pädagogik – similarly argued that education means an exercise of power over people; first of all of the parents over the 'nonage' children who are not capable of living by themselves, of the Masters in their schools, on the order of society, of the board of examiners, on the internal build up and the aims of education. Flitner already distinguishes two psychologically different forms of this submission and speaks of the silent violence of morals and religion and the severe and ascetic discipline which is rational and planned. The authority which starts from morality needs, according to Flitner, no further justification.

The general introduction to this volume already stressed that the implications concerning the educational context of the 'traditional' position were spelled out very clearly in its 20th century form, by the Dutch philosopher of education, Langeveld (1946). Suffice it to remark here that this kind of elaboration is analogous to the discussion of the concept of autonomy which Anglo-Saxon philosophy of education has been concerned about. R.S. Peters (1964, 1966 & 1967) for instance, develops the concept of education as initiation and offers furthermore (together with Hirst, 1974a) a 'transcendental' justification of its content.

In reality it is the criticism of the Enlightenment tradition itself, that has been the basis of the criticism of its educational counterpart. Why should reason and reason alone decide what to do, and moreover (and more correctly) how can such rational thinking – not embedded in reality – be thought of as possible at all? Phenomenology, existentialism, neo-marxism and so on, criticise the over-ambitious rational project. Within education discussions centre for instance upon how to decide when adulthood has been reached and whether all adults ever reach it. Numerous criticisms are also spelled out concerning the hidden means-end reasoning in Kant's ideas. 'To become human', is difficult to conceive of, so it is argued. Isn't one human from the beginning? The time had come to look for alternatives and to conceive education differently. Those alternatives were offered from the end of the 19th century onwards, starting with the child-centred movement (among others Neill, A. Freud, Decroly, Freinet) and with the so-called 'Geisteswissenschaftliche Pädagogik' of which Bollnow, Flitner, Nohl, Litt and Weniger are the best known representatives. More recently the child-centred interest is taken up by authors such as Rogers and Gordon, whilst the 'hermeneutic' tradition has generated authors such as Klafki, Habermas and Mollenhauer. I will only go into some of the characteristics of these positions in as much as they play a part in my overall argument, which I trust will not be damaged, by the sketchiness of the outline of these positions.

As an example one may look into the position of the French pedagogue Célestin Freinet. He argued that the tasks of the child in the traditional school could not be conceived as real work ('travail'), as they are not conceived from the position of the child. Their labour is after all only the result of estranging pressure far from one's conscious activities. 'Work' nevertheless is for Freinet the only way humans can express themselves. The education by means of work he argues for is therefore not just using 'work' as a means, it is the point of departure for a culture in which 'work' is in the centre "...*le point de départ d'une culture dont le travail sera le centre*' (Freinet, 1946, p. 209). One speaks of 'work', Freinet argues, each time there is a physical or intellectual activity which answers to a natural need of the individual and which satisfies itself. The knowledge acquired at school is senseless so long as it does not belong to the 'living' child. Freinet therefore advises us: "Il faut tout passer par l'expérience de la vie [One has to pass everything through the experience of life]" (Freinet, 1946, p. 196). It will be clear that the emphasis is not as much on facts to be memorized, but on the zeal of the individual, on creative and active capacities, and on the possibility belonging in human nature to move on and to realize oneself maximally. Clearly, Freinet argues, if one does not give enough room to the child's own activity, she or he will turn away from his or her environment but nevertheless will try to achieve what is ordered by her or his 'instinct'.

Generally 'progressive' educators accepted the child as an equal partner, his or her opinion to be taken into account. Education itself became then a process to be characterized as consideration or deliberation. According to Rogers (1969) and Gordon (1975), the educator (the parent and the teacher), is first of all the adviser of the child, the facilitator of what he/she really wants. It is the pupil who is learning, who has to master for himself, starting from what she or he already knows and according to real interests. It is the child who is from the beginning responsible for his or her learning. If she or he doesn't already know what is good for oneself, how could one ever decide, argues Rogers. Gordon on the other hand stresses the importance of keeping communication-channels open. Parents should therefore first of all listen to their children. Active listening, presupposes also the acceptance of the other in order to help him or her to overcome a problematic situation. Since the success of authors such as Rogers and Gendlin, many in the educational context became convinced of the necessity to start a relationship with children based on authenticity, acceptance and empathy. These attitudes are considered as a condition in order to bring the child in relation with its own stream of experience. Basically, for these authors, educational actions are analogous to therapeutic interventions. Parents should not impose their values on their children, but ought to respect the children's values. And it is not because parents and children are not factually in an equal power-relationship – as the parents generally make the final decisions concerning overall family matters, but also concerning what children are allowed to do – that this inequality is justified. On the contrary, the actual helplessness does not justify the power-relationship. Consequently, parents are not responsible for what their children do, children are themselves responsible and the educational project in a way has, so one could say, been watered down. Now the educator resembles more a counsellor who is at the child's disposal and in so far as it is still there, the project is framed according to the child's interests.

This position anticipated the one in which the concept of 'experience' is used within social philosophy and more generally within social sciences as the 'critical resort' out of which the dissatisfaction with the present, sometimes combined with more specific suggestions for change, is expressed. Personal experience

functions here as a critical touchstone of the present situation, thus making possible personal and societal emancipation. This concept has many 'meanings'
some of which will be dealt with and criticized. Also, more recently, the Anglo-
Saxon educational literature concerning schooling, refers to 'one's own experience', Schon's 'reflective practitioner' being the paradigm case (1983). Here and
elsewhere one deals with 'reflection-in-action' for instance and with 'learning by
doing and developing the ability for continued learning and problem solving
throughout the professional's career'. In this case the concept of 'experience' is
used as a kind of corrective to the theoretical approach (doing as opposed to
simply knowing).

It is clear that the concept of 'experience' plays a crucial role in these elabora-
tions, but doubtful however whether this concept can be understood in an
organic way, i.e. as something that works from inside and develops from there
the individual's understanding of self, others and the surrounding world. This
would require a metaphysical concept of development like plants developing
from seeds. All that is essential and which will determine its future shape, is
already there. The question is therefore whether it is possible for an individual to
discover within him/herself what he/she really wants. In a way the closed cogito,
rightly criticised in my opinion, is taken up here again. Values do not seem to be
first generated in the mind of an individual, but have to be thought of from the
beginning as bestowed upon us by 'significant others'. Besides this there is also,
as already mentioned in the general introduction to this volume, the issue that
whether the values parents and teachers enhance have only the same significance
for them as the possibly contradictory values their children and pupils accept.
Furthermore there is the question how they could avoid initiating their children
in the values they live by, and therefore they will, so it seems, inevitably – in
opposition to what the progressive educators want – influence the child in an
important way. Quite evidently progressivism is a broad tradition that contains
many shades of view within it, not all as 'extreme' as I have indicated.

More generally, the initiation metaphor is blamed for the reproductive character that has to be allocated to it, at least at first sight. This conservative bias is
linked to Wittgenstein's philosophy which is reproached for not leaving enough
room for what is new. Moreover it is accused of wanting to maintain all order.
That this matter is of crucial educational importance was recently again highlighted by Helmut Peukert who asks himself what can be done to prevent a new
Auschwitz, to obstruct the appearance of the destructive tendencies of a certain
type of rationality. The central question, he argues:

"... seems to be whether we will be successful in developing organs that have an increased perception of our society and its self-destructive possibilities, and in creating democratic institutions
for a morally reflected self-control and self-transformation that do not destroy freedom" (Peukert,
1994, p. 10).

He asks in other words for the way we can, and have to think about education, in
order not to be confronted again by the dreadful situations from the past. Simply
relying on individual experience will not do, as Hamlyn, following Wittgenstein,
has already pointed out:

"The fatal and wrong suggestion is that the child starts by distinguishing its own experience, because if the child is initially confined to its experiences there is no way of this so that it can come to have knowledge of a world independent of itself. It could not even come to have any conception of such a world" (Hamlyn, 1978, p. 95).

But there seems to be more than a simple refusal of a rough use of the concept of 'experience', which is incidentally not denied by Hamlyn. There is indeed a possibility of criticizing what 'is there'. To put this in Wittgensteinian terms, it is possible that the river-bed changes, at least from time to time. For some this seems to put the idea of initiation itself at risk. It will therefore be important to develop in a subtle manner the concept of 'experience', in order to do justice to the possibility of criticism and at the same time to embeddedness in a culture.

In my opinion, as was stressed earlier, Wittgenstein, by the way he deals with 'meaning' and 'intention', and by his insistence on the fact that the individual does not lose himself in the intersubjective though being carried by it, and lastly by the indication that the intersubjective criteria finally are accepted and recognised by the individual, offers just that subtle balance.

It is important to stress that not only relatively unimportant issues have been the focus of criticism on the basis of the concept of 'experience', but that certain values also have been rejected. How this process has to be thought of is at stake here. It will be argued that child-rearing and education itself have to be described in terms of passing on 'what one stands for' because one *cannot* do otherwise. The conception of 'offering' a content within the context of education and child-rearing, will thus not be given up. To argue this the possibility and the pretext may be sought in the concept of 'experience', starting from a well-known quotation from Wittgenstein:

"*I*, L.W., believe, am sure, that my friend hasn't sawdust in his body or in his head, even though I have no direct evidence of my senses to the contrary. I am sure, by reason of what has been said to me, of what I have read, and of my experience. To have doubts about it would seem to me madness – of course, this is also in agreement with other people; but *I* agree with them (C, # 281).

Wittgenstein poses the problem here concerning the relationship between the individual and the community in terms of how an expression materialises. To put this quite simply – and because of that partly incorrectly or at least incomplete – is it what an individual thinks about it that is correct, or is it what a community in consensus claims, that will count? If the experience of an individual is at stake, then one has to indicate in what ways such an experience can be thought of; how, in other words, the 'contribution' of the others has to be conceived. Is it a matter of adapting the individual to 'what others say', rather than the way the consensus has to be thought of, which is problematic? After all how can we think that 'the others' decide what is the case without allocating a place for the individual's contribution? And if it is claimed concerning the first (conceived in its most extreme form), that every individual will decide for himself 'what is the case', then one has to explain how a consensus, perhaps even language itself, is possible. The effect of the intersubjective is dealt with extremely succinctly in what is known as the 'private language argument'. Compared to the chapter in this volume by van Haaften, in which this argument is also under scrutiny, a detailed somewhat different interpretation will be offered.

'PRIVATE LANGUAGE' AND 'EXPERIENCE'

In the 'private language argument' Wittgenstein shows that the community of language-speakers is a necessary condition for using a language. At the core we find the concept of 'following a rule' which contains both the possibility of speaking in accordance with the rule and of transgressing it. The strong message is that a private language is impossible, because of the impossibility of an ostensive definition with a private mental object. Furthermore the language community is important because it determines the 'normal use', in other words what it means to follow a rule. The central part of the argument given in the *Philosophical Investigations* is to be found in # 293. If one accepts the possibility of a private language, claiming that communication is possible, then, Wittgenstein states, the private object cannot have any substance and it has to be characterised as 'idle' (cf. PI, I, # 132). The 'private object' cannot play any role in the mechanism of conversation. If on the other hand it is claimed that it can play a role, then communication becomes impossible. The 'naming relationship' as conceived by the private linguist, has nothing to do with explaining what is involved in knowing the meaning of a word, nor with what is intended with it. Nevertheless it seems that one needs private experience, as some kind of paradigm to give meaning to a concept. The defender of a private language tries to explain what he means with a word by indicating a mental object. 'That' gives meaning to his words, but nothing can be said about it. What seems to be an explanation at first sight, proves on closer examination to be an illusion. The moral of the 'private language argument' is not that one cannot follow a rule privately – as we often just do that, though if complex rules are involved it will take a lot of effort to understand these if there is no personal interaction involved. Nor is it that one cannot follow rules no one knows the existence of, as that can also be done by many for instance in the writing of a diary. It is that there is no such thing as 'private rules', rules which in principle cannot be understood by our fellow human beings. These alleged rules would have to use 'private ostensive definition' which from impossibility of access to the 'private samples' in principle cannot be communicated. The acceptance of just that, lies nevertheless at the heart of idealism and solipsism. The 'private linguist' insists that his experiences are private in two different meanings: epistemically and 'from him'.

The doctrine of epistemic privateness is made explicit by the demand that only the individual can know whether he or she is in pain and that others can only assume it. To this Wittgenstein answers that it is partly wrong and partly nonsense. In the usual meaning of 'I know' it is wrong. Others know as well that I am in pain on the basis of my pain-behaviour. That only I can *know* this, is nonsense, because it is not meaningful for an individual to doubt whether one is in pain. It is not the proximity of the experience, but the 'grammar' that excludes doubt here. There is only limited truth in the doctrine of epistemic privacy, as one can say from someone that one is completely transparent, one can also say that she or he is a complete mystery to us. This is the case if one is confronted with someone from an alien culture as the reasons why one behaves in a certain way can be a complete mystery for the outsider. What one thinks can be private, in the sense of not being known to others, but this is no reason to pre-suppose something totally impenetrable or exclusively private. There is no meta-physical border which limits one's possible knowledge at the portal of the mind of others.

The second kind of privateness from which confusions arise, concerns the fact that 'experiences are from someone'. Someone else cannot have my pain. Wittgenstein comments on this: "... the subject of pain is the person who gives it expression" (PI, I, # 302). Do I not know differently that I am in pain by feeling it, instead of by looking at it? That also is confusing, as saying that 'I know I am in pain', doesn't mean anything unless one wants to indicate that there is something like 'being in pain' which is different from 'asking whose pain it is'. And the supposed difference between 'being in pain' and 'feeling pain', is a distinction which cannot meaningfully be made. The defender of a 'private language' who claims that no one can 'have' this pain, does not say anything more than that there cannot be a chair where there already is one, and as such does not say very much. That someone else cannot 'have' my pain, is a 'grammatical' expression. Incidentally, private ownership of experiences is not limited to mental experiences, but applies also to smiling or sneezing. From the fact that another person cannot have my experiences, it does not follow that nothing can be said about it. In this sense the expression 'Experiences are private' can be compared with 'Patience – a game of cards – is played by oneself'. Both are grammatical (cf. PI, I, # 248).

That our experiences are private, either epistemically or in the sense that someone 'has them', excludes 'only' that one can be certain or in doubt in 'con-fessing' certain experiences. Hintikka comments on this:

> "In other words, Wittgenstein's point is not that I cannot remember what my private experience was like, but that such an act of remembering cannot be a move in a language-game that would link my private experience to its name. The apparent epistemological problems he raises are thus merely an expositional device to dramatize semantical facts of life" (Hintikka, 1986, p. 259).

Wittgenstein does not claim (cf. PI, I, # 270) that experience is left out as irrele-vant, but that it cannot be spoken of unless by means of something public. He definitely does not deny the possibility of private experiences.

It is time now to indicate how there is a place for the above-mentioned critical resort of 'experience'.

A RISK-CONCEPTION OF COMMUNICATION

In the consequence of the criticism that has been dealt with, one can see though a possibility to think 'newness' and language acquisition as well as a way to think nonsense (gibberish) differently. The crucial element always is to indicate for the others (the competent language users – also for myself at a later moment) the reasons for using a concept in a certain way and why certain consequences for our acting have to be linked with it. The problem that is raised here, is whether apparently new reasons can be really new, or whether one is instead condemned to a reiteration of old ones. All that given, the acceptance of the possibility of communication, presupposes that already something is shared by those who are involved. How can the blind alley to which the 'private language argument' superficially seems to lead be overcome? I will quote extensively some sections of Wittgenstein's work:

> "I am not more certain of the meaning of my words than I am of certain judgments. Can I doubt that this colour is called "blue"? (My) doubts form a system. For how do I know that someone is in doubt? How do I know that he uses the words 'I doubt it' as I do? From a child up I learnt to judge like this. *This is* judging. This is how I learned to judge; *this* I got to know *as* judgment. But isn't experience that teaches us to judge like *this*, that is to say, that it is correct to judge like this? But how does experience *teach* us, then? *We* may derive it from experience, but experience does not direct us to derive anything from experience. If it is the *ground* of our judging like this, and not just the cause, still we do not have a ground for seeing this in turn as a ground. No, experience is not the ground for our game of judging. Nor is its outstanding success" (C, ## 126–131).

Our use of words, our doubting and judging, Wittgenstein argues, are the result of what we have learned. Not experience, nor success of our judging, determine the way in which we judge. This is part of a certain 'form of life' to which the others and I belong and which is in itself maintained by them and me. Wittgenstein expresses this as follows:

> "If experience is the ground of our certainty, then naturally it is past experience. And it isn't for example just *my* experience, but other people's, that I get knowledge from. Now one might say that it is experience again that leads us to give credence to others. But what experience makes me believe that the anatomy and physiology books don't contain what is false? Though it is true that this trust is *backed* up by my own experience" (C, # 275).

As stressed in the general introduction, Wittgenstein's theory of meaning neither advocates a position of pure inwardness nor of pure outwardness. Right from the beginning, what one could call an element of risk, is present in the way communication is thought of. The consistency of meaning Wittgenstein argues for is free of essentialism. Though every situation is in some sense new, the different meanings of a concept are linked with each other through family-resemblances. In order to be understood, the present use may not radically be different from the former ones. It is within the *normal* context that the meaning of a concept is determined. The others and I proceed in this way. There is neither for them, nor for me an absolute point of reference, neither an internal nor an external one. The community of language speakers forms the warrant for the consistency of meaning. What is there is a constant stream of language in which 'meaning' again and again is realized not separated from the past. This seems to me the real meaning of 'meaning as use'. In order for the others (and for myself at a later moment if I wrote something down for instance) to understand, consistency is needed. This consistency is 'carried' and maintained by the community of language-speakers who speak the same language. They help me, and I can be continuously questioned by them concerning what I mean and how such is understood (by them), and moreover can be corrected.

A certain meaning of words and expressions can be held fast for a certain period, but quite evidently it will evolve as part of a living language because the language itself evolves. Neither the primacy of the subject, nor the primacy of the collectivity is at stake here, but a community of language-speakers to which they and I belong. In this community certain people say things and others (want to) understand what is said and done. And it is continuously made clear what is meant (intended) and what is understood, in reactions to what is said, and also misunderstood. The context in which one has learnt to speak, namely by in some sense to imitate and thus to illicit a certain response, will remain present in our speaking through associations with certain sounds, thoughts and circumstances. This indication is only relativistic at the first sight. The contrary really is the case, but it does take fully into account the anti-essentialism present in section 292 of the *Philosophical Investigations*:

> "Don't always think that you read off what you say from the facts; that you portray these in words according to rules. For even so you would have to apply the rule in the particular case without guidance".

This interpretation is analogous to Luise and David McCarty's position (1991) that a concept is not made explicit by a word. Language cannot be controlled in such a way:

> "Language, to use Wittgenstein's expression, is not just vast, it is unsäglich (immeasurable). We do not control it; it controls us" (p. 247).

The problems we have dealt with concerning meaning are related to the two following questions. Firstly, how can something be learned if one's understanding is limited to what one already knows? How for instance is an historic understanding developed with a child if this is a new kind of understanding for the child, and 'to understand' really means to be able to go on? And secondly, how can one think of really new content, for this presupposition is needed to criticize radically what 'is there'?

SEEING, SEEING-AS AND SPEAKING

The association between 'meaning' and the *way* one experiences something is made by Wittgenstein explicitly in the *Philosophical Investigations*. Given its importance I will quote it extensively.

> "In the triangle I can see now *this* as apex, *that* as base – now *this* as apex, *that* as base. – Clearly the words "Now I am seeing *this* as the apex" cannot so far mean anything to a learner who has only just met the concepts of apex, base, and so on. – But I do not mean this as an empirical proposition. "Now he's seeing it like *this*", "now like *that*" would only be said of someone *capable* of making certain applications of the figure quite freely. The substratum of this experience is the mastery of a technique. But how queer for this to be the logical condition of someone's having such-and-such an *experience*! After all, you don't say that one only 'has toothache' if one is capable of doing such-and-such. – From this it follows that we cannot be dealing with the same concept of experience here. It is a different though related concept. It is only if someone *can do*, has learnt, is master of, such-and-such, that it makes sense to say he has had *this* experience. And

if this sounds crazy, you need to reflect that the *concept* of seeing is modified here. (A similar consideration is often necessary to get rid of a feeling of dizziness in mathematics.) We talk, we utter words, and only *later* get a picture of their life" (PI, II, p. 208e–209e).

Here Wittgenstein indicates the importance of 'seeing something as', which cannot be inferred from experience. He points out that 'the picture of their (the concepts') life' can only be drawn afterwards. Moreover, it is made clear that the vocabulary used to speak about our 'inner experiences', does not refer to 'inner states', of which the existence can only be spoken of by the individual person. 'First person present tense' expressions do not refer but are expressive. This also makes the apparent impossibility clear that the subject cannot be mistaken about them, and it furthermore indicates the only sense in which one's experiences and thoughts are only known to the subject. As Peacocke argues:

> "This is just one of many kinds of cases in which to fall under a psychological concept is to have an ability. Not only should understanding and following a rule be so regarded, but also should the enjoyment of colour experiences" (1982, p. 162).

A description of the abilities associated with psychological states is usually done by an implicit reference to human practices and is based on human agreement. Wittgenstein accepts that if someone has mastered the English language concerning pain-behaviour, she or he is disposed to (ceteris paribus, as this disposition can also be oppressed) use sincerely the expression "I am in pain" in the same circumstances (ceteris paribus) as one is disposed to express non-linguistic pain-behaviour. Peacocke calls this the 'mastery claim'. Wittgenstein accepts, according to Peacocke, also a further theory concerning the way the expressions are materialized: "... that a disposition to utter this sentence replaces certain primitive, non-linguistic manifestations of pain" (1982, p. 163). He distinguishes psychological states which are dispositional (such as knowledge, understanding, intention) from mental states which are 'undergoings'. The last mentioned, of which impressions and images are examples, have a certain duration and intensity. A particular problem confronts us here as expressive behaviour and 'first person expressions' can both be associated with dispositions as with mental states. Wittgenstein denies that the meaning of the word 'pain', even in a minor way, is determined by an association between an ostensive definition of 'the word' and something 'it refers to'. If it is correct to indicate in Wittgenstein's philosophy a non-referential conception of the pain-language, in terms of expressive language, it is important to understand this in a certain way. He quite evidently indicates that in certain contexts "I am in pain" functions as a cry, in the sense that it is not a report of what happens. Language is expressive, he writes in *Zettel*, # 472, "The first person of the present ((is)) akin to an expression". This 'being akin', first of all is to be found in the fact that through the association of a natural expression of pain, the word 'pain' gets a certain meaning. A connection is made more with this than with that natural expression, as a consequence of which a word becomes the name of a certain sensation.

Wittgenstein furthermore claims that expressions such as "I am in pain" are themselves part of the pain-behaviour and are of the same nature as cries.

Therefore, they cannot be separated unless in special cases in which one oppresses the expression or in cases in which one pretends. In this sense expressivity is at stake, not only in the way Peacocke indicated it in terms of 'expressive non-descriptive', because that might tempt us to think that pain is not a real event. Foot comments on Peacocke's position in this way:

> "He (Wittgenstein) has no objection to speaking of describing one's sensations, images or state of mind, and he says that even a cry which is "too primitive" to be called a description may nevertheless serve as one (PI, II, p. 189)" (Foot, 1983, p. 188).

As a cry may be a kind of complaint but not always is, the same goes for "I am in pain": it *can* be a description but is not always so. The opposition referring/non-referring is therefore of a different kind than the opposition between descriptive and non-descriptive. Pain is non-referring but therefore not always non-descriptive, as Wittgenstein states:

> "And yet you again and again reach the conclusion that the sensation itself is a *nothing*". – Not at all. It is not a *something*, but not a *nothing* either! The conclusion was only that a nothing would serve just as well as a something about which nothing could be said. We have only rejected the grammar which tries to force itself on us here" (PI, I, # 304).

The possibility to describe does not presuppose a radical separateness between 'what I say' and 'the object', and does not presuppose in this sense a reference. Therefore a non-referring language-use is at stake, as to accept the reference would imply accepting a separateness. The idea of a pre-linguistic network can also be found in the position of Pears, who argues that in case of lack of it:

> "...there would be no way of stopping the regressive search for critical authentication" (Pears, 1989, p. 271)..."I think that simple animal facts about human beings, neural and behavioral, are the foundation of Wittgenstein's later philosophy" (Pears, 1989, p. 271).

That a certain experience can be described as 'from the subject', seems to follow from 'the animal facts' on which concepts are imbued by competent language users. Pears continues:

> "The crucial point, on which Wittgenstein's whole argument relies, is that it is a false intellectualization of the subject's predicament to suppose that he cannot use the pre-linguistic network until he is in a position to describe it" (Pears, 1989, p. 273).

So far three elements to which Wittgenstein draws our attention have been discussed. Firstly, he indicates the importance of a certain perspective linked with what one has learned. At the same time he clarifies that the use of words in some sense only leads to their 'meaning' afterwards. Finally he is interested in the nature of first person expressions, to be conceived as descriptive but non-referring. Here also he stresses that it is not necessary to describe the pre-linguistic network in order to use it. This insight I will now connect with the idea of 'associations of meanings' after which I have indicated a parallel with 'seeing something'. When we look at an object then we sometimes see that, although it has not been changed while we were looking, the *way* we see it has. We see it differently though we see that it is not different from the way it was (an example might be from looking to a jigsaw of lines to looking to the representation of a face). What constitutes this change? Wittgenstein gave attention to this matter which is linked with the issue of 'experiencing the meaning of a word'. Several things are at stake here (cf. Budd, 1987, p. 2). One can indicate the organisation of the image from the perspective of the person. Also important is the question of whether it is 'seeing' instead of 'interpreting', whether it is something we 'go through' or something we 'do'. Credit to the first is the fact that the image does not change, that it is not dependent on the will, but on the contrary in some sense is completely isolated from it. Against this is the fact that an individual's particular seeing is a state which can change rapidly. Concerning this Wittgenstein writes:

> "It is seeing, *insofar as* ...
> It is seeing, only insofar *as* ...
> (That seems to be the solution)" (RPP, I, # 390).

Clearly the insistence on the particularity of the situation goes along with the passivity of the individual. The correct use of the word 'seeing' which has connotations with experience is not limited to the perception of coloured surfaces but bears also upon seeing similarities between faces:

> "The point here is not that our sense-impressions can lie, but that we understand their language. (And this language like any other is founded on convention)" (PI, I, # 355).

'Seeing' and 'seeing as' has to do with having gone through certain processes of learning, and concerning that Wittgenstein states:

> "Is there such a thing as 'expert judgment' about the genuineness of expressions of feeling? – Even here, there are those whose judgment is 'better' and those whose judgment is 'worse'.
>   Correcter prognoses will generally issue from the judgments of those with better knowledge of mankind.
>   Can one learn this knowledge? Yes; some can. Not, however, by taking a course in it, but through '*experience*'. – Can someone else be a man's teacher in this? Certainly. From time to time he gives him the right *tip*. – This is what 'learning' and 'teaching' are like here. – What one acquires here is not a technique; one learns correct judgments. There are also rules, but they do not form a system, and only experienced people can apply them right. Unlike calculating-rules.
>   What is most difficult here is to put this indefiniteness, correctly and unfalsified, into words" (PI, II, p. 227e).

Again, judging and learning to judge is 'tied' to the community to which one belongs: one learns to judge correctly and what is implied in a correct judgement. The different aspects of what was discussed come together in what is understood as 'the experience of the meaning of a word'. Wittgenstein indicates that his analysis of 'experience of noticing aspects' is only a move towards a different aim, namely 'experiencing the meaning of a word' (PI, II, p. 210) and that the importance of the discussion of 'aspect blindness' concerns the relationship between the concepts 'seeing an aspect' and 'experiencing the meaning of a word' (PI, II, p. 214 also p. 218). He stated:

> "... for a *large* class of cases – though not for all – in which we employ the word "meaning" it can be defined thus: the meaning of a word is its use in the language" (PI, I, # 43).

'My' experience with the meaning of a word can be different from situation to situation and relates also to my own past. My own experience can 'colour' the experience I have of the meaning of a word. In the *Philosophical Investigations* Wittgenstein suggests (PI, II, p. 216e–217e) that there is a primary and a secondary meaning. The first one to be indicated by 'use', and the second one, to be differentiated from any metaphorical use, refers to 'what it means to me'. Certain situations will demand that a word is placed within a context before I can experience its meaning. Here both what a word evokes, and what it evokes with me, are at stake. To put this in other words, 'meaning' is largely a matter of use, but it is I who use a word.

'Newness' and the Possibility of Criticism

In the following quotation Wittgenstein expresses the subtle balance between the 'linguistic community' and 'the experiencing individual':

> "I remember that sugar tasted like this. The experience returns to consciousness. But, of course: how do I know that this was the earlier experience? Memory is no more use to me here. No, in those words, that the experience returns to consciousness..., I am only transcribing my memory, not explaining it.
>
> But when I say "It tastes exactly like sugar", in an important sense no remembering takes place. So I do *not have grounds for* my judgment or my exclamation. If someone asks me "What do you mean by 'sugar'?" – I shall indeed try to show him a lump of sugar. And if someone asks "How do you know that sugar tastes like that?" I shall indeed answer him "I've eaten sugar thousands of time" – but that is not a justification that I give myself" (RFP, II, # 353).

Wittgenstein seems to suggest that being unable to give a justification to say certain things, is not quite the same as denying that I can state why I say certain things. Outside of what I associate in an experience, there is only the confirmation or the denial of my fellow human beings. An individual has neither an ultimate criterion nor 'ground' to decide whether his experience can be expressed in a certain way.

'New meaning' is possible firstly because situations are never quite identical. There are always different particularisations, and always a 'performing' of the meaning which has to take place. This is the crux of the possibility of looking differently at something. Starting from the pre-linguistic material, there is also the 'personal colour' of the meaning of a concept. My associations have to do with my experiences, with my own past. This means that on the basis of what we intersubjectively share, there can originate a personal 'colouring' which can be communicated to others. 'Meaning' is conceived here as the result of intersecting circles, in which each circle stands for the meaning of a word which has been used before now. 'Meanings' never exist completely separated from each other, but are linked through family-resemblances. The circles intersect with each other. In this sense it is possible that with the use of paraphrase I can express something that is new 'for me'. Hence it is possible that a new meaning emerges. Finally it is possible that this new meaning questions what is actually the case. But it will be clear that this can only be done with fragments of the past. In this sense newness can be thought without becoming incomprehensible and criticism can be given without losing its point of application. The criticism goes back to my experience and to the experience of the others and is expressed in a medium that can only be thought of as intersubjective. This medium literally precedes the use, but it is at the same time a use which is, in its turn, intersubjectively situated: it is regulated by the-others-and-each-individual-of-them. In that use 'meaning' is established and through its use future use is put at stake. In this sense it can be understood that Wittgenstein speaks of change of our concepts:

> "Do I want to say, then, that certain facts are favourable to the formation of certain concepts; or again unfavourable? And does experience teach us this? It is a fact of experience that human beings alter their concepts, exchange them for others when they learn new facts; when in this way what was formerly important to them becomes unimportant, and *vice versa*. (It is discovered, e.g. that what formerly counted as a difference in kind, is *really* only a difference in degree.)" (RFP, II, # 727).

The crucial role of the individual is again made clear by Wittgenstein where he ties the concept of 'imagination' strongly to that of 'intention'. He draws our attention to the fact that images are subdued to the will (and not in any psychological sense), and that 'to imagine' can be done intentionally. These images tell us almost nothing of 'the world': "The concept of imagining is rather like one of doing than of receiving" (RFP, II, # 111).

Finally it can be indicated in what sense people are bound together to 'what is'. People are firstly bound together to what is 'given' by 'science and education', by its *being there* and *being there for us* of the things. Smith (1987) points at the vagueness of the concept of 'experience'. It can mean both the world with which we are confronted and as what we make of it. To speak of consciously experiencing one's experiences:

> "... is to insist on the possibility of staying in touch with your experience in two senses: first in admitting what is 'given', thrown as it were before your feet on life's journey, into your subjectivity and consciously fitting it into the pattern of what things mean to you; and secondly in not forgetting that behind your interpretation there is that which you interpret, which may by its nature impose limits to what you can make of it without passing into fantasy or wishful thinking" (Smith, 1987, p. 40).

And he refers to 'experiential learning' as equivalent with 'attaining receptivity', opposed to the manipulative dealing with the world. In using the second meaning of 'givenness', it was made clear how 'newness' can be thought of. Quite evidently this leaves us with the problem of the justification of it, which is, though not completely different, still another matter. It will be clear that the weaker type of justification of education and child-rearing which was earlier argued for, need not be given up. To argue that it is an initiation into what is important for us, need not imply that no criticism is possible. Rather it supplies us with the necessary elements which make criticism possible at all. Neither the teacher nor the parent can start as from something that is valuable to them. 'Carried' by the community it is also that what an individual needs to give shape to one's experiences. The individual experience is not the beginning, but neither is what there is now or ever has been, the final destination.

Reminiscent of the difference for Wittgenstein between 'meaning' and political action, in this sense a concept of education appears that is not necessarily directed at lifting someone up out of one's social class. Indeed, in the end, philosophy, education and philosophy of education ought to have this individual blend, *pace* an unavoidable touch of conservatism. Only in the rightful modesty realising that philosophy cannot change the world, it leaves everything, but the individual, as 'it' is.

What Wittgenstein would have said about personal autonomy

STEFAAN E. CUYPERS[1]

University of Leuven, Belgium

INTRODUCTION: A WITTGENSTEINIAN OUTLOOK ON PERSONAL AUTONOMY

In section 122 of the *Investigations* Wittgenstein writes:

"A main source of our failure to understand is that we do not *command a clear view* of the use of our words. – Our grammar is lacking in this sort of perspicuity. A perspicuous representation produces just that understanding which consists in 'seeing connections'. Hence the importance of finding and inventing *intermediate cases*.

The concept of a perspicuous representation is of fundamental significance to us. It earmarks the form of account we give, the way we look at things. (Is this a 'Weltanschauung'?)" (PI, I, # 122).

This means that the positive task of philosophy lies, according to Wittgenstein, in the construction of a perspicuous representation ('übersichtliche Darstellung'). Hopefully, 'nothing is hidden' in the end when we are in the command of such a clear view. But in the beginning everything lacks perspicuity.

My topic in this chapter is the understanding of the *nature* and the *importance* of personal autonomy, especially in regard to educational practice. To this end Wittgenstein himself seems to be of little help. Nowhere in his works can one find a perspicuous representation of personal autonomy. Although Wittgenstein briefly remarked upon the issues of the subject and the person, especially in the context of solipsism (e.g. TLP, 5.63–5.64; BB, p. 61–74), he never tried to see the connections between the concept of personal autonomy and other clarifying concepts such as that of the will. Moreover, Wittgenstein never elaborated a philosophy of education and, a fortiori, never explored the role of (the ideal of) personal autonomy in an educational setting. Of course, this is not at all surprising, since Wittgenstein invested the bulk of his philosophical energy in semantical, epistemological and ontological topics. One can therefore wonder what, if anything, Wittgenstein has to say on the way we look at personal autonomy and educational practice.

Notwithstanding the fact that Wittgenstein never explicitly dealt with the philosophy of education, Hamlyn (1989) recently suggested that Wittgenstein's pure philosophical views can have illuminating implications for the philosophy of education. The application of his semantical, epistemological and ontological views to traditional issues in educational theory such as learning and understanding can readily provide a counterbalance to theoretical accounts which are too mentalistic and too individualistic in the interpretation they give of these processes. If one takes Hamlyn's advice seriously, it is to be expected that what Wittgenstein has to say in philosophy in general will equally be fruitful when

127

Studies in Philosophy and Education **14**: 251–265, 1995.

applied to other less epistemological and more ethical concepts in the philosophy of education, among which there is the concept of personal autonomy. The
fact that these concepts are less epistemological or ontological and more ethical
or existential does not exclude the possibility of an applied Wittgensteinian philosophy in advance. Thus, while one cannot reconstruct in any direct way
Wittgenstein's view on ethical or existential topics, one can try to construct *a
Wittgensteinian outlook* on such topics as personal autonomy and its role in educational practice. That is at least what I shall try to do in this chapter. My 'übersichtliche Darstellung' will then offer not so much what Wittgenstein actually
said as what he *would have* said about the nature and the importance of personal
autonomy.

The application of Wittgenstein's pure philosophy to the topic under consideration might seem at first sight unfruitful and even impossible. Indeed, an analysis of the concept of personal autonomy seems blatantly incompatible with the
currently predominant interpretation of Wittgenstein's later philosophy, the philosophy consolidated in the *Investigations*. This interpretation has come to be
known as the *Community View* (cf. especially Kripke, 1982). In this view the
Cartesian privilege of the first person is radically abolished, while the primacy
of the third person is firmly installed in its place, especially in regard to semantics. The individual person, considered in isolation, lacks the capacity to constitute meaning and rule-following. Instead, it is argued that social agreement in
forms of life and social customs (uses, institutions) (cf. PI, I, # 241 & 199) are
necessary for the very possibility of meaning and rule-following. Consequently,
if applying Wittgenstein's pure philosophy comes to the same thing as applying
the Community View, then a Wittgensteinian outlook on personal autonomy
does not seem feasible. For it is commonly thought that social interference in
whatever way poses a serious threat to personal autonomy. According to this
widespread view, 'autonomy' and 'community' are mutually exclusive terms in
the sense that the creativity of the autonomous individual is thought to be suffo-
cated by the conformism of the community. How can a person be called
autonomous, if what (s)he is and does necessarily depends upon the judgements
of other people, if her or his identity is radically moulded under the influence of
the social environment?

However, I shall try to show that Wittgenstein's general picture as outlined by
the Community View on the *Investigations* is only inconsistent with a narcissistic and corrupt conception of personal autonomy. This conception has to be considered as a deviant form of the more moral and ideal conception of personal
autonomy as *authenticity*. The moral ideal of authenticity is not at all at variance
with the Community View on the human condition. Quite on the contrary, true
personal autonomy presupposes the impact of other people's attitudes and the
larger communal context. Thus, although social dependence is usually regarded
as incompatible with personal autonomy, this dependence on other people's
opinions and social frameworks is not so much an impediment as it is a *constitutive* contribution to authentic autonomy. Hence, a Wittgensteinian outlook on
personal autonomy seems possible after all. To develop this theme I have, sur-

prisingly perhaps, not to start from scratch. My construction of this outlook as well as its defence is based upon two major views in contemporary philosophical anthropology, namely Frankfurt's *hierarchical model of the self* and Taylor's *moral psychology*. In an important sense, which will hopefully become clear during my construction, what Wittgenstein *would have said* about personal autonomy is to a large extent the same as what Frankfurt and Taylor *actually say* about it.

THE USE OF 'I' AS SUBJECT AND THE HIERARCHICAL MODEL OF THE SELF AND ITS AUTONOMY

Although Wittgenstein in his later period possibly changed, or at least relaxed, his views on solipsism, he never changed his views on the self or the subject. From beginning to end, his philosophical anthropology remained through and through *anti-Cartesian*. Thus, in the *Tractatus* Wittgenstein states:

> "The thinking, presenting subject; there is no such thing.
>   If I wrote a book 'The world as I found it', I should also have therein to report on my body and say which members obey my will and which do not, etc. This then would be a method of isolating the subject or rather of showing that in an important sense there is no subject: that is to say, of it alone in this book mention could *not* be made" (TLP, 5.631).

And again, near the end of *The Blue Book* he writes:

> "We feel then that in the cases in which 'I' is used as subject, we don't use it because we recognize a particular person by his bodily characteristics; and this creates the illusion that we use this word to refer to something bodiless, which, however, has its seat in our body. In fact *this* seems to be the real ego, the one of which it was said, 'Cogito, ergo sum'" (BB, p.69).

Parfit claims that Wittgenstein's rejection of the Ego Theory directly implies that Wittgenstein *would have* agreed with the empiricist Bundle Theory of self-identity (cf. Parfit, 1984, p. 273). Facing a choice between two views on a person's self-identity, Wittgenstein would have rejected the Cartesian view that the self-identity of a person involves the identity of her or his soul-substance and, consequently, he would have accepted the alternative empiricist view that a person's self-identity consists in the continuity of the bundle of her or his experiences. However, Wittgenstein's anti-Cartesianism does not in and of itself implicate empiricism with regard to the constitution of the self. Wittgenstein clearly distinguishes between two different uses of the word 'I': its use as subject and its use as object (BB, p. 66). Most importantly, 'I' in its use as subject is irreducible to 'I' in its use as object, in which case it refers to the person's body (BB, p. 74). Now, as Nagel convincingly argued, if the first person pronoun is used to refer to the bundle of experiences, then 'I' cannot be used as subject, but only as object (cf. Nagel, 1986, p. 32–37; 54–66). To adapt Wittgenstein's first sentence of the above quoted passage from *The Blue Book*: In the cases in which 'I' is used as subject, we equally don't use it because we recognize a particular person by her or his *psychological* characteristics. The bundle of experiences belongs as much to the objective world as the person's body. The psychological I would certainly be mentioned in the book 'The world as I found it'. But, of course, because we do use 'I' *as subject*:

> "There is [therefore] really a sense in which in philosophy we can talk of a non-psychological I. . . .
>
>   The philosophical I is not the man, not the human body or the human soul of which psychology treats, but the metaphysical subject, the limit – not a part of the world" (TLP, 5.641).

Wittgenstein's notion of 'the metaphysical subject' raises difficult semantical and ontological questions about self-reference and self-constitution. In our attempt to apply Wittgenstein's pure philosophy to more ethical and existential issues, these intricate problems can luckily be set aside. Suffice it to say that the metaphysical subject is neither a soul-substance nor a bundle of experiences: it's a non-Cartesian as well as a non-psychological self. A Wittgensteinian outlook on personal autonomy must at least be compatible with this negative ontology of the self. Positively we can say, I think, that when we talk in philosophy about the metaphysical subject as the limit of the world we are talking, as Nagel (1986, p. 62, note 3) claims, about *subjectivity*. Although 'I' in its use as subject does not refer to a special entity which has its seat in a person's body, it still *expresses* or *indicates* the subjectivity of a person. The fact that in an important sense there are no such *things* as subjects does not preclude the fact that in another equally important sense there really exist centres of subjectivity. *Pace* Malcolm (1988), to admit the existence of subjectivity in the world does not amount to the same thing as endorsing Cartesianism again.

   The best model to represent the essential subjectivity of the person is, I think, the *hierarchical model* of the self (cf. Frankfurt, 1971 & 1987; Cuypers, 1992). This model comprises two major elements. First: since subjectivity always involves self-consciousness, and since the structure which 'I' in its use as subject expresses necessarily entails reflexivity, we can draw a hierarchical distinction between mental states (events, processes) of the *first order* and those of the *second or higher order*. Second: taking into consideration our endeavour to render Wittgenstein's pure philosophy useful for the ethical and existential domains, we are not so much interested in the 'theoretical' part of the mind as in its 'practical' part. A person's essential subjectivity is therefore more germane to her or his *will* than to her or his reason; the existential essence of a person has more to do with her or his *volitions or desires* than with her or his beliefs. If we are interested in the ethical dimension and the meaning of a person's life, we are particularly concerned with the structure of her or his motives and the pattern of her or his actions which flows from that motivational structure. Hence, taking the two elements together, we can say that the hierarchical model of the self represents the essential subjectivity of the person in that it concentrates on her or his motivational structure which is composed of first-order and second-order desires. As an example of such a complex volitional structure, consider a corpulent weightwatcher who not only desires to be slim, but also does not desire that (s)he desires to eat sweets.

   In terms of this model's central notion of a *hierarchy of desires* different central notions in philosophical anthropology can fruitfully be analysed (cf.

Frankfurt, 1988). Among these anthropological notions the most salient are self-evaluation, autonomy, self-identification, authenticity, self-constitution, ego-ideal, self-change, internal conflict, self-fulfilment and weakness of the will. Here I will only highlight self-evaluation and the autonomy of the self (cf. Cuypers, 1992).

When a person cares about her- or himself, (s)he cares about her or his will because her or his identity – what (s)he is – is particularly constituted by her or his volitional character. Out of a special self-love, a person normally isn't indifferent to the structure of her or his will. This means that (s)he takes an evaluative attitude towards her or his own volitions. It is this capacity for reflective *self-evaluation* that is manifested in the formation of second-order desires. When a person takes a pro-attitude towards a certain part of her or his own will, (s)he forms a positive desire of the second order in regard to a certain desire of the first order. And conversely, when a person takes a contra-attitude, (s)he forms a negative desire of the second order. Now, in the event that a person forms a positive second-order desire in regard to a first-order desire, we can also say that (s)he identifies her- or himself with her or his will. And, if a person can reflectively identify her- or himself with her or his desires of the first order, then (s)he has a positively *free* will. In other words, when there exists a conformity of a person's first-order desires to her or his second-order desires, (s)he enjoys *autonomy*. (S)he determines her- or himself, if (s)he has a will (s)he wants to have. But if (s)he has a will (s)he does not want to have, (s)he is estranged from her- or himself. To put it succinctly, autonomy is volitional harmony. Or, to keep faith with the etymology of the term, auto-nomy is self-rule: a person rules her- or himself by evaluating her or his desires of the lower order according to her or his own desires of the higher order. This self-evaluation amounts to *self-government*: the government of a person by the person her- or himself.

Admittedly, the hierarchical model of the use of 'I' as subject is certainly not a standard Wittgensteinian picture. Although it models the reflexive will which is the seat of moral significance, it's still much too psychological:

> "Of the will as the subject of the ethical we cannot speak.
> And the will as a phenomenon is only of interest to psychology" (TLP, 6.423).

Nonetheless, the suggested model is, I think, at least compatible with the use of 'I' as subject, especially in a moral context. Moreover, this model does not presuppose the picture theory of meaning which definitely informs the quoted passage from the *Tractatus*, but rather it invites the view that meaning is use. Be that as it may, in order to interpret other more existential remarks of Wittgenstein, the hierarchical model seems right on the mark:

> *"Nobody can truthfully say of himself that he is filth.* Because if I do say it, though it can be true in a sense, this is not a truth by which I myself can be penetrated: otherwise I should either have to go mad or change myself" (CV, p. 32e).

In this quoted passage from *Culture and Value* Wittgenstein is surely commenting on self-evaluation, (the lack of) autonomy and self-change in a much more psychological setting and against a moral background.

Besides the problem of a possible infinite regress, the most notoriously troublesome aspect of the hierarchical model of the self and its autonomy is the problem of *normativity* (cf. Cuypers, 1992). The difficulty which pertains to the authority which second-order desires apparently have in the hierarchical model of self-evaluation is this. By taking pro-attitudes or contra-attitudes of the second order towards her or his desires of the first order a person evaluates her or his volitional system. But where do these evaluative attitudes get their authoritative or normative power from? Second-order attitudes are on this account, after all, just like the first-order desires they evaluate, *simply desires*. Going up one level does not automatically confer an evaluative authority upon desires of the second order; desires, of whatever order, can never have of themselves a special normative status. The difficulty here is not so much that there is a possibility of a regressive ascent, but rather that nothing about the level of desires gives them any special authority with respect to self-evaluation. Watson (1975) has brought this difficulty eminently to light and has suggested that in order to meet it a distinction should be made between desiring and *valuing*, between a volitional and a *valuation system*. To have an evaluative authority, higher order attitudes or desires must be grounded in a person's values which themselves cannot simply be reduced to her or his desires. Hence, the question of normativity boils down to the question as to what *constitutes* a person's valuation system.

THE COMMUNITY VIEW ON MEANING AS SIGNIFICANCE

It is to this important question of normativity, I think, that a distinctively Wittgensteinian answer can be suggested. To be sure, no straightforward answer of Wittgenstein, or even broadly Wittgensteinian answer, is readily available. My construction of a Wittgensteinian outlook on the normativity of self-evaluation starts from a rough analogy between meaning *as sense (and reference)* on the one hand and meaning *as significance (or value)* on the other hand. A Wittgensteinian picture of autonomy only manifests itself when Wittgenstein's semantical views on meaning in language are applied to *existential* meaning or 'the meaning of life'. Again, the distinction between the two modes of meaning-(fullness), I have in mind, is that between meaning as external referential or semantic relation and meaning as personal significance, relevance, importance, value, mattering (cf. Nozick, 1981, p. 574). Roughly speaking, philosophers of language and logic – and so Wittgenstein himself – concentrate on semantic meaning, while philosophers of man and morals as well as educational theorists attend to personal meaning. When we talk about the meaning of linguistic entities such as the word 'cow' and the sentence 'The cat is on the mat', the first mode of meaning is under consideration. But when we say, for example, '(S)he means a lot to her or him' or 'The principle of equality means a lot to socialists', the second mode of meaning is at issue. Of course, it is this second mode of meaning(fullness) – meaning as value – that is at stake in the problems of self-evaluation and autonomy. A person who says of her- or himself that "(S)he is filth" and, consequently, whose volitional structure is not indifferent to her or him, cares about the meaning or value of her or his life.

The question as to what constitutes a person's valuation system, or generally speaking, meaning as value can now be treated analogously to the question as to what constitutes meaning as sense. To this latter semantic question it is very plausible, as I mentioned at the outset of this paper, to give the answer of the so-called *Community View*. According to this view's interpretation of Wittgenstein's *(anti-)private language argument*, the normativity of meaning as sense cannot be accounted for unless the authority of the linguistic community is invoked. In a nutshell, the line of argumentation goes like this (cf. also Smeyers & Marshall, Introduction to this volume). The concept of semantic meaning is normative: "The relation of meaning and intention to future action is *normative*, not *descriptive*" (Kripke, 1982, p. 37). However, a single person considered in isolation is utterly incapable of constituting normative meaning: "In particular, this point applies if I direct my attention to a sensation and name it: nothing I have done determines future applications (in the sense of being uniquely *justified* by the concept grasped" (ibid., p. 107). Therefore, the normative concept of meaning is social: "... if the individual in question no longer conforms to what the community would do in these circumstances, the community can no longer attribute the concept to him" (ibid., p. 95).

Now, if there is something to gain from the analogy between meaning as sense and meaning as significance, then a distinctively Wittgensteinian answer can be suggested to the initial existential question as to what constitutes a person's evaluational system. This answer, surprisingly perhaps, can be found in Taylor's work on the nature of the moral self. Although he himself only rarely brings out his allegiance to a broadly Wittgensteinian framework (cf. Taylor, 1989, especially p. 35; 38), Taylor implicitly but clearly develops a Community View on *personal* meaning, and even gives an (anti-)private *significance* argument in support of this view. It is to Taylor's central ideas about the issues of self-evaluation and autonomy – ideas which have, to my mind, a recognizable Wittgensteinian flavour – that I now turn. In my construction of this Wittgensteinian outlook on personal autonomy, I will focus on Taylor's minor study *The Ethics of Authenticity* (1991) instead of on his major study *The Sources of the Self* (1989) because the former recapitulates the basic view and the main arguments of the latter in a more formal as well as more accessible way.

THE NEED FOR RECOGNITION, HORIZONS OF SIGNIFICANCE AND FORMS OF LIFE

Confronted with the problem of normativity, the modern Western, liberal, educated and secular (wo)man unhesitatingly opts for the currently obvious solution. The straightforward answer to the question as to what constitutes a person's valuation system is, of course, that the person her- or himself determines her or his own values. This *self-determination of values* directly flows from moral subjectivism and soft relativism both of which are offshoots of radical individualism, the hallmark of modernity. To say that the modern (wo)man is the self-determining or autonomous (wo)man has become a tautology:

"...everyone has a right to develop their own form of life, *grounded on their own sense of what is really important or of value*. People are called upon to be true to themselves and to seek their own self-fulfilment. What this consists of, each must, *in the last instance, determine for him- or herself. No one else* can or should try to dictate its content" (Taylor, 1991, p. 14, my italics).

The valuation system of a modern person must therefore be grounded in a *radically free choice or decision of her or his own*. For, in her or his self-evaluation an autonomous person can neither submit her- or himself to a pre-established religious or moral authority nor to any socially prevalent system of values and norms. (S)he has the absolute right of self-creation in regard to the manner as well as the matter or content of her or his life.

Unmistakably, this modern individualism of self-fulfilment collides head-on with a Community View on personal meaning or value. However, the individualistic and even narcissistic conception of personal autonomy is, according to Taylor (1991, p. 15–16), only a debased and travestied expression of a more adequate conception of being true to oneself. And this more moral and ideal conception of having one's own original way, for which he uses the phrase 'the ideal of *authenticity*', does incorporate a Community View on the constitution of a person's valuation system. Not only is such a Community View compatible with the ideal of authenticity, it is even a conceptual prerequisite of being in true contact with oneself. In short, atomistic autonomy which radically excludes social interference is a deviant form of authenticity which only flourishes in a certain social context. In this way, Taylor's retrieval of the ideal of authenticity from our modern culture of narcissism and self-indulgence comes to the same thing as elaborating a Community View on the *nature* and *importance* of the higher ideal behind the egoistic and hedonistic practices of people in the age of modernity.

As against the reactionaries who try to knock down all forms of individualism in contemporary society, the importance or worthiness of authenticity can be defended in terms of its essential relation to *the good life and human happiness*. Taking into consideration the human aspirations as such, the validity of authenticity as an ideal in human life is self-evident:

"...in articulating this ideal [of authenticity] over the last two centuries, Western culture has identified *one of the important potentialities of human life*. Like other facets of modern individualism...authenticity points us towards *a more self-responsible form of life*. It allows us to live (potentially) *a fuller and more differentiated life*, because more fully appropriated as our own.... at its best authenticity allows *a richer mode of existence*" (Taylor, 1991, p. 74, my italics).

Indeed, the role of authenticity in the modern Western world is unquestionably constitutive of what it means to lead a distinctively human life. Brought into existence as much by the Enlightenment as by Romanticism, the ideal of authenticity is here to stay, for better or for worse. The pessimists who try to debunk all appeals to self-realization too readily forget that individualism does not in and of itself bring a loss of meaning and a fading of moral horizons – the 'disenchantment' of the world – in its wake. But, of course, they are right to point out the dangers of the subjectivist turn which the pursuit of self-fulfilment quite recently took.

As against the boosters of the contemporary culture of narcissism who happily embrace its liberating relativism and subjectivism, the self-defeating structure of radical autonomy or self-determining freedom can be convincingly demonstrated. Such a demonstration directly follows from an articulation of the nature of the ideal of authenticity in terms of a *Community View on personal meaning or significance*. By way of rational argumentation, Taylor tries to show that the corrupt self-centred forms of being true to oneself are in the end narrow and shallow because these forms destroy the very possibility of the conditions of leading an authentic life. His overall argument consists of two mutually support- ing parts: first, the more concrete considerations from *the need for recognition*, and second, the more abstract considerations from *horizons of significance*. It is these latter considerations which constitute, to my mind, an (anti-)private signifi- cance argument that runs parallel to Wittgenstein's famous (anti-)private lan- guage argument in semantics and epistemology. Taylor's general argument takes as its premise our shared human condition and then tries to remind us of certain general features of human life in support of his argumentation (cf. Taylor, 1991, p. 32; 56). This procedure calls to mind a well-known methodological point of Wittgenstein:

> "What we are supplying are really remarks on *the natural history of human beings*; we are not contributing curiosities however, but observations which no one has doubted, but which have escaped remark only because *they are always before our eyes*" (PI, I, # 415, my italics).

One general fact about our shared human condition which Taylor tries to remind us of is that the definition of our identity essentially depends upon the recogni- tion we get from – what George Herbert Mead called – *significant others* (cf. Taylor, 1991, p. 33). Persons are not like self-contained monads. The existential identity of a person – her or his self-esteem – is not built in a monological, but in a *dialogical* way. Through the medium of languages of expression, the exchange between the self and the other constitutes the *narrative* identity of the self (cf. Taylor, 1989, p. 35; 47). Of course, it is almost a commonplace to say that human beings are deeply involved with other human beings. However, the involvement with other people in the definition of our identity is not only a temporal genetical, but also an everlasting structural feature of our lives. Moreover, the reference to other people in the delineation of 'who we are' is not so much extrinsic and instrumental, as it is intrinsic and constitutive. Our deal- ings with other selves cannot be thought of on the model of a social contract between fundamentally isolated individuals. Quite the reverse is the case, for always we are already caught in an original social web of attitudes and reactive attitudes upon which our identity as individuals depends:

> "Then we should think, . . . of the kind of importance we attach to the attitudes and intentions towards us of those who stand in these [personal] relationships to us, and of the kinds of *reactive* attitudes and feelings to which we ourselves are prone" (Strawson, 1962, p. 6).

Or, to put the same idea otherwise, in the making and sustaining of our identity, we really take other human beings seriously: "My attitude towards him is an attitude towards a soul ... " (PI, II, iv).

The *recognition* by others which we get or which is withheld from us expresses their *evaluative attitudes* towards our identity and character. Herein resides, I think, a first step towards a Wittgensteinian solution of the problem of normativity. For, to keep in view the social dependence of a person's identity is to bear in mind that a person identifies her- or himself with the pro- and contra-attitudes of other people and that (s)he subsequently takes these attitudes towards her or his own motivational structure. This is to say that a person's valuation system in terms of which she or he evaluates desires and preferences is basically constituted by the valuation system of the community lived in. The socio-psychological mechanism behind such a form of self-evaluation can be explained in terms of – what Charles Horton Cooley called – the idea of *the reflected or looking-glass self* (cf. Cuypers, 1992). The self-image of a person is the reflected image of her or him in the eyes of other people. Now, we *need* this recognition or misrecognition by others in order to evaluate ourselves, primarily because of the decline of traditional hierarchical society in which ascribed social roles fixed a person's identity once and for all (cf. Taylor, 1991, p. 47). When traditional religious and political frameworks collapse, we have to appeal to the authority of other people to keep our mental sanity and an appropriate sense of our identity. Without the evaluative attitudes of other people we should be completely in the dark about our *true or real* personal worth. Our self-esteem has to keep track of the esteem of others. Briefly, the emergence of the ideal of authenticity in the age of modernity, together with the impossibility of a monological identity, create the explicit need for recognition by other people:

> "... the development of an ideal of inwardly generated identity gives a new and crucial importance to recognition. My own identity crucially depends on my dialogical relations with others" (Taylor, 1991, p. 47–48).

Hence, if having one's own original way is reduced and degraded to a self-centred autonomy that does not acknowledge the need for recognition by others, then one of the major possibility conditions of the ideal of authenticity is itself destroyed. The denial of the social dependence of our identity is therefore self-defeating.

But does not this Community View on self-evaluation imply the eradication of all creativity and the justification of sheer conformism? Furthermore, if the second-order attitudes or desires of the self considered by itself are normatively impotent, what then gives the evaluative attitudes of other people a special authoritative power? Exactly why, one perhaps wonders, isn't it possible to determine values and norms all by oneself? All these and similar worries in the end boil down to the one fundamental question: *Why is private significance impossible?* It is in answering this question that – what I have called – Taylor's (anti-)private significance argument is in place (cf. Taylor, 1991, p. 35–41).

"All options are equally worthy, because they are freely chosen, and it is choice that confers worth" (Taylor, 1991, p. 37). This soft relativism and its underlying subjectivism about value vigorously reject the impact of all valuation frameworks which transcend the self. The possibility of private significance is evidently a consequence of radical individualism. Thus, the self all by itself determines its values and norms in that it fixes 'what has significance' by radically free choice, or by decision, or by just feeling that way. However, if in my self-definition and self-evaluation *anything goes*, then my identity and personal worth become insignificant or trivial. Extreme individualism is therefore self-destructive. For, to be significant means to be set apart or to make a difference. But if radically free choice is the crucial justifying reason, then any option is on the same level with any other option, and consequently, no one option stands apart. Before choice confers importance upon an option, all options are, *ex hypothesi*, without importance. Since valuation frameworks anterior to choice are excluded, no option is of itself more worthwhile than any other option. But if everything can in principle become significant, then nothing has any special significance. If everything can make a difference, then nothing actually does. If any option we choose is all right, then no one option can make a special difference. Self-chosen difference becomes insignificant or trivial. It is *just crazy* to think that your choice, decision or feeling can determine what is significant.

The untenable nature of private significance can be shown in yet another way (cf. Taylor, 1977). According to the hypothesis under consideration, the higher-order attitudes in a person's self-evaluation are expressive of self-chosen values. But these putative evaluative attitudes are really either only *factual* preferences or merely *arbitrary* options. For, if there are no prior value-criteria whatsoever by reference to which a radically free choice is made, then such a choice is either based upon the strongest attraction of one preference among other alternatives or made without regard to preferences at all. Consequently, a special normative status can never accrue to such higher-order attitudes. A radically free choice is, after all, just a wanton movement of the mind without any special authority. Here self-determining freedom or radical autonomy collapses into *anomy* and thus the initial problem of normativity reappears again (cf. Cuypers, 1992). In sum, a single individual, considered by her- or himself and in isolation, cannot just by *fiat* constitute normative significance because whatever is going to *seem* significant to her or him *ipso facto is* significant. But that only means that we cannot talk about *significance* at all. Interestingly, this parallels Wittgenstein's conclusion in regard to the impossibility of private meaning (as sense) and rule-following:

"And hence also 'obeying a rule' is a practice. And to *think* one is obeying a rule is also not to obey a rule. Hence it is not possible to obey a rule 'privately': otherwise thinking one was obeying a rule would be the same thing as obeying it" (PI, I, # 202; see also # 258).

Consequently, in my self-definition and self-evaluation I have to take as a background a sense of what is significant *independent of my autonomous will*. My identity and personal worth only take on importance against a background of intelligibility or – what Taylor calls – a *horizon of significance* (cf. Taylor, 1991, p. 37). A horizon of significance is a valuation system of a historically grown community. It consists of the authoritative principles, rules, values and norms which are expressive of the normative and socially prevalent conception of the good life. Such inescapable frameworks within which we define ourselves and determine our self-worth are not chosen but discovered: "Horizons [of significance] are given" (Taylor, 1991, p. 39). Of course, this line of thought immediately brings another famous remark of Wittgenstein to mind: "What has to be accepted, the given, is – so one could say – *forms of life*" (PI, II, xi). If there is some truth in my suggestion that Taylor basically offers an (anti-)private significance argument, then 'forms of life' are indeed necessary for authentic personal autonomy:

> "Otherwise put, I can define my identity only against the background of things that matter [a horizon of significance]. . . . Only if I exist in a world in which history, or the demands of nature, or the needs of my fellow human beings, or the duties of citizenship, or the call of God, or something else of this order *matters* crucially, can I define an identity for myself that is not trivial" (Taylor, 1991, p. 40–41).

Hence, if being true to oneself is reduced and degraded to a self-centred autonomy that shuts out horizons of significance, then another of the very possibility conditions of the ideal of authenticity is itself destroyed. Since authenticity presupposes significance, and since the constitution of significance ultimately depends upon 'forms of life' (cf. also Smeyers & Marshall, Introduction to this volume), it follows that authenticity necessarily requires valuation frameworks which transcend the self.

Finally, in order to further indicate the direction in which the distinctively Wittgensteinian answer to the question of normativity leads, we can bring the two parts of the Community View on authenticity and self-evaluation briefly together. For an adequate self-evaluation a person needs the recognition of other people. Identity and self-esteem crucially depend upon their evaluative attitudes. But, of course, in their measured evaluation of a person's character, concrete other people do not express their own idiosyncratic values, but the valuation framework of the community at large. The authority of other people's evaluative attitudes is only *derived from* the authority of the community's horizon of significance or 'form of life'. This highest court of appeal has an original or special normative status because it *transcends* a person's evaluation as well as other people's evaluation of her or him. Horizons of significance not only transcend the self *but also the other*. The fact that horizons are given at least means that they have some sort of dynamic life of their own. The status of such a transcendent valuation framework can partially be clarified – in keeping with the Wittgensteinian spirit – by saying that a horizon of significance is neither a relativistic or conventionalistic framework in a Humpty-Dumpty sense nor an absolute or separated framework in a Platonic sense. A 'form of life' in so far as it pertains to common principles, rules, values and norms is a normative framework which is neither fully immanent nor strongly transcendent. A horizon of significance refers to *inherited traditions and customs* of valuing to which both the person who asks for recognition and the other people who give or deny it are subordinated. The authenticity of the self is therefore constituted against an inherited background of intelligibility by an 'ongoing conversation' between the self and the other.

CONCLUSION: THE IDEAL OF AUTHENTICITY AND EDUCATION

Admittedly, my construction of a Wittgensteinian outlook on personal autonomy only offers a rough sketch of a perspicuous representation of this important educational issue. But if there is some truth in my 'übersichtliche Darstellung', then the central claim which the Community View on personal autonomy and significance makes with regard to education in general is, I think, that education can be best construed as *initiation*. Thus, education fundamentally comes to the same thing as the complex process of the initiation of social selves in a given form of life on which they ultimately depend for their self-realization and life-fulfilment. This basic claim – education as initiation – echoes, of course, the position of Peters on the matter: "...education consists essentially in the initiation of others into *a public world* picked out by the language and concepts of a people and in encouraging others to join in exploring realms marked out by *more differentiated forms of awareness*" (Peters, 1966, p. 52, my italics).

The fact that it is possible to adequately formulate a Wittgensteinian outlook on personal autonomy and education in general does not mean in and of itself that such an outlook is also a *justifiable* position to take in contemporary philosophy of education. In particular, a Wittgensteinian philosophy of education seems at first sight to be exposed to the objection of *inherent conservatism or conformism*. To lower the temperature of this steamy issue, I would like to give two concise but important replies. First: the Wittgensteinian outlook on personal autonomy only offers an anthropological view which belongs to an adequate account of the metaphysics of personhood. As such it remains *neutral* in regard to the particular ethical and political contents which are conferred upon the formal possibility conditions of authenticity in a particular society. Horizons of significance and dialogical relationships are present in 'nice' or democratic as well as in 'grim' or totalitarian societies. There is nothing intrinsically conservative about the structural possibility conditions of authenticity. Second, and more importantly: the significance *itself* of being critical of and opposed to the demands of external conformity crucially depends upon a *wider* horizon of significance that promotes authentic self-realization and self-fulfilment as worthy ideals. As the (anti-)private significance argument shows, the very sense of criticism and opposition presupposes the value of a *tradition* of critique. In primitive and closed societies there is not even the possibility of being critical; only in our modern Western society is such a possibility created and preserved. Even the capacity for being critical is not something that a single individual, considered by her- or himself and in isolation, could bring about and continue to maintain. Since criticism and opposition depend upon a Community View there is nothing inherently conformistic about it.

It goes without saying that personal autonomy is one of the most important educational ideals, if not the most important one. In conclusion, I will therefore briefly explore the role of personal autonomy and authenticity in an educational setting. The Wittgensteinian outlook on personal autonomy which I tentatively extracted from Frankfurt's hierarchical model of the self and Taylor's moral psychology leads up to the following overall definition of authenticity:

> "Briefly, we can say that authenticity (A) involves (i) creation and construction as well as discovery, (ii) originality, and frequently (iii) opposition to the rules of society and even potentially to what we recognize as morality. But it is also true, as we saw, that it (B) requires (i) openness to horizons of significance... and (ii) a self-definition in dialogue. That these demands may be in tension has to be allowed. But what must be wrong is a simple privileging of one over the other, of (A), say, at the expense of (B), or vice versa" (Taylor, 1991, p. 66).

Now, what is wrong with much contemporary educational practice and pedagogical theory is indeed that they stress (A), while altogether forgetting the import of (B). Not only proponents of liberal education, but also defenders of classical schooling in the tradition of Kant and Herbart often start from the self-evident principle that children and pupils are either actual or potential autonomous beings in the *radical* sense. These educational practitioners and theorists certainly do not deny the temporal and factual dependence of autonomy on the impact of other people's attitudes and the larger communal context. But they nevertheless presume that the individual child or pupil remains *in principle* the independent creator of his volitional character as well as his values. However, if the Wittgensteinian picture of personal autonomy which I drew is plausible, then this exclusive emphasis on the self-determining freedom of youngsters – the exaltation of (A) over (B) – is fully unwarranted, and even self-defeating. Again, if the (anti-)private significance argument is valid, then any conception of being true to oneself which staves off horizons of significance and dialogical relationships is fundamentally distorted or corrupt. The ideal in educational practice and the starting-point of pedagogical theory can therefore not be personal autonomy of the radical self-determining type, but *must* be authenticity in the above defined sense. The fundamental educational ideal in the motivational or volitional field is thus not so much autonomy, as it is authenticity. This constitutes, I think, a fruitful and promising result of an applied Wittgensteinian philosophy with regard to the ethical or existential domain. Of course, those in sympathy with a Community View on personal autonomy and significance should guard against the opposite failure, namely the privileging of (B) at the expense of (A). Whatever future development of a Wittgensteinian outlook on personal autonomy must therefore respect *the fundamental tension* in the ideal of authenticity because such a tension belongs to the very nature of the self itself.[2]

NOTES

[1] Senior Research Assistant National Fund for Scientific Research (Belgium).
[2] I would like to thank Paul Smeyers for his friendly encouragement to write this paper and James Marshall for his thought-provoking criticisms of my 1992 paper to which the present paper only gives a partial reply. And I am most grateful to my colleague Stuart Rennie for his amiable companionship over the last two years.

Why We Should not Speak of an Educational Science

PAUL STANDISH

University of Dundee, United Kingdom

Why should anyone be inclined to speak of an educational science? What is science being contrasted with? What purpose might an educational science serve? These questions raise issues of both descriptive and programmatic kinds. The descriptive issue concerns how far what currently goes on in the study of education is appropriately seen as science. The programmatic has to do with the agenda for the future direction of the subject. In the following pages the target for a Wittgensteinian attack will come into view as an appropriate vocabulary is gradually marshalled.

It is worth saying something briefly about the connotations of 'science'. The term itself has a recent history which separates it from *Wissenschaft*. Current usage is uneven especially insofar as the employment of the term in debate about disciplines may be at odds with more everyday parlance. Thus in the latter, human or social 'science' is a clear borrowing from the natural sciences, where procedures and standards have been set which the human sciences attempt to emulate. It is appropriate also to flag the ambiguity of 'education'. This can refer to the practice of education, in both institutional and non-institutional forms, and to its academic study. It is with the latter that the question of an educational science is primarily concerned. The argument for an educational science might be extended to encompass the practising teacher in the way that the hospital doctor is a practitioner of medical science. But if this move is made it leaves problematic the relation between the teacher and the subjects which are taught.

It may be sensible not to equivocate over terminology. The important issues here are with how education is to be understood and practised as a discipline. Nevertheless there are circumstances which may make the question of terminology one of key importance. It may be, for example, that prestige attaches to anything called science in such a way that funding is conditional on this. This is one reason why someone might be inclined to speak of an educational science.

Related to this is the fact that what appear to be possibilities of science also dovetail neatly with the prevalent (scientistic) concern with accountability. Thus an educational science might, for example, operate with, and propagate the use of, statements of objectives of a behavioural and measurable kind. If the positivism which prevailed in philosophy earlier this century has been superseded, it is clear that it retains its hold over many other aspects of contemporary life. With this comes a revering of science as the embodiment of certain intellectual virtues: science epitomizes rigour and disinterestedness, a proper concern for

143

Studies in Philosophy and Education **14**: 267–281, 1995.

explanation and evidence, and a securing of foundations for thought; it requires expertise. These factors also might attract someone to the possibility of an educational science.

The implication is not, it is assumed, that there might be a number of different educational sciences such as the psychology of education, all coming under the umbrella of education alongside other non-scientific facets of study. Similarly the question of how far education is made up of contributing disciplines from, for example, the established social sciences is not at issue here. The placing of education as a science may involve two major moves. One is that education is contrasted with humanities or arts. The separation from the humanities means that, for example, the way that history studies the life of a culture will not be seen as appropriate to education; the separation from the arts means *inter alia* that the type of creativity and imagination found in literature or the practical arts will be thought inappropriate to the more technical problems which education encounters, where the need is for efficient means towards pre-determined ends. The other move is towards seeing education as a unified discipline. It is this which first needs attention.

What actually goes on in education, as studied in universities, is diverse. Three typical cases can be identified. First, a researcher in education may be concerned with the disinterested observation of current practice. Often, however, what presents itself as a focus for research will arise out of an interest in improvement in some aspect of current developments. Second, the work of a student of education may be more narrowly instrumental in kind, where teaching techniques (directed towards agreed, imposed, or tacitly assumed ends) are developed. Third, the academic working in education may pursue a questioning of the practice of education and an enquiry into the very concept, considering its aims and its place in human life, or aspects of these questions. Education (in this third dimension) shades into questions addressed more or less directly in other subjects – most directly perhaps in philosophy, extensively but obliquely in the humanities, tangentially in science. Some of these questions explore the nature of the good life.

There is a curious asymmetry between the study of education and other disciplines. For any academic discipline one can speak of being educated in it; there is an obvious strangeness about being educated in education – though this must be what happens. This is a potential source of confusion, not least in essays like the present one. But this may say something more deep about the possibilities of such a subject. In other disciplines one is never outside the practice of education; where educational studies involve a questioning of the practice and concept of education this is quintessentially part of educational practice! Education *qua* subject must be a part of education *qua* practice. This indicates its unusual breadth and pervasiveness. Philosophy of education itself reflects something of this in that, unlike the (plausibly analogous) philosophy of health care, for example, there is no major branch of philosophy which is not relevant to it. With the breadth and pervasiveness of education, however, there is a certain amorphousness – a loosely connected set of practices and modes of enquiry – which threatens the cogency of any attempt to establish a unified and tidy conception of it as a subject.

A complicating factor is the way in which education may be an amalgam of more pure disciplines. Thus some questions which arise in education are appropriately addressed by the methods of psychology or of history. Such a conception was behind the curriculum for teacher education with its foundational disciplines. But this amalgam of contributing subjects could never be said to exhaust the nature of education, where time and attention are given to a plethora of matters concerning teaching and the running of a school. Nor does it convincingly encompass those narratives and visionary tracts – from *The Republic* to *Deschooling Society* – which illuminate the consideration and planning of educational practice.

There is a strong case then for seeing education as unlike other subjects, especially because of the difficulty of setting limits to it in any tidy way. Against this unpromising background it must be asked what criteria must be fulfilled if the subject is to count as a science. The situation of the human sciences will be considered as a potential best case for an educational science.

The everyday naive conception of science, which has been implicit thus far, is the outcome of logical empiricism. Crucial to it is the belief that the world can be observed in a way which is not dependent on subjective concerns. Observation which is independent in this way is value-free and universal in its claims; the legitimacy of its findings is based on the idea of a correspondence between the descriptions it offers and what is observed to be the case. Understood in this way, science embodies standards and procedures which are in tension with the practice of a social science, especially with regard to the issue of relativism and the relationship between evidence and explanation.

With the demise of positivism, however, the logical empiricist view of science has been widely rejected. The background to this is the growing recognition that the data of science are theory-dependent. Thomas Kuhn's position emphasizes the subject-relativity of scientific practice. It introduces the idea of 'normal' science to identify those times when sufficient agreement about method coalesces to enable research to proceed without a continued and incapacitating questioning. The conceding of the subject-relativity of scientific procedures removes one crucial barrier between natural and social science. For some writers this breakthrough is decisive. Thus Richard Rorty sees no crucial difference in method (Rorty, 1980). All that can be said is that natural science has been found to achieve periods of normality more often than social science, where methodological disputes are never far from the surface.

The rejection of logical empiricism need not, however, lead to this conclusion. That this is so can be seen by identifying a further more problematic difference between the natural and the social sciences. This hinges on how far the objects of observation are independent of the descriptions which it will be appropriate to use about them. The objection here is that the social groups which are observed cannot be understood or analyzed without employing the concepts inherent in their own practices. In hermeneutic terms human beings will be seen as necessarily self-interpreting and no analysis which is not fundamentally attuned to this fact will be adequate.

In *The Idea of a Social Science* Peter Winch details this Wittgensteinian objection (Winch, 1958). The natural scientist, according to Winch, proceeds by observing regularities in the natural world. But the idea of a regularity depends upon criteria for without these how can two occurrences be judged the same? What generates the criteria is the practice of science, in which the individual researcher participates. As Winch puts it, "to understand the activities of the scientific investigator we must take account of two sets of relations: first, his relation to the phenomena which he investigates; second, his relation to his fellow scientists" (ibid., p. 84).

The social scientist's practice, however, cannot be like this. Winch gives the example of the parable of the Pharisee and the Publican (Luke 18, 9). The Pharisee says, "God, I thank Thee that I am not as other men are"; the Publican, "God be merciful unto me a sinner". Are these men doing the same thing? Are they both praying? To answer this it will be necessary to consider the concept of prayer and this is not a scientific but a religious question. Questions of this kind are internal to the phenomena being observed in a way that questions concerning natural objects are not.

Applied to education, this reasoning reveals a sort of circularity. Inherent in the practices studied by the educational researcher are educational concepts – of teaching and learning, for example. The difference in the operation of the concepts in the respective activities of the researcher and the classroom teacher is in part a matter of self-consciousness. This point does not deny the hermeneutic objection. It shows how acknowledging it further exposes the curious self-referential nature of education.

Something of this complexity is recognized by Wilfred Carr in *The Idea of an Educational Science* (Carr, 1989). Developing ideas from Habermas, he asserts that "a critical educational science would not be a science *about* education but a science *for* education. Understood in this way, the aims of education and the aims of educational science would be one" (ibid., p. 35). What is advocated is "nothing other than an elaboration of the mode of social and moral life of which it would be an integral part" (ibid., p. 36). Central to Habermas' notion of communicative rationality is the idea of the realisation of the rational discourse which is implicit in everyday human language. Such a realisation is crucially linked to democracy and to the achievement of personal autonomy. It would yield, on Carr's account, an educational science in which the method of critique would be addressed to existing practice to confront it with some shared understanding of educational values. The process would be dialectical so that the values themselves would be clarified and developed in the light of particular practices. Education would be *par excellence* the arena within which the possibilities of democracy were worked out.

Striking features of this position are its faith in rationality and its aim of enlightenment, drawing from Habermas' identification of the basic human interest in emancipation. This is achieved through a reflexively acquired self-knowledge whereby individuals are "more consciously aware of the social or ideological roots of their self-understanding" (ibid., p. 33). The attention to practice which is a key feature of this approach accords well with Wittgenstein's thought but the preoccupation with rationality and enlightenment and the concern with making things explicit pull in a different direction.

This emphasis on the explicit marks a difference which is thematic in Hubert Dreyfus' discussion of theoretical and practical holism (Dreyfus, 1980). Both types are characterized by the importance they attach to the background to all experience. This background is a context which necessarily extends beyond any description which could be given. In the theoretical version, all understanding is taken to be epistemic. The background is a belief system. Any of these background beliefs, though not all, could in principle be brought to light. Practical holism, on the other hand, pictures the background in a non-cognitive way, as behaviour. Such background behaviour is non-analyzable, not to be objectified. The outcome of training, it is rightly seen in terms of skills. (This conception of skills is, of course, very different from the generic context-free skills currently in vogue in education.) In Heidegger's terms the background involves a *Vorhaben*: correctly understood, this prompts appreciation of the way that circumstances *have us*. In the micropractices which constitute backgrounds there is preserved something which enables human beings *to be*. Such practices require an agreement in judgments, where this is a common response to circumstance and not a shared deliberation and debate. In these terms Wittgenstein is appropriately seen as a practical holist.

Foundationalist modes of thinking, such as logical empiricism, fail on this view to recognize the background. Properly regarded, the background may be seen as that which preserves; its reality something to which a religious attitude might be directed. This might take the form of a focusing of our contemporary cultural practices while evidence is assembled of an alternative understanding of human beings implicit in our micropractices but suppressed by our everyday concerns (ibid., p. 23). It would be a resistance against the nihilism engendered where the objectifying practices of the Enlightenment eclipse or disperse these micropractices.

When the issue between theoretical and practical holism is related to the natural and the human sciences, it raises the question how far the decontextualizing of theory, the abstraction from the background, can be consistent with the purpose of the study. Dreyfus' argument is that in the natural sciences the background is external to the science while in the human sciences it is internal. In a different way, however, both types of science are dependent on a background: this is the background of skills from which the scientist draws. Such skills are not learned through textbooks but picked up in apprenticeship, perhaps by working through exemplary problems. Moreover, these background scientific skills presuppose our everyday practices and discriminations so that they cannot be decontextualized like the context-free properties they reveal (ibid., p. 16). In the findings of the natural scientist this background can be effectively excluded whereas in those of the human scientist it cannot. This is because there is a con-

tinuity in the latter between researcher and researched such that the observation
acknowledges the reality of the background from which the research itself
draws. The research inevitably calls into question the ground the researcher is
standing on. The suspension of this acknowledgement, which worked effectively
in natural science, can no longer be sustained.

There are then two major arguments against the assimilation of human and
natural science. The argument from Winch stresses the contextual nature of what
is studied in the impossibility of gaining understanding without reference to the
self-interpretations of the human beings who are studied. The argument from
Dreyfus focuses more on the researcher: the human sciences cannot work suc-
cessfully without acknowledgement of the background and this in turn calls into
question the researcher's own situation. The emphasis on particularity and
context and the denial in practical holism that human behaviour is formalizable
in terms of strict rules together weigh heavily against the development of grand
theory of the kind exemplified by the work of Habermas.

These objections indicate the sorts of opposition to the idea of an educational
science which are raised by the work of Wittgenstein but the potential range of a
critique drawn from his work is more complex. I shall address the matter in three
ways: first, through his attack on certain positions which the claim of science
would seem to hold; second, through various remarks on culture; third, through
his stance regarding the nature of ethics. It is in keeping with the holistic character of Wittgenstein's thought that these are not water-tight divisions.

It is apparent that no uniform characterization of science can be given. But it
is reasonable to draw from what has been said so far certain characteristics. Thus
science – at least, as commonly understood – is typified by generality, universality, freedom from context, a faith in rationality and logic, the commitment to
theory and system, quantifiability, and explicitness. This is not a definitive list; it
is designed to show the sorts of criteria which education as a science would vari-
ously need to satisfy. In what follows these will be seen recurrently to be the
objects of Wittgenstein's attack.

Wittgenstein's attitude to the possibilities of science is closely bound up with
his conception of philosophy and with what appropriate methods in philosophy
might be. His later views are reached by an overt rejection of philosophy as the
Queen of the Sciences, the view held by Russell, but also by overturning central
tenets of his own earlier position.

David Pears remarks that Wittgenstein's method is more art than science
"because the nuances of particular cases are not caught in any theory" (Pears,
1971, p. 105). The failure of the net (TLP, 6.34) indicates Wittgenstein's growing suspicion of large scale and systematic theory. The idea of logic as something sublime, at the bottom of all the sciences, is an emblem of universality and
foundationalism. Ordinary language then seems a pale shadow of the real thing.
But the most that could be said, Wittgenstein now suggests, is that logic is constructed *out of* ordinary language. Attention needs to be turned away from the
slippery ice of logic, in its crystalline purity, and towards the rough ground of
ordinary language: we need friction in order to be able to walk (PI, I, # 107).

The preconceived idea of the primacy of logic can only be removed by turning the whole examination round: the axis of reference of the examination must be rotated, but about the fixed point of our real need (ibid., # 108).

If the examination is turned round, it will be directed upon the ordinary circumstances of our language. But what form will the examination then take? Wittgenstein's method is to focus on different language-games, the sorts of things we say in different segments of our lives, in what Dreyfus perhaps means by 'micropractices'. In reaction to the early work, this repeatedly draws attention to context. The emphasis is on the particulars of experience. To some extent a precept is provided which is applicable to science itself. For here too error is likely to arise where a seemingly recurrent feature leads to the hypostatization which subsequently directs investigation. The diagnosis of 'shock' in victims of war – as Wittgenstein discovered in his work at Guy's Hospital during the War – is a case in point (cf. Monk, 1990, pp. 445–7). The particulars of experience are not to be identified as the discrete data of experience but to be understood in language-games. A feature of these is their incommensurability: they contain their own criteria.

Wittgenstein's aim is not, as supposedly in science, the establishment of propositions of the highest level of generality but the achievement of an *Übersicht*, a perspicuous representation or overview. What is required is a "clear view of the use of our words" (PI, I, # 122; cf. Z, # 447). It is not by abstracting common elements from a variety of cases but by seeing connections and identifying intermediate cases that this will be achieved (PI, I, # 122). This attention to the way we speak has been called "a subtle kind of positivism" (Pears, 1971, p. 38). But such a characterization draws the attention away from the ways in which the examples are used and from the purpose of the investigation. As Wittgenstein expresses the matter:

> "It was true to say that our considerations could not be scientific ones. It was not of any possible interest to us to find out empirically 'that, contrary to our preconceived ideas, it is possible to think such and such' – whatever that may mean. (The conception of thought as a gaseous medium.) And we may not advance any kind of theory. There must not be anything hypothetical in our considerations. We must do away with all *explanation*, and description alone must take its place. And this description gets its light, that is to say its purpose, from the philosophical problems. These are, of course, not empirical problems; they are solved, rather, by looking into the workings of our language, and that in such a way as to make us recognize those workings: *in despite of* an urge to misunderstand them. The problems are solved, not by giving new information, but by arranging what we have always known. Philosophy is a battle against the bewitchment of our intelligence by means of language" (PI, I, # 109).

The investigation is not just towards phenomena but towards "the '*possibilities*' of phenomena" (ibid., 90). Whatever might count as *empiria*, Wittgenstein's concern is with the phenomena as understood within a grammar. These will not normally be mere objects of perception but something understood in terms of an appropriate range of response. Where objects of perception are cited these will emerge from a practice of science which divests ordinary experience of its normal actions and reactions. Such a scientific outlook will be privative; it will never be foundational in the way in which Wittgenstein had once imagined.

Wittgenstein's use of examples is then located (in a sense) between the peculiarly philosophical alternatives of empiricism and rationalism: the examples, pointing beyond themselves, reveal possibilities of thought. Essence is found in their grammar. And grammar is not to be underpinned by reference to 'data' for grammar is autonomous.

This last point indicates a further way in which the suggestion of empiricism is ill-founded. This is that many of the examples which are given are of imaginary language-games, sometimes exaggerated or impossible, cases which, through juxtaposition with our ordinary experience, point towards the limits of intelligibility of segments of grammar.

While such connections can lead towards the achievement of an *Übersicht*, analogy also provides a valuable technique. Baker and Hacker show how the germs of this notion in Wittgenstein's thought can be found in his reading of Hertz and Boltzmann where the value of fruitful analogy, rather than the seeking of ultimate explanations, is acknowledged in respect of science itself (Baker and Hacker, 1980, pp. 297–8). That natural science makes progress through analogy does not deny its other fundamental points of difference from the human sciences.

The *Übersicht* is in keeping with the holistic character of Wittgenstein's thought. It is manifestly not an exhaustive explanation; it is necessarily partial, covering a limited domain of our experience or a limited segment of grammar. The "craving for generality" (BB, p. 18), with its contemptuous attitude towards the particular case, is to be resisted and the *Übersicht* is set against any ideal of an over-arching theory. Understanding does not require and sometimes precludes the holding of a theory.

The *Übersicht* is closely linked with the idea of seeing aspects. Wittgenstein deals with this extensively in Part II, xi of the *Philosophical Investigations*. In the puzzle picture of the duck-rabbit (PI, II, p. 194) it is not the addition of a datum which allows the alternative picture to be seen but the dawning of an aspect such that the structural role of each part of the picture is quite different. A key point here is the primacy of (non-deliberative) interpretation. What is first seen is a duck or a rabbit. It is not the case that we first 'see' the visual data and then construct from these one or the other meaningful image. It would be closer to the truth to say that it is through abstracting from the picture of the duck or the rabbit that we can identify the lines which make it up. And this move is a privative one along the lines of the procedures of science. But even through this abstraction we do not arrive at any atomism of visual data. For what is to count in our observation will itself be determined by further interpretations, as, for example, to do with the idea of a drawn line. Theories of causality cannot explain these matters of significance.

The duck-rabbit is unusual as a reading of the drawing can go either way: normally an interpretation forces itself on us. Even a proof in mathematics is not recognized as the logical deduction from a series of propositions but as something which we *see*. Not seeing a pattern will mean that we do not know where we are or how to go on; seeing it will be the result of a training not in generic skills but in correct judgements.

Similar to the error of assuming that meaning must be built up from primary elements is the fallacy that where a term is used across a diverse range of cases there must be some underlying factor which is shared. It suggests that language functions through a correspondence with reality and that this reality is, as it were, already partitioned in a way which awaits the application of language. It betokens a metaphysics which is under Wittgenstein's constant attack, a metaphysics which the doctrine of meaning as use is calculated to dissolve.

Related to this is the suspicion of the explication of a phenomenon in terms of defining characteristics (sometimes known as *Merkmal*-definition), which is foundational for a prevalent conception of science. Wittgenstein's satire here extends to Socratic method:

> "As for his arguments, they're too formal, too neat. There's no groping. It's X or Y or Z. It's not X, not Y. So: Z. When you're looking for something you go and look closely, if you think D is in a certain place, and if it isn't there you look somewhere nearby" (Bouwsma, 1986, p. 60).

The metaphysics of substance and attributes settles neatly into the grammar of predication; but Wittgenstein's world is one where things are connected by something like family resemblance and divided according to their varying uses and contexts.

Against the Augustinian picture of learning a language through ostensive definition, Wittgenstein sketches a picture where mature practice is preceded by training: the subtle range of emotion in the adult has its antecedents in the exaggerated facial expressions the parent displays to the infant. Training emerges within a shared way of life in which what is learned far outstrips what is taught. Much must remain inexplicit. The background of skilled behaviour which is thereby achieved is not a matter of deliberation or explicit theory: the skills are contextual and largely non-cognitive enabling us to know how to go on. The background is not normally to be negotiated. The criteria of successful performance are internally related to our forms of life. Instead of a raw confrontation with some external reality, our nature, as Stanley Cavell provocatively explores the matter, is convention (Cavell, 1979, p. 111). The agreement in judgements which makes this possible is not deliberative but a congruence in response, and this is to be understood in part at a physiological level. It is this which constitutes the system of reference which makes translation possible (PI, I, # 206). This is a world apart from the rationality central to Habermas' thought.

The discussion so far has shown how Wittgenstein's conception of science and its limits is at odds with logical empiricism and that it calls into question assumptions about explanation, generalization, and systematic thought. The key role played in this by the exploration of language – the extensive, piecemeal, grammatical exploration of psychological concepts in Wittgenstein's later work – is exemplary for any study in the human sciences, where the phenomena are intrinsically linguistic. An approach of this kind is not scientific: in the 'science' of psychology Wittgenstein finds "experimental methods and *conceptual confusion*" (PI, II, p. 232).

The inappropriate use of experimental methods is an object of Wittgenstein's criticisms elsewhere. The attempt to understand an unfamiliar cultural practice through the construction of a hypothesis and the drawing of conclusions may veil what is going on. The procedure of explanation suggests to the anthropologist that what is then impressive in the practice is the result of his investigation. This is seen in the dazzling and sensational nature of some anthropological research. But, Wittgenstein asks, "if he can draw the conclusion himself, how should the conclusion make an impression on him? What makes the impression must surely be something *he* has not done" (GB, p. 17e). Rather he is *led* to the conclusion by the impression the phenomenon makes from the start. The practice is impressive without any explanation. The explanation does not so much dissolve the sense of mystery as obscure it, encouraging our belief in some unknown law behind practices. The satisfaction which the explanation purports to offer is achieved if we "put together in the right way what we *know*, without adding anything" (GB, p. 2e).

Understanding the practice will depend on maintaining the sense of mystery through an awareness of its "inner life" (ibid., p. 14e). By this Wittgenstein means:

> "all those circumstances in which it is carried out that are not included in the account of the festival, because they consist not so much in particular actions which characterize it, but rather in what we might call the spirit of the festival: which could be described by, for example, describing the sort of people that take part, their way of behaviour at other times, i.e. their character, and the other kinds of games that they play" (GB, p. 14e).

The inner nature is not a hidden presence but the embeddedness of the festival in this background.

It follows that understanding will be achieved by attention to the material in its particularity. This may become more vivid through setting like cases side by side; but it will be obscured where an underlying factor is thought to exist. Description of a practice which is borne of this attention to the particular can paradoxically contain the unutterable; in the attempt to state this directly, in contrast, it is lost.

Frazer in *The Golden Bough* sometimes sees *errors* in cultural practices. This is to assume that the practices must be based on opinion. This way of thinking also distorts the understanding of practice and in turn makes inaccessible the non-cognitive background which our lives must have. It also limits our ability to recognize the role which myth plays in human lives. Different possibilities of understanding here are brought out in the contrasting approaches of Fraser and Freud. That Freud's dream interpretations reveal something deep is shown by the way they are compelling. They are compelling in the way of tragedy, the sense of inevitability acknowledging something, beyond the realms of science, which is not explanation but which frames the way in which things are understood. That inevitability was once recognized in speaking of God and Fate where these constituted an order untouched by the revelations of empirical observation; these notions were less the result of experience than its precondition. Their replacement by a faith in science is already lamented in the *Tractatus* (6.372).

Recovering something of what has been lost through the primacy of science involves a restoring of culture as an *Ordensregel*, a monastic order (CV, p. 83). That culture is first and foremost an observance redirects attention from the idea of a conscious working out of things to the preserving of practices. Following a rule, knowing how to go on (in Wittgenstein's non-cognitive way), logically precedes any deliberation; culturally it is more central. The conservatism here is a conserving of practices which can be destroyed but which cannot be rationally reconstructed or replaced. Wittgenstein's conservatism is not a straightforward matter. When he became a school teacher, he was inclined towards an egalitarianism which put him at odds with the Catholic Church but, on the other hand, deeply sceptical of the secularism which characterized the School Reform Movement. The latter antipathy is a reflection of a belief that faith in social progress subdues religious sensibility (cf. Monk, 1990, pp. 188–189). The notion of obedience is then opposed to that liberalism which prizes freedom of choice but not subservient to a supreme authority. In their variety Wittgenstein's investigations demonstrate the "grammatical dispersal of authority", in J. C. Edwards' apt phrase (Edwards, 1990, p. 227). The element of conservatism already noted is partly a manifestation of a Spenglerian cultural pessimism but there is no suggestion of a complacent acceptance of the *status quo*. Recognizing the need for radical change, Wittgenstein complains that nothing is more conservative than science itself: "Science lays down railway tracks. And for scientists it is important that their work should move along these tracks" (Rhees, 1984, p. 202).

Theorisation is a temptation. It carries the allure of an expertise which transcends the bounds of context and brings with it a vocabulary of 'super-concepts'. Thus in education, 'motivation', 'play', development', 'creativity', 'imagination', 'learning', 'aim', 'objective', 'competence', 'skill' acquire a bogus aura of significance. Wittgenstein would bring these words back to the ordinary circumstances of their use (PI, I, # 116). Theorization may emerge where an unclarity about the meaning of words leads to expression in the *form* of a scientific question: this is a typically metaphysical question (BB, p. 35). The urge to theorize is perhaps telling, however, in that it is symptomatic of a reaching after significance, a significance which the decline of observance denies us.

Wittgenstein's remarks here show something about the way culture and cultural practices are to be understood. Any Wittgensteinian approach to education must incorporate this richness of conception. The descriptive accounts provided by the anthropologist and the student of education in turn play their part in the student's own cultural definition. The boundary between the descriptive and the programmatic in education is seldom clear and the proactive nature of this definition with regard to matters of policy is particularly evident.

At this point the nature of the ethical demands of education comes more obviously into view. If theorization and generalization are to be avoided, how is education to address such matters? Wittgenstein speaks with a robust pragmatism of the need to be 'business-like'. He quotes Goethe: "In the beginning was the deed". The note of radicalism reflects the Kierkegaardian nature of his ethics.

Putting an end to all the idle talk in ethics does not prevent us from getting things done; indeed it may be a condition for authentic engagement. But the irrelevance of theory must be recognized and paradox confronted: our urge to say something true in ethics seems to involve running up against the limits of language, a tendency which Wittgenstein deeply respects (LE, p. 12). This acknowledgement points towards the thinness of the conceptions of certainty and of truth which drive science, something recognized by Wittgenstein already in the *Tractatus*. At the end of the *Lecture on Ethics* Wittgenstein comments on the special importance of speaking in the first person in such matters. There is in ethics no counterpart to the disinterested relation to truth which characterizes scientific knowledge. Neither can one's relation to ethical truth be one of indifference as it might be in the case of other matters of fact. Something is at stake. To speak the truth in such matters one must be at home with it. The voice of the first person has a peculiar weight in this. And I am certain when I resist putting my hand into the fire. The engagement indicated in such contexts is not touched where truth is understood in theories of correspondence or in theories of ethics.

There can be no doubt that any Wittgensteinian conception of education would have to take account of engagement in this sense. It may be possible to limit some questions within education to a technical level. But it is worth considering the limited range of technical knowledge in teaching in contrast to the way the ethical intrudes at almost every point – over what should be learned, over how it should be taught, over how people should be treated, over who should decide... This dubious balance between the technical and the ethical is found in medicine also but there, governed more clearly than education by the aim of normal functioning, the pervasive importance of technical know-how is clear. In contrast to this guiding aim the essentially projective nature of education can be seen.

Such projection occurs against a background which is richly challenging at an ethical level. That this level is challenging does not mean that it is amenable to theorization. It is neither conducive to generalization nor wholly available to overt scrutiny. Similarly it would be a mistake to think that the need for perspicuity would sanction an education which was primarily concerned with conceptual clarification. There is only a limited sense in which philosophy leaves everything as it is; education must do more. So how can education proceed? There is a problem in that, for all its cultural sensitivity, the individualistic and Kierkegaardian nature of Wittgenstein's ethics does not map easily onto matters of institutional policy and collective responsibility.

Sometimes, Wittgenstein says, the question 'Why?' is to be suppressed (PI, I, # 471). Similarly, explanation must come to an end somewhere. To some extent this happens in periods of normal science. It happens also where culture is an observance. Seeking explanations in such contexts involves a reduction whereby practices are thought to be understandable in terms of matters of opinion.

The nature of the suppression will vary but it must not occur in such a way that practices atrophy. Engagement is crucial in preventing this: one needs to give oneself fully to one's work and to be present in one's words. Words are not inert instruments at one's disposal but internal to the way one is. It may be that in large scale bureaucratic institutions this presence in one's work and words is hard to achieve. Such organizations are in part outcomes of that systematic acontextual way of thinking which Wittgenstein attacks. In them there would be a place for calculated polemic where sincerity and seriousness in one's language fall on deaf ears. But it would be a mistake to pretend that the picture is clear or consistent here. Wittgenstein's desire – however ill-informed – to work as a labourer in Stalin's Russia suggests something rather different, something perhaps to do with the catharsis of radical change.

The ambivalence between conservatism and radical change begins to be resolved when it is recognized that we can only experience a change against the background of a culture which we have been initiated into. The catharsis which Wittgenstein seeks is to be provided not by rational planning but by a change of aspect. Just as we may fail to see the duck in the duck-rabbit picture, we may, more seriously, fail to see the point of a joke or to appreciate a piece of music: we may be aspect-blind. We may then fail to see the meaning in someone else's life or in an alternative way of doing things. To overcome this we need a *complete* change of view. The hope of achieving this depends on a closer attention to things in their particularity. Imagination will be significant in the drawing of examples and analogies helping us to see connections which reveal new aspects. For Wittgenstein, art – the art of Tolstoy, say – has more to offer here than science.

There is no single method in philosophy, and neither is there in education. But there are methods and these may work as a kind of therapy, undoing the knots in our understanding. It is difficult to see how anything so pervasive but diverse as education could warrant something other than this piecemeal and flexible approach. Sometimes these methods will involve changes of aspect: to enable us to gain a clear view of a facet of learning; to enable us to understand the circumstances of an individual or of a social group; to enable us to see other possible ways of doing things, perhaps altering the horizons of our understanding of what education can be. Such dissolutions and resolutions do not settle things finally but recurrently, clearing the way for engagement. For what education is is always to be struggled with, never comfortably to be settled. The picture here is at odds with anything which could be called science.

Suppressing the question 'Why?' may be a move towards resisting tidy explanation and in this a stage in something like the recovery of the childhood of the mind. It is possible to explore the resonances of a vocabulary found in Wittgenstein, and in Wittgensteinian exegesis, in a way which is richly suggestive for education. Stanley Cavell says that in the face of the questions of philosophy, which are questions of education, we are as children (Cavell, 1979, p. 189). The figure of the child – and of child-like beings struggling to build – is important. Wittgenstein has contempt for the system-building of so much modern thought; the edification which he brings about is appropriately seen as a building of a different sort. And this is a metaphor which accords well with education. For the life of the culture is renewed through education to give us our bearings. The processes of its entry and renewal are inseparable from education. This can never be a building from scratch; it is perhaps something like the finding (or the founding) of that home where we can speak for ourselves. We forever require education – where perspicuity will be more important than explanation, where knowing where we are (and how to go on) will be a requirement of authentic engagement. This is a spirit in which Wittgensteinian studies in education might proceed.

But Wittgenstein sees philosophy also as a means of combatting the myth-building tendency in our language. (A persistent abuse of Wittgenstein's work is its reduction to slogans.) If the preceding reading, going beyond the letter, is consistent with the spirit of the text, it may nevertheless be that, expressed in these terms, this spirit is difficult to realize in studies in education. Let us turn to ask what pointers are offered by the present account for the three cases of the researcher into current practice, the trainee teacher, and the academic enquiring into the concept of education.

Wittgenstein's practical holism shows the way towards a more accurate understanding of successful practice. The accomplished teacher would be seen as working with a complex and flexible range of skills. These would not for the most part be consciously exercised but would operate in the background. Some might have been acquired as 'tips for teachers' and some from textbooks. Most, however, would be the result of a training in correct judgments. In other words they would depend on the building up of experience of related cases, partly through the teacher's own work and partly through the observation of others, and these would pass scarcely noticeably into the teacher's accustomed behaviour. In some respects such skills would not be sharply differentiated from the teacher's behaviour in everyday life. But in the successful teacher these would be assembled and focused in an unusually sensitive way.

Skilled performance of this kind would be characterized by its responsive adjustment to context. Thus it would be consistent with Wittgenstein's thought that the teacher should be acquainted with the history of education and with its specific development in the local context. This would extend to an awareness of the social circumstances of the school and to the situation of individual children. The training of teachers would require attention to the particular case but it would also keep in view those larger traditions of engagement and enquiry of which the practice is a part.

For teacher and researcher alike understanding would be limited if it lost sight of the particularity and the diversity of practice. Both would be in varying degrees caught up in the practice in question. This is to admit a sort of relativism, but a relativism qualified by the recognition that diverse cultural practices are at some point varying responses to certain "very general facts of nature" (PI, II, p. 230). Understanding these practices cannot be achieved solely through the specialised concepts the researcher shares with colleagues but must involve the ways of speaking internal to the classroom and to the subjects which are taught. It may be enhanced through analogy where parallel practices in different schools and different cultures are held in view. What is jeopardized is the project of a systematic account – of the sort offered perhaps by a 'psychology of education' or by curriculum theory – dedicated to explanation and to uncovering underlying laws. What can be aimed at is the perspicuous description of a limited part of what is going on in school.

For those involved in a questioning of practice and policy and an enquiry into the concept of education Wittgenstein's work offers an unsettling challenge. Wittgenstein provokes reflection but he warns against large-scale theorizing. His rich exploration of so many aspects of thinking and learning yields a picture which is at odds with the systematic. This undermines the taxonomy of educational objectives and the tidy statement of aims. But Wittgenstein's work also testifies to ethical engagement and the patient struggle which is evident in his investigations shows something of how education might proceed. The difficulty and the frequent inconclusiveness of what can be said should not divert those studying education from engaging with these questions. It is in such a spirit that studies in education should proceed. This is a spirit which is stifled by the idea of an educational science.

Wittgenstein and Aesthetic Education

NICK McADOO

The Open University, Great Britain

AESTHETIC NECESSITY

In the *Tractatus*, it is clear that the aesthetic along with the related notions of the ethical and 'the riddle of life', pose a major challenge to that work's bleak atomistic metaphysics. In a world that is no more than "the totality of facts" (TLP, # 1.1) and where the only kind of 'necessity' is a logical one (TLP, # 6.37) the apparent power of the aesthetic to 'shape up' the contingent material of the world into expressive configurations revealing their own kind of 'necessity' must remain quite obscure – for what could one *say*, from the *Tractatus* point of view, about Van Gogh's chair, Hokusai's wave or Monet's poplars? Only such aesthetically unenlightening facts as that they picture a pipe and some tobacco resting on the artist's chair, a giant wave about to engulf a fishing boat and an avenue of poplar trees by a river.

The *Tractatus*, however, as is well known, does not follow the positivist path in assigning the aesthetic (along with the ethical) to the waste paper basket of the merely emotive, but rather locates it in the enigmatic realm of the 'mystical' that "*shows* itself" (TLP, # 6.5292) only when language falls silent. This is the siren song that beckons to us from beyond the furthest horizon of "the world" understood as "the totality of facts", drawing us on with the promise of transfiguring these facts into an expressive and meaningful whole, like a work of art:

> "The contemplation of the world sub specie aeterni is its contemplation as a limited whole. The feeling of the world as a limited whole is the mystical feeling" (TLP, # 6.45).

According to recent commentaries by Ray Elliott (1993) and B.R. Tilghman (1991), what such perceived aesthetic unities hint at for Wittgenstein, as they did also for Kant in *The Third Critique*, is a realization of what it would be like for life to have meaning. Now clearly, if one *could* 'show' in this way that both nature and art can 'shape up' for us into such epiphanies whose 'rightness' is one that is neither logical nor scientific, then this would give art educators the kind of justification for their subject of which they must dream. However, not only is this early attempt to find a place for the aesthetic dogged by familiar metaphysical problems such as those raised by the dualistic 'picture theory of meaning', but a further difficulty arises even when Wittgenstein recasts the aesthetic into the 'ordinary language' framework of his later writing. This is the familiar one to which Proust alludes when the hero of *Remembrance of Things Past* reflects on the depth of his reaction to a musical phrase in Vinteuil's septet:

159

Studies in Philosophy and Education **14**: 283–293, 1995.
© 1995 *Kluwer Academic Publishers. Printed in the Netherlands.*

"There was nothing to assure me that the vagueness of such states was a sign of their profundity rather than of our not having learned yet to analyze them ... And yet that happiness, that sense of certainty in happiness ... " (Proust, 1972, p. 242).

Thus, however strong our feeling at the time that there is a non-reducible significance about aesthetic experience, there is always, over our shoulder, the spectre of the positivist, explaining away all such claims by reference to a hidden cause – sometimes in terms of the object (e.g. the tree is only 'golden' because the leaves have stopped photosynthesizing) but more commonly in terms of the subject (e.g. tracing it back to a 'mechanical' association of ideas in the manner of 'emotivist" psychology or to an invariant causal connection between our tastes and our culture class and gender, as in some sociological accounts). Ironically, while the positivists were quite happy to demystify *aesthetic* claims in this way, they were somewhat less then happy at the idea that similar contingent processes might also underlie the very nature of rationality itself!

Commenting on this problem some sixteen years later in *Lectures and Conversations on Aesthetics*, Wittgenstein (having in mind the examples of James Jean's scientific demystification of the universe and Freud's sexual explanation of a 'beautiful dream'), offers the following warning:

"The attraction of certain kinds of explanation is overwhelming ... In particular, explanation of the kind "This is really only this" (LA, p. 24).

– as witness the undoubted satisfaction that the Positivists (like the more recent Structuralists) took in showing how aesthetic discourse reveals, not the art object but the conditioned subject (see e.g. Ayer, 1962, p. 114). However, for Wittgenstein as for Proust, the possibility that all aesthetic response may in reality, have only a prosaic, causal origin, simply cannot be squared either with the importance that we attach to it or with the kind of certainty that we feel when we say, e.g. of a piece of music, that it sounds "just right" (LA, p. 3). Still less can it be reconciled with our ability to recognize the *tremendous* in art, as when some extraordinary work like a Shakespearean tragedy or Miles Davis trumpet solo sweeps aside all our normal notions of 'correctness' and yet we still feel that somehow there is a 'rightness' about it (LA, p. 8) – as Kant also recognized in distinguishing between art which is "neat and elegant" and art which has *geist*, in *The Third Critique* (Kant, 1966).

THE PROBLEM OF AESTHETIC RELATIVISM

The most problematic conclusion of all to arise from the causal thesis is that the aesthetic realm must be irredeemably subjective, or at least irredeemably relative to the outlook of my culture, class, gender etc. This is the commonplace view that a foolhardy student ventures to put to Wittgenstein: "If my landlady says a picture is lovely and I say it is hideous, we don't contradict one another" (LA, p. 11). Wittgenstein can barely conceal his annoyance:

"In a sense you do ... this is just the stupid kind of example which is given in philosophy ... Suppose the landlady says: "this is hideous", and you say: "This is lovely" – all right, that's that" (LA, p. 11).

The inanity of the imagined 'discussion' between student and landlady may be seen to arise because the student has taken as his model for aesthetic discourse the kind of 'language game' normally reserved for airing our tastes in food and drink. Usually, we are quite happy to live with the fact that e.g. our partner likes cheese and onion crisps and we don't and that's an end to it. However, if all talk about art were as inconsequential as this, then not only would aesthetic education be quite pointless but indeed so would *any* talk about art – agreement being then as arbitrary as disagreement.

So how does Wittgenstein show aesthetic educators and art lovers in general "the way out of the bottle"? Two questions really need answering here: (i) Can there be any kind of non-arbitrary 'force' to our aesthetic claims? (ii) What is the *importance* to us of the aesthetic? While a positive answer to the first is clearly a necessary condition for the very intelligibility of 'aesthetic education', it cannot be a sufficient one to justify its existence because it tells us nothing in itself about the importance of art in our lives. Why, in the end, should Wittgenstein's "*tremendous* things in art" (LA, p. 8), matter to us any more than his 'everyday' example of choosing the cut of a suit? (LA, p. 5) Certainly, we cannot appeal in any straightforward way here to the original *Tractatus* proposition that "ethics and aesthetics are one" (TLP, # 6.421) – not in the face of those many counter-examples of people whose refined powers of aesthetic judgment are just not matched by a similar sensitivity towards other human beings. Let us start, however, with the first question.

NATURAL REACTIONS AND CULTURAL BACKGROUND

Clearly, for Wittgenstein, the answer is not to be found in a hopeless pursuit of some essence of "the Beautiful" (LA, p. 1) with its illusory promise of necessary and sufficient conditions. Still less can it lie in a "science of aesthetics" (LA, p. 11) of the psychological or sociological kind since, as we have already seen, it is *this* line of argument that has created the problem in the first place. Given then that aesthetic appreciation can be inferred neither logically nor scientifically, what is left to sustain that feeling of aesthetic necessity that grips us so strongly, from time to time, in our dealings with works of art and the environment?

It may come as something of a surprise after all that has been said, to find that Wittgenstein is quite prepared to concede the contingent *origins* of aesthetic (*and* ethical) understanding, locating them, of all places, in the infant's spontaneous expressions of pleasure and disgust in response to food!

> "If you ask yourself how a child first learns 'beautiful', 'fine', etc., you find it learns them roughly as interjections . . . A child generally applies a word like 'good' first to food . . . The word is taught as a substitute for a facial expression or gesture" (LA, p. 2).

Does this mean that Wittgenstein has decided, after all, to go down the primrose path of behavioural psychology? Not at all! The point is rather the familiar 'transcendental' one that aesthetic learning, like any other form of learning (including that of logic and mathematics), must depend initially on unlearned starting points, for if all learning depended on previous learning then its initial appear-

ance in early infancy would be inexplicable. Here, it is of the utmost significance that one finds in infants, presumably the world over, an abundance of
spontaneous agreement in pleasurable reactions to bright colours, rhythms,
musical sounds, dancing movements etc. As Wittgenstein says of such reactions
in general, including those with a proto-aesthetic character:

> "The origin and the primitive form of the language game is a reaction; only from this can the more
> complicated forms grow. Language – I want to say – is a refinement; 'in the beginning was the
> deed'" (CV, p. 31).

Commenting on this remark, Norman Malcolm reports Wittgenstein as saying:
"Not merely is much of the first language of a child grafted onto instinctive
behaviour – but the whole of the developed, complex employment of language
by adult speakers embodies something resembling instinct" (Malcolm, 1981,
p. 2). Such natural reactions just are 'given'. That is how we find ourselves to be
and *all* areas of understanding share these contingent origins. However, it is of
the utmost importance to Wittgenstein's position that we should here distinguish
between our *primitive* and *educated* feelings for the language game in question.
Unless we can do this, we must remain the 'creatures of habit' from which we
originated – all our 'talk' about art signifying no more than does the wagging
tail of a dog at mealtimes!

> "Would it matter if instead of saying "This is lovely", I just said "Ah!" and smiled, or just rubbed
> my stomach? As far as these primitive languages go, problems about ... what their real subject is
> don't come up at all" (LA, p. 3).

So where is this 'educated' feeling to come from, that can transform the arbitrary 'necessity' of a knee-jerk reaction into the measured and thoughtful gaze of
aesthetic judgment? Clearly, it must first appear with the 'dawning' of language,
although if Malcolm's interpretation of Wittgenstein is correct, there will never
be a complete transformation. This is because even our most 'educated' responses will have to contain the involuntary element that links them, as by an
umbilical cord, to the spontaneous reactions of earliest infancy.

Furthermore, our initiation into language may also seem to bring with it yet
another kind of contingency – namely, the socio-historical world into which it
plunges us. The 'later Wittgenstein' is no autonomist in aesthetic matters, for in
Lectures and Conversations it is spelled out clearly that only against a background of the conventions, traditions, attitudes, beliefs and practices that go to
make up a culture can we even begin to make sense of works of art in all their
variety and plenitude: "To describe ... what you mean by a cultured taste, you
have to describe a whole culture" (LA, p. 8).

However, whereas we *have* to presuppose that all human beings are united as
a species by the universality of their natural (i.e. unlearned) reactions to the
world in earliest infancy, nonetheless, as Wittgenstein reminds us in his subse-
quent discussion of European and African traditions in art (LA, pp. 8–9), what
happens when language gets to work on such reactions is that they soon give
way to cultural beliefs and practices that are often very diverse. Does this mean
that our 'educated' appreciation of art in terms of our mastery of such a back-

ground is, in the end, no more than a culturally conditioned phenomenon revealing once again, not an objective world of art and aesthetic value, but yet another set of 'knee jerk' reactions, standing this time in an invariant causal relationship to our class, culture, gender etc.?

Now in one way, it would be quite amazing if people's tastes in art did not, by and large, reflect the circumstances of their birth and upbringing, even when they were reacting against it. However, in another way, to see this as the whole story would be, for Wittgenstein, to confuse two very different kinds of explanation, as when some sociologists are tempted to say that a statement such as: "I like the Monet because of the way the light falls on the water" really only means something like: "I enjoy the Monet landscape because I'm a white, middle-class escapist". The two explanations may not be wholly incompatible in a 'duck/ rabbit' sense, but there is a crucial difference: 'causal' accounts like the former, simply cannot explain the *directedness* of our gaze towards that particular object. As Wittgenstein points out in considering the case of aesthetic dissatisfaction:

> "We have here a kind of discomfort which you may call "directed"... There is a "why?" to aesthetic discomfort not a "cause" to it" (LA, p. 14).

The point here is that if all such experiences simply stood in an invariant causal relation to the work of art, then the work itself would drop out of the picture in so far as any other object that produced the same effect could be substituted without loss. For example, we can always ask of the 'music lover' who only listens to a particular minuet "to get this and that effect": "And doesn't the minuet itself matter? – hearing *this*: would another have done as well?" (LA, p. 29).

AESTHETIC JUDGMENT

An 'educated' aesthetic judgment for Wittgenstein then, is one that is freely directed towards its object rather than just being 'pushed from behind' by the weight of our inherited reactions and culture. Paradoxically however, it is the latter that make the former possible, for to believe, as do some teachers and students, that appreciation is most 'liberated' when most free from the background of language and culture is to display the same kind of innocence as Kant's 'light dove': "(who), cleaving the air in her free flight, and feeling its resistance, might imagine that its flight would be still easier in empty space" (Kant, 1964, p. 47).

How then, do we learn to appreciate? First, one just has to learn a few basic rules either by imitation and practice, "as in music you are drilled in harmony and counterpoint" (LA, p. 5) or, as is more often the case, intuitively, simply by listening to a lot of music – as infants learn to produce well-formed sentences without any explicit knowledge of grammar. As with learning in any sphere, it does not make sense to question the application of the rules until you have first learned them. Infants do not start by questioning whether e.g. painting should be figurative or non-figurative, rather they learn a basic notion of what counts as 'painting' from within the culture. However, in learning the rules "I develop a feeling for the rules" (LA, p. 5) which, as in all areas of understanding, is capable of over-riding any mechanical application of them. This is because, in the end, it is always judgment that 'gives the rule' and not vice-versa, although very straight-forward human activities may have the *appearance* of being the other way round, as when we work out elementary calculations or wire up a plug. Nonetheless, in so far as the proper role of 'judgment' in *any* sphere of human activity is to be the final arbiter when it comes to interpreting and apply-ing the rules, then judgment itself cannot be rule governed. It is learned, there-fore:

> "not ... by taking a course in it, but through *experience*. – Can someone else be a (person's) teacher in this? Certainly. From time to time they give (one) the right tip. – This is what "learning" and "teaching" are like here. – What one acquires here is not a technique; one learns correct judg-ments. There are also rules, but they do not form a system, and only experienced people can apply them right. Unlike calculating rules" (PI, II, p. 227).

Aesthetic education commences then, as we enter into the ebb and flow of expe-rienced art lovers' most spontaneous talk about works of art. Such 'educa-tive' talk will, of course, be informed by acquaintance with the many and often complex 'rules' of art, such as those of fugue, sonnet, twelve bar blues, haiku, and traditions like those of Cubism, Metaphysical poetry and New Orleans jazz, but what it *really* centres on is a feeling for their interpretation and application. Is the pile of bricks in the art gallery a 'work of art'? Only judgment can decide!

Such appreciative activity, according to the *Lectures and Conversations*, seems to take two basic forms: Firstly, there is that which focuses on the more 'techni-cal' side of the work and expresses itself in the language of "correctness" (LA, pp. 4–5), as when I say "that chord sounded just right!". The 'force' of such claims may seem to have a quasi-logical character although this tends to come apart at the seams in our dealings with what Wittgenstein calls the 'tremendous' in art when, as in the case of responding to a Gothic Cathedral: "what we do is not at all to find it correct – it plays an entirely different game with us" (LA, p. 8). I shall return to this at the end.

Secondly, there is that which aims to *characterize* the work in some way, as when: "I might choose between calling a melody 'lovely' and calling it 'youth-ful'" (LA, p. 3). What is interesting about this latter type of judgment, as Wittgenstein points out, is our tendency to characterize works of art in a vocabu-lary drawn from our life-experiences rather than from the limited range of 'pure' aesthetic words like 'beautiful' and 'lovely'. (LA, p. 3) Typically, we find our-selves saying: "the music is sad/cheerful/profound etc.", although to get around the *logical* divide between the aesthetic and non-aesthetic use of such terms here, we find ourselves using them in an extended or 'secondary sense', (PI, II, p. 216; see also Hanfling, 1991), with their normal truth-criteria held in abeyance. The music cannot itself *literally* feel e.g. sadness, nor can its sad aspect be a spur for the listener to leap into action as would be the case in real life, for in art all emo-tions are inescapably linked to a feeling of contemplative pleasure. Nonetheless, in so far as it only makes sense to call the music 'sad' if I feel there to be *some* connection with the standard meaning of the word, then Wittgenstein can be seen as offering an important way out from the narrow formalism inherent in the first type of judgment (for a detailed examination of this issue see Scruton, 1974 and McAdoo, 1992). In calling the form of the music 'sad' I imply a *continuity* between this aesthetic aspect and the rest of life.

EXPERIENCING THE MEANING

Nonetheless, such aspects as 'sounds just right' and 'sad' are clearly not *there* in the same way as are the work's obvious 'everyday' aspects, such as 'that's a tune' or 'that's a loud chord'. If they were to show or yield themselves as readily as does the familiar everyday world then, as Ray Elliott (1993) has pointed out, we would all be walking around like angels, in a permanent state of aesthetic grace and the 'everyday' world would melt away! As all art lovers know, however, the 'givenness' of aesthetic experience waxes and wanes in a way that the familiar everyday features of the world do not. Anyone with normal intelligence and eyesight can see that Monet's painting depicts poplar trees, but to see the *flowing dance* of their slender trunks requires something more. As Wittgenstein points out:

> "You could play a minuet once and get a lot out of it, and play the same minuet another time and get nothing out of it. But it doesn't follow that what you get out of it is then independent of the minuet" (LA, p. 29).

Now of course in one way, what you get out of it will inevitably depend on possessing a knowledge of the culture. However, in another way, the possession of such necessary background knowledge as we may need (especially with art from another culture) will only ever be a necessary and not a sufficient condition for aesthetic insight because one may have all such knowledge at one's finger tips and yet *still*, on occasions, not be able to *hear* the 'gracefulness' in the melody. So what is the difference between seeing the poplar tree and seeing the same tree (whether in nature or in art) as 'graceful'?

The account that seems tailor-made to explain this phenomenon (although surprisingly, Wittgenstein never explicitly links it to aesthetics) is the key distinction in the *Philosophical Investigations* between "continuous seeing" like seeing a triangle, and the "dawning of an aspect", as when we see a mountain in the same triangle (PI, II, pp. 193–217). Now although there is a sense in which *all* perception must start off as 'aspect perception', what characterizes the familiar 'everyday' variety is that it soon turns into the habit-laden, quasi-automatic form of 'continuous seeing' – rendering the world secure but banal. As we have already seen, however, *aesthetic* aspect perception does *not* work like this, but is always ultimately dependent on having a heightened experience that does not always come. In this respect, there does seem to be a kind of continuity between the original *Tractatus* view of the aesthetic as something that can be *shown* but not said, and the *Investigations* view of the 'dawning of an aspect' as something that, in the end, just *appears* to us. Of course, as the 'later Wittgenstein' constantly reiterates here: "what is at issue is the fixing of concepts. A concept forces itself on one" (PI, II, p. 204).

Nonetheless, in so far as "the flashing of an aspect seems half visual experience, half thought" (PI, II, p. 197), one still has to *experience* the aspect for oneself in order to see the point of the concept under which it falls. Thus, I can be staring at a Cubist still-life with the *thought* that what I ought to be seeing is a miraculous crystalline structure, yet the harder I try to see this, the more insistently does it reveal to me only a rather bent bottle and tortuously twisted guitar surrounded by a jumble of unrelated shapes! The problem is, however, that even if I *do* come to see the aesthetic aspect, I cannot *say* anything more about it than I could before. So how then, are such 'aspects' to be communicated?

PERSUASION

Again, it may come as something of a surprise to find that Wittgenstein sees the real 'force' of aesthetic argument, in the absence of ready-to-hand inferential rules, as an essentially *persuasive* one:

> "Here it occurs to me that in conversation on aesthetic matters we use the words: "You have to see it like *this*, this is how it its meant"... "You have to hear this bar as an introduction"... "You must phrase it like *this*" (PI, II, p. 202).

Now for many, the idea of 'persuasion' will inevitably be associated with 'manipulation' and the arbitrary abuse of power. But the real point here is that, in the absence of inferential conditions, persuasion is *all that we have got* to get our point across. This *is* the aesthetic language game. For Wittgenstein, what must ultimately preserve it from abuse is that, as with all aspect-perception, we can no more bend the appearance of the work of art to our will than we can force other people to see what has 'dawned' for us in the work, if they cannot see it:

> "But how is it possible to *see* an object according to an *interpretation*?... as if something were being forced into a form it did not really fit. But no squeezing, no forcing took place here" (PI, II, p. 200).

On the other hand, the persuasive role of aesthetic description would be unintelligible if there were not a voluntary element somewhere along the line. As Wittgenstein argues later on: "Seeing an aspect and imagining are subject to the will. There is such an order as ... "Now see the figure like *this*" (PI, II, p. 213).

However, this does not contradict Wittgenstein's earlier point about the involuntary nature of the "dawning of an aspect" if we understand it, not in terms of the impossible situation of forcing oneself to see the point when one does not, but rather in terms of disciplining oneself to attend more closely to the interpretation being offered – noticing details that one might hitherto have missed or misunderstood or cultural and artistic conventions of which one was hitherto ignorant etc. In this respect, no aesthetic claims are incorrigible, although such limitations need to be distinguished from what Wittgenstein calls "aspect-blindness" (PI, II, p. 213) which may simply be a natural limitation, like colour blindness, that all of us, to a greater or lesser extent, just have to accept.

Where the persuasive side of aesthetic discourse does become a problem is when people, instead of trying to attend more closely to the interpretation, try to *simulate* appropriate responses – much as one forces oneself to laugh at a joke that one does not understand. In so far as such simulated responses are linked to powerful, though aesthetically irrelevant motives like a desire to come up to a required academic standard, it may be hard at times, for students themselves to tell whether their responses are genuine or not, as when they try to convince themselves that they are really seeing what, in reality, has not emerged for them at all, or perhaps, only partially.

Nonetheless, if *I* can hear the 'rightness' or the 'sadness' in the music and if you come to hear it as well, then that makes two of us, and that is a start! This must surely be how 'aesthetic communities' come about in the first place as someone is 'struck' by a new combination of sounds, colours or words and tries to get others to see it:

> "The rules of harmony, you can say, expressed the way people wanted chords to follow – their wishes crystallized in these rules ... "(LA, p. 6).

Then the rules take on a life of their own as their inherent 'logic' is worked out. As the composer Webern put it:

> "We know of the Greek modes, then the church modes of bygone ages. How did these scales come about? They are really a manifestation of the overtone series. As you know, the octave comes first, then the fifth, then in the next octave the third" (Webern, 1963, p. 12).

THE IMPORTANCE OF ART

The problem with *all* such autonomous accounts of art as Webern's, however, is that in limiting the scope of art to attractive but non-signifying patterns they are quite unable to explain the enormously important role that art seems to play in so many people's lives. Of course much of this importance is related to the thematic content of art, especially in the case of literature, but this is of no help in characterizing the special nature of our *aesthetic* as opposed to our general human interest in the arts. Fortunately, as we saw above, the answer is ready-to-hand in Wittgenstein's acute observation that aesthetic discourse typically draws on a non-aesthetic vocabulary to characterize aesthetic form – as when the music strikes us as 'brooding', 'profound', 'cheerful' or 'bursting with energy'. It would seem then, that the continuity between art and life is written into the aesthetic language game (see Sibley, 1962; McAdoo, 1992).

Whether or not such aspects as 'dawn' for us in art may also, on occasions, hint at some kind of ethico-religious insight into the 'meaning of life', as Wittgenstein speculated in the *Tractatus*, is a further metaphysical question. Ray Elliott (1993) has argued that Wittgenstein never saw his later 'critical' position as entirely superseding the earlier 'speculative' one. His main evidence for this is that Wittgenstein emphatically excludes the 'tremendous' in art from the usual concern of the aesthetic 'language game' with 'correctness':

"One wouldn't talk of appreciating the *tremendous* things in Art . . . The entire *game* is different. It is as different as to judge a human being and on the one hand to say "He behaves well" and on the other hand "He made a great impression on me" (LA, p. 8).

But here, of course, we reach the limits of language, as may be seen in the following account of a 'tremendous' piece of music:

"I should like to say: "These notes say something glorious, but I do not know what." These notes are a powerful gesture, but I cannot put anything side by side with it that will serve as an explanation" (PI, I, # 610).

In the circumstances, the best he can manage is an expressive gesture – "a grave nod" (PI, I, # 610).

AESTHETIC EDUCATION

What food for thought then, does Wittgenstein offer art educators? First of all, he confirms what in fact most parents and nursery teachers know already – namely, the importance of very young children's 'primitive' aesthetic reactions for their later development. Of course, children have to discover that adults recognize the importance of such reactions, just as adults have then to help children find the words to express them. Everything follows from this two-way relationship. However, it is equally true that if aesthetic education is ever to evolve, then sooner or later, the more serious cultivation of aesthetic judgment has to be separated from its origins in the relativistic conception of 'taste' (which arises, as we have seen, from its associations with our taste in such things as food, drink and clothes).

It is also central to Wittgenstein's account that the aesthetic language game depends on sustaining connections with the rest of our lives. Thus, a feeling for interpreting and judging works of art (including the students' own work) arises not just from an educated awareness of the traditions, conventions and innovations that give art shape, but also from the related 'common sense' judgments of our everyday life – as when our ability to recognize the authentic note of sadness in a work of art links quite naturally with our ability to tell whether someone really is sad or only pretending.

However, what of those magical, concentrated acts of judgment directed at the 'tremendous' in art? Although such experiences more than justify the whole of aesthetic education, they clearly need the most careful handling. Nothing can be more off-putting or wrong-headed than the impression given by some teachers that art consists primarily of 'great moments' to which only the 'chosen few' are privy! Too often, this leads to students rejecting art altogether, or even worse, faking such responses through the cultivation of what they take to be 'arty' behaviour, thus destroying their chances of ever really experiencing the work. Just how teachers manage to harness the persuasive powers of language in a non-manipulative way in order to bring about the 'dawning' of such aspects is beyond the scope of this paper, although I would refer all readers to Frank

Sibley's classic examples of aesthetic discourse in action in his celebrated paper, *Aesthetic Concepts* (Sibley, 1962, pp. 81–83).

Finally, perhaps everyone in art education needs reminding from time to time of just what an extraordinary philosophical curiosity their subject is. How is it, for example, that art can give aesthetic shape to the extremities of human suffering, as does the war poetry of Wilfred Owen? Or again, why should we find ourselves gazing so long and lingeringly at Van Gogh's painting of what, after all, is only a very ordinary chair? "Don't take it as a matter of course, but as a remarkable fact", says Wittgenstein, "that pictures and fictitious narratives give us pleasure, occupy our minds" (PI, I, # 524). For aesthetic education, this is *the given* from which everything else flows.

Wittgenstein, Education and Religion

TERENCE H. McLAUGHLIN

University of Cambridge, United Kingdom

Wittgenstein's remarks about religion are neither systematic, complete nor wholly transparent. Nevertheless, they interestingly illuminate a number of central philosophical issues relating to the religious domain and to education in religion.

Any exploration of this illumination confronts the difficulty of establishing a reliable account of what Wittgenstein's views on religion actually were. This is a task of no mean complexity (see, for example, Barrett, 1991; Hudson, 1975; Keightley, 1976; Kerr, 1986; Malcolm, 1993; Phillips, 1993; Sherry, 1977; Shields, 1993; Rhees, 1969, Ch. 13; Winch, 1987, Ch. 6, 8, 9; 1993). One aspect of this task is the need to distinguish the views of Wittgenstein himself from those of philosophers who have developed a more fully worked out philosophy of religion influenced by him (e.g. Phillips, 1965, 1970a, 1971, 1976, 1986, 1988, 1993). Another problem which arises is the need to select from among a wide range of potential issues for discussion.

In this paper I shall confine myself to exploring the educational significance of a number of central themes relating to religion which are recognisably Wittgensteinian in the sense that they are to be found in, or as plausible developments of, Wittgenstein's work. My discussion will tend to focus upon elements found in Wittgenstein's later philosophy, although it should be noted that the sections of the *Tractatus* concerned with 'the inexpressible' are of significance for religious questions, as is the issue of the continuity of Wittgenstein's thought on religious matters between his earlier and later work (on Wittgenstein's early thought in relation to religion and the question of continuity see, for example, Barrett, 1991, Chs. 1–5, 12–13; Hudson, 1975, Ch. 3, pp. 151–152). For reasons of space, the selection and the characterisation of the themes with which I deal, and the extent to which they can properly be ascribed to Wittgenstein himself, will receive less discussion than they deserve. Nor will I be able to consider in detail the extensive criticism to which this general perspective has been subjected (on this see, for example, Cook, 1988; Mackie, 1982, Ch. 12; O'Hear, 1984, Ch. 1; Trigg, 1973, Ch. 2). However, in the discussion of its educational significance, a number of considerations relevant to the evaluation of the perspective will become apparent.

An interesting preliminary indication of this significance can be gained by reference to a general view concerning education in religion which is currently very influential, and which can be briefly sketched.

Studies in Philosophy and Education **14**: 295–311, 1995.

EDUCATION IN RELIGION: A CONTEMPORARY VIEW

It is widely agreed among contemporary philosophers of education, and educationalists more generally, that education in religion, at least in the common schools of a pluralistic liberal democracy, should aim not at the fostering of religious belief and practice in students but at their achievement of *understanding* in this domain. Education qua education is seen as unconcerned with whether students are, or become, religious believers or unbelievers, or, more broadly, religious persons. The forms of commitment it seeks to bring about are those of the educated, rather than the religious, person. It is therefore seen as quite wrong for educators to present or teach a particular religion *as if it were true*. Or, to put the point more precisely, it is insisted that students must be made aware that the domain of religion, though one worthy of engaged attention, involves uncertainty and controversy and the question of religious faith and practice is therefore a matter for personal reflective evaluation, decision and response.

Although the precise arguments articulating such a perspective are varied, one general conception of education in religion in which it is embodied is very familiar (cf. Hirst, 1972, 1974a, esp., Ch. 3, 1974b, 1981, 1984, 1985; Hull, 1984; Schools Council, 1971; Sealey, 1985; Smart, 1968; Great Britain Parliament House of Commons, 1985, Ch. 8). This conception is supported by a range of equally familiar arguments concerning the uncertain and controversial epistemological and ethical status of religious beliefs, the distinction between public and private values in a pluralistic liberal democratic society and the requirements of a conception of education which has as its heart the crucial importance of critical, reflective and appropriately independent judgement by individuals as part of their achievement of a form of personal autonomy (McLaughlin, 1992 including footnotes 4, 5, 7, 9, 15, 18, 25, 47). Although this view is explicitly addressed to the form of education in religion appropriate for the common schools of a pluralistic liberal democratic society, it also calls into question the character and legitimacy of education in religion in religious schools (ibid.).

This general view of education in religion needs to be properly understood. In ruling out the teaching of any particular religion as if it were true, for example, the view is not expressing hostility to religious faith as such, but seeking to achieve for individuals an appropriate degree of objectivity of judgement and scope for self-determination. In stressing the need for personal reasoning and decision in religion, neither a paradigm of reasoning alien to the domain, nor a utopian conception of the autonomy of the individual need be assumed. Nor need the complexity involved in achieving understanding in the religious domain be overlooked or oversimplified. The significance of the 'internal' perspective, for example, is typically acknowledged. This is seen, for example, in a well known passage from a Schools Council report: "Religion cannot be understood simply from the outside. It is like stained-glass windows in the cathedrals. You see them from the outside, and they are nothing, grey and colourless. You see them from the inside, and they are wonderful, full of life and colour. Unless they are understood as seen from the inside religious dogmas and rituals seem grey and sapless, if not absurd" (Schools Council, 1976, p. 49). Since this general view rules out the formation and maintenance of faith, attempts are made to satisfy the requirements of this 'internal' perspective through such strategies as sympathetic imaginative participation (Smart, 1973).

For ease of reference, I shall describe this general view of education in religion as an LR – Liberal Rational – one, without entering into discussion of the complexities inherent in the use of such a label.

The extent to which this view actually underpins contemporary educational policy and practice is unclear (on this issue in relation to England and Wales see, for example, Jackson, 1992). However, at the theoretical level, even when properly understood, the view gives rise to a number of prominent questions and difficulties which are rich in implication for educational practice. What is involved in achieving objectivity of judgement in religious matters? To what extent can understanding in religion be achieved by those who do not have religious beliefs and live a religious life? Can the demands of the 'internal' perspective be adequately satisfied by strategies such as 'sympathetic imaginative participation'? Is religious understanding essentially particular rather than general in character? How are 'understanding' and 'truth' to be understood in the religious domain? In presenting religion as an uncertain and controversial matter calling for personal reflective decision and response are central elements of the life of religious faith misrepresented?

These are all matters on which Wittgenstein's discussion of religion throws some light. As is obvious, the Wittgensteinian perspective offers a challenge to many of the underlying philosophical assumptions (e.g. Hirst, 1985; Cooper, 1993) on which the view which has just been sketched depends, not least, perhaps, its conception of the rational human agent (cf. Kerr, 1986, Chs. 1, 3–6). The nature of this challenge can be seen in the themes considered below.

WITTGENSTEIN ON RELIGION

There has been much speculation about Wittgenstein's own religious beliefs, attitudes and commitments (Malcolm, 1993, esp. Ch. 1; McGuinness, 1988; Monk, 1990) occasioned in part by remarks of his such as: "I am not a religious man but I cannot help seeing every problem from a religious point of view" (quoted in Rhees 1984, p. 79), and the nature and significance of characteristically religious perspectives in Wittgenstein's general approach to philosophy have been explored in a number of recent studies (Malcolm, 1993, esp. Ch. 2–7; Shields, 1993; Winch, 1993).

Wittgenstein's remarks about religious belief are not confined to his rather brief academic discussions of the matter (e.g. LA). References to religion are scattered throughout his work (see especially CV) and much of interest can be gleaned from his diaries (McGuinness, 1988; Monk, 1990) and from the recollections and reports of those who knew him (e.g. Rhees, 1984, esp. the conversations reported by M.O'C. Drury, pp. 76–171).

From this wide range of material, varying in significance and complexity, a number of distinctively Wittgensteinian themes can be identified which illuminate the LR view of education in religion.

(1) The Status of Religious Faith and Practice

One of the starting points for the LR view is an anxiety about the uncertain epistemological status of religious beliefs. This is seen in Hirst's claim that: "...as there is no agreement in our society on the truth of any body of religious claims, nor even how we might in principle judge such beliefs to be true, we have no justification for teaching any body of such claims *as a body of established knowledge*" (Hirst, 1970, p. 213).

Leaving to one side at this point the issue of what it is appropriate to teach, it is clear that, for various reasons, this description of the status of religious faith and practice is uncongenial to a Wittgensteinian perspective.

That this is so is seen in the reaction of D.Z. Phillips to Hirst's claim that there are (at present) no public criteria in religion to distinguish the true from the false. Accusing Hirst of a 'misplaced scepticism', Phillips points to the criteria within religious traditions which do exist. Anticipating Hirst's response that such tests constitute tests merely for orthodoxy and not for truth (Hirst, 1970, p. 214), Phillips accuses Hirst of making demands which arise from inattention to the actual character of religious beliefs. Although Phillips misunderstands Hirst in interpreting him as seeking criteria of truth external to the religious domain (Phillips, 1970b, p. 12), his accusation stands in relation to the demands which Hirst in fact does make, which insist *inter alia* upon a distinction between 'accepted public rules' for the use of religious language and 'tests for truth' making possible the objective adjudication of alternative religious claims (Hirst, 1970, p. 214; 1985). For on Phillips' view religious beliefs are not conjectures or hypotheses at all; much less ones which can be objectively adjudicated or about which believers and non-believers can share a common understanding and disagree. Rather they are distinctive ways in which life can be seen and lived out in the light of commitments which have an absolute character. 'Truth' in the religious domain is concerned with the possibility of commitment to the religious life. Thus Phillips insists: "...religious beliefs are not a class of second-best statements, hypotheses awaiting confirmation or conjectures longing to be borne out. They are a body of truths, in the sense I have been talking about, which have played an important part in the history of mankind, and by which many people still regulate or attempt to regulate their lives" (Phillips, 1970b, p. 12).

Aside from the question of the extent to which Phillips' general position can be regarded as similar to that of Wittgenstein himself, contained in this statement are a number of central Wittgensteinian themes which require exploration (for a brief general overview of such themes from Phillips' perspective see Phillips, 1993, Introduction).

(II) The Distinctiveness of Religious Commitment

In the notes of Wittgenstein's 'Lectures and Conversations on Aesthetics, Psychology and Religious Belief' (LA) taken down by his students, we find a number of remarks about the distinctiveness of religious commitment: To hold a religious belief is not to hold a (mere) opinion, for example about whether there is a German aeroplane overhead (LA, p. 53) but to have an unshakeable belief, which will show in the believer: "... not by reasoning or by appeal to ordinary grounds for belief, but rather by regulating for all in his life" (ibid., p. 54), involving sacrifices and risks which would not be made for beliefs which are better established. Wittgenstein comments: "... there is this extraordinary use of the word 'believe'. One talks of believing and at the same time one doesn't use 'believe' as one does ordinarily. You might say (in the normal use): "You only believe – oh well ... " Here it is used entirely differently; on the other hand it is not used as we generally use the word 'know'" (LA, pp. 59–60). Hilary Putnam makes the point that Wittgenstein cannot be supposed here to be claiming that religious belief is always free from doubt, but that, whilst belief may alternate with doubt, it 'regulates for all' in the believer's life (Putnam, 1992, p. 145).

Wittgenstein points out that religious commitment is not based on reason and evidence in a normal way. "Reasons look entirely different from normal reasons. They are, in a way, quite inconclusive. The point is that if there were evidence, this would in fact destroy the whole business" (LA, p. 56).[1] Religious beliefs involve the use of 'pictures' with their associated 'technique of usage', which rules out as inappropriate talk of (say) 'eyebrows' in relation to 'the eye of God' (LA, p. 71). In religious belief: "The expression of belief may play an absolutely minor role" (LA, p. 55) in contrast to the way it is embedded in the believer's thoughts and life. Religious belief is unique in that, in contrast to other kinds of belief, failure to believe is seen as something bad (LA, p. 59). Further, religious believers and unbelievers are not involved in clear-cut disagreement and contradiction. Of a person who thinks of illness in terms of punishment, Wittgenstein remarks: "If I'm ill, I don't think of punishment at all. If you say: "Do you believe the opposite?" – you can call it believing the opposite, but it is entirely different from what we would normally call believing the opposite. I think differently, in a different way. I say different things to myself. I have different pictures" (LA, p. 55; see also LA, pp. 55–59).

In his recent discussion of these lectures, Hilary Putnam takes them to exemplify in a powerful way the need for us: "... to take our lives and our practice seriously in philosophical discussion" (Putnam, 1992, p. 135), and cautions against a too hasty classification of Wittgenstein's conception of religious belief as incommensurable, 'non-cognitive', relativist or (given that there is no 'essence of reference') non referential (ibid., Ch. 7, 8). Nor should Wittgenstein too hastily be described as providing a reductionist account of religious belief. Of the notion of a 'picture' Wittgenstein says: "It says what is says. Why should you be able to substitute anything else? ... If I say he used a picture, I don't want to say anything he himself wouldn't say. I want to say that he draws these conclusions" (LA, p. 71). Although this matter is difficult to interpret, Cyril Barrett claims that, however unorthodox they may appear, Wittgenstein's views on religion are rooted in a traditional theology and philosophy of religion (Barrett, 1991, p. xiii. On the application of Wittgenstein's ideas to theological questions see, for example, Kerr, 1986, Ch. 8).

(III) Religion and Practice

In a remark published in 'Culture and Value' Wittgenstein claims that: "Christianity is not a doctrine, not, I mean, a theory about what has happened and will happen to the human soul, but a description of something that actually takes place in human life" (CV, p. 28), which is echoed in his remark that "... the *words* you utter or what you think as you utter them are not what matters, so much as the difference they make at various points in your life. How do I know that two people mean the same when each says he believes in God?... *Practice* gives the words their sense" (CV, p. 85, cf. C, # 229). For Wittgenstein, what matters in Christianity is not 'sound doctrines' but a change of life (CV, p. 53). Considerations such as these lead into the familiar Wittgensteinian emphasis upon religion as a 'language game' and 'form of life'.

Wittgenstein's conception of these notions needs no detailed recapitulation here (on their application to religion see, for example, Barrett, 1991, Ch. 6–10; Hudson, 1975, Ch. 2 II, 5) nor the related account of Wittgenstein's move from his earlier abstract, static and uniform theory of the nature of language in the *Tractatus* to a conception of it as a 'set of tools' for use in various contexts and for various purposes, meaning being connected to use. 'Language games', consisting of language and (crucially): "...the actions into which it is woven..." (PI, I, # 7) 'forms of life', make possible (among other things) agreement in judgements, and are significantly distinct in virtue of their own rules or 'logical grammar' (PI, I, # 373; cf. PI, I, # 664) and their own activities.

A number of issues arise in relation to these notions. Those of particular significance to religion include the nature of the grounding of the religious language game and form of life, the question of the 'reality' with which these are concerned and the relationship between religious understanding and religious practice.

(IV) The Grounds of Religious Belief

On the grounding of language games and forms of life in general, Wittgenstein writes: "The origin and the primitive form of the language game is a reaction; only from this can more complicated forms develop. Language – I want to say – is a refinement, "in the beginning was the deed" (CV, p. 31) – "...it is our *acting*, which lies at the bottom of our language-game" (C, # 204). Language games, and their related forms of life, are not based on 'grounds' but are rather entrenched in our life and thinking, held fast by surrounding beliefs (C, # 144; cf. C, ## 140, 141, 225) and supported by such attitudes as 'acknowledgement' (C, # 378), acceptance (PI, II, xi, p. 226; CV, p. 16; C, # 559), respect (appropriate for a picture which is at the root of our thinking: CV, p. 83), 'observance' (for Wittgenstein, culture is, or presupposes, an observance: CV, p. 83) and trust. "If I have exhausted the justifications I have reached bedrock, and my spade is turned. Then I am inclined to say: "This is simply what I do"" (PI, I, # 217).

Consistent with this perspective, Wittgenstein holds that the religious form of life is not concerned with empirical hypotheses (see LA; cf. Phillips, 1976) or grounded in evidence (cf. C, # 336) or metaphysical theories about the nature of the world, but on certain basic or primitive reactions to our 'natural-historical setting'. As Fergus Kerr puts it: "The very idea of God depends on such brute facts as that, in certain circumstances, people cannot help shuddering with awe or shame, and so on" (Kerr, 1986, p. 183). Wittgenstein's account of how religious faith may become possible for a person echoes his account of religious faith as a form of trusting not superstitious fear (CV, p. 72; cf. C, # 509). He writes: "Life can educate one to a belief in God. And *experiences* too are what bring this about; but I don't mean visions and other forms of sense experience which show us the 'existence of this being', but e.g., sufferings of various sorts. These neither show us God in a way a sense impression shows us an object, nor do they give rise to *conjectures* about him. Experiences, thoughts, – life can force this concept on us" (CV, p. 86) (cf. "...faith is faith in what is needed by my *heart*, my *soul*, not my speculative intelligence... What combats doubt is, at it were *redemption*" (CV, p. 33)).

Given that standards of explanation, intelligibility and justification are internal to particular language games and forms of life, the search for external standards, including 'grounds' is, in Wittgenstein's view, illusory (Brown, 1969; cf. Barrett, 1991, Ch. 9; cf. in contrast, Hepburn, 1987). The extent to which Wittgenstein's perspective on these matters can properly be described as relativistic has given rise to considerable discussion (Barrett, 1991, Ch. 7; Putnam, 1992, Ch. 8; Smeyers, 1992).

(V) Religious Truth and Reality

Rush Rhees claims that if people come to love God: "...this has to do with the life they lead and in which they take part" (Rhees, 1969, p. 122). It is in a religious life, including activities such as worship, that the reality of God can be found. But what is the nature of this reality? As we saw earlier, Wittgenstein holds that this is something very distinctive. "If the question arises as to the existence of a god or God, it plays an entirely different role to that of the existence of any person or object I ever heard of" (LA, p. 59). One of the distinctive features of the use of religious pictures to which Wittgenstein draws attention is the absence of a 'technique of comparison' in the case (say) of a picture of God creating Adam, in contrast to that available in the case of a picture of a tropical plant, where the thing depicted can be compared to the depiction (LA, p. 64).

For D.Z. Phillips, coming to see that there is a God does not amount to discovering that an additional being exists; it is *seeing the point of* or *discovering* the religious way of life. For Phillips, the reality of God is embodied and lived out in the religious attitude. To participate in the love of God, he argues, is to adopt the perspective of 'the eternal'. A central feature of such an attitude is an independence of the believer from 'the way things go': no empirical event can affect his or her love of God. This is part of the 'grammar' of the concept 'God', a feature which Wittgenstein associated with 'being safe whatever happens' (cf. Malcolm, 1993, p. 7) on the part of the religious believer. Phillips seems to equate believing in God with participating in the religious attitude, 'the eternal', and living according to it. He writes: "The God-given ability to give thanks in all things *is* the goodness of God" (Phillips, 1970a, p. 209); "To *use* this language is to worship, to believe in God" (ibid., p. 69). Thus, for Phillips, a man who finds God has not found an object but: "... he has found God *in* a praise, a thanksgiving, a confessing and an asking which were not his before" (Phillips, 1976, p. 181).

On this view, religious beliefs are neither metaphysical theories nor factual hypotheses; they do not postulate 'transcendental' reality of an ontological or metaphysical kind. The language is not *referential* in the sense that it is about an *object:* God, but expressive of the values contained in the religious attitude to life "... it is a grammatical confusion to think that this language is referential or descriptive. It is an expression of value. If one asks what it says, the answer is what it says itself" (Phillips, 1976, p. 147). Phillips rejects the 'exclusive simple choice' implicit in the suggestion that talk of God must either literally refer to a fact or object or be metaphorical (cf. Phillips, 1988, pp. 317–325) and has delineated in considerable detail the character of the religious life that emerges on his view. (For an application of this approach to the notion of prayer see Phillips, 1965 and to the concept of immortality see Phillips, 1971; see also Moore, 1988).

Phillips has vigorously rejected the charge that his approach reduces religion to either morality (he opposes Braithwaite's reduction of religion to an adjunct of moral behaviour: Phillips, 1993, Ch. 4, esp. pp. 45–46) or to language games. For Phillips, "... the meaning of God's reality is to be found in His divinity, which is expressed in the role worship plays in people's lives. This does not imply that God's reality, divinity or worship, can be equated with language-games; that is not what they *mean!*" (Phillips, 1970a, p. 130).

To think otherwise, claims Phillips, is to confuse "... a linguistic context with what is said" (ibid.). An exploration of the 'depth grammar' of religious beliefs, at least 'non-superstitious' ones, reveals their non-metaphysical character. Phillips' position is illuminated by the contrasts he draws between it and the views of the proponents of 'Reformed epistemology' (Phillips, 1988) and recent 'non-realist' theorists of religion (Cupitt, 1980, 1984; see also Dawes, 1992; Freeman, 1993; D. Hart, 1993).[2]

Whether Phillips' approach does justice to Wittgenstein's own views on the matter, and is acceptable in itself, has invited considerable debate. W.D. Hudson, for example, although influenced by Wittgenstein, holds that the object of religious belief is constituted by the concept of 'transcendent consciousness and agency'. In relation to the reality of this concept, he stresses, against Phillips, the need and possibility of a perspective and a status which is, in important respects, 'external' to the religious form of life (Hudson, 1975, pp. 164; 175–193). Similarly, Cyril Barrett finds fault with Phillips' account of the 'something' to which religious life, on the Wittgensteinian view, refers (Barrett, 1991, Ch. 13; see also Brummer, 1993).

(VI) Religious Understanding and Religious Practice

A central element in Wittgenstein's approach to religion is the close connection, which emerges in all that has been outlined above, between understanding in religion and religious practice. As D.Z. Phillips puts it: "...there is no theoretical knowledge of God" (Phillips, 1970a, p. 32).

Two related questions which arise here are whether religious understanding is *impossible* without religious practice and whether the believer and unbeliever understand each other. On the former question, Phillips has rejected claims that he holds such a view. Whilst certain forms of religious understanding presuppose belief, other forms of religious understanding do not, and the possibility of elucidating religious belief to non-believers is open (Phillips, 1986, pp. 10–12). On the question of whether the believer and the unbeliever understand each other, Wittgenstein's comments may serve to discourage a dogmatic answer to the question: "You might say 'well if you can't contradict him, that means you don't understand him. If you did understand him, then you might'. That again is Greek to me. My normal technique of language leaves me. I don't know whether to say that they understand one another or not" (LA, p. 55; see also Bambrough, 1991; Barrett, 1991, Ch. 8, 9; Brown, 1969; Putnam, 1992).

WITTGENSTEIN AND EDUCATION IN RELIGION

A considerable task of exegesis and interpretation is required for the achievement of a full critical understanding of Wittgenstein's views on religion. The precise meaning and import of these views are unclear and disputed, and there is much that is puzzling and unresolved. In the absence of a much more extended discussion, only general lines and directions of implication for education in religion can be indicated. On the basis of the elements of those general views which have been outlined, however, a number of significant implications for education in religion and, in particular, the LR conception of that task, can be discerned.

Educational practice in general, and therefore education in religion, is not, of course, and cannot be, determined solely by philosophical considerations. The LR conception of education in religion, for example, is articulated as much by social and cultural realities as by philosophical argument, and the implications of this point will be returned to in due course. However, Wittgenstein's perspective on religion, through its capacity to influence the way in which education in religion is conceptualised, is potentially one rich in implication for the way in which education in religion is conducted.

*(I) Wittgenstein and the LR Conception of Education in Religion: Some
Preliminary Points*

Wittgenstein's general approach clearly calls into question a number of the
major features and philosophical underpinnings of the LR conception. From a
Wittgensteinian perspective, it is no longer possible (for example) to maintain a
sharp distinction for educational purposes between fostering religious belief and
practice and developing religious understanding; the presentation of religion as
uncertain and requiring rational assessment, decision and commitment misrepre-
sents some of the central distinctive features of the domain; religious truth and
reality are seen as requiring a much more subtle and nuanced elucidation, and so
forth (for general implications for the general 'Liberal Rational' view of education of a broadly Wittgensteinian critique see Lloyd, 1980). Hirst's recent work
stressing the significance for education of initiation into certain substantive social
practices (Hirst, 1993) can be regarded as a step in the right direction from the
Wittgensteinian point of view, although its evaluation from that perspective
depends heavily on how Hirst's continuing, though modified, commitment to the
notion of rational critical assessment is to be understood. One issue which has
emerged is the question of whether, on a Wittgensteinian view, education in religion in a recognisably LR sense is impossible (Marples, 1978). Proponents of
such a view neglect, however, the possibility of kinds and degrees of understanding and the significance of the religious imagination (cf. Hepburn, 1992).

At the very least, however, Wittgenstein's view of the nature of religious
belief and practice inhibits an over-confident articulation of the LR view, and
places it squarely in the context of the engaged persuasive discussion referred to
by Marshall and Smeyers in their introduction to this volume.

*(II) Some General Requirements of a Wittgensteinian Approach to Education in
Religion*

A number of requirements for education in religion can be plausibly deduced
from the Wittgensteinian point of view.

The most basic requirement is to accurately portray the distinctive character
of religious belief as understood from the perspective. Wittgenstein writes: "An
honest religious thinker is like a tightrope walker. He almost looks as though he
were walking on nothing but air. His support is the slenderest imaginable. And
yet it really is possible to walk on it" (CV, p. 73). What is involved in illuminating this sort of perception for pupils is complex and underexamined. One aspect
of this complexity arises from the fact that, because of the nature of the development of the understanding of pupils, many religious notions in their characteristically Wittgensteinian form will need to be presented to pupils initially in
straightforwardly realist and literal terms (Astley, 1993, 1994, pp. 170–185).

A related requirement from the Wittgensteinian perspective is the need
to avoid the treatment of religion in an unduly abstract or context-free way
(Phillips, 1970b, p. 16), although there is a tension between an acknowledgement by the perspective on the one hand of the general salience of particularity

and on the other of its acceptance that there is no 'essence' or single normative form of religion.

Another conclusion that can be safely drawn from the Wittgensteinian perspective is that education in general has an obligation to combat our tendency to: "... remain unconscious of the prodigious diversity of all every-day language-games because the clothing of our language makes everything alike" (PI, II, xi, p. 224). Education must "teach us differences" (cf. Malcolm, 1993 pp. 43–47). One interesting task here is that of helping students to distinguish between religious and scientific beliefs, and to come to an understanding of the proper relationship between them (cf. Winch, 1987, Ch. 9).

(III) Confessionalism

One requirement that might be deduced from Wittgenstein's general view of religion is to see education in this domain as requiring a confessional approach viz. one which proceeds from, and seeks to develop and sustain commitment to, a (particular) religious faith.

There are elements in Wittgenstein's position which lend strong support to this conclusion. Wittgenstein writes: "It strikes me that a religious belief could only be something like a passionate commitment to a system of reference. Hence, although it's *belief*, it's really a way of living, or a way of assessing life. It's passionately seizing hold of *this* interpretation. Instruction in a religious faith, therefore, would have to take the form of a portrayal, a description, of that system of reference, while at the same time being an appeal to conscience. And this combination would have to result in the pupil himself, of his own accord, passionately taking hold of the system of reference. It would be as though someone were first to let me see the hopelessness of my situation and then show me the means of rescue until, of my own accord, or not at any rate led to it by my *instructor*, I ran to it and grasped it" (CV, p. 64). Given that religious believers do not come to believe on the basis of reasons and proofs, Wittgenstein comments: "Perhaps one could "convince someone that God exists" by means of a certain kind of upbringing, by shaping his life in such and such a way" (CV, p. 85, cf. C, # 107).

In addition to statements such as these, support for a confessional approach to education in religion can be derived from a number of other central elements in Wittgenstein's position. For example, Wittgenstein observes: "Religion says: *Do this! – Think like that!* – but it cannot justify this and once it even tries to, it becomes repellent; because for every reason it offers there is a valid counter-reason. It is more convincing to say: "Think like this! however strangely it may strike you"" (CV, p. 29). Further: "Christianity is not based on a historical truth; rather, it offers us a (historical) narrative and says: now believe! But not, believe this narrative with the belief appropriate to a historical narrative, rather: believe, through thick and thin, which you can only do as the result of a life. *Here you have a narrative, don't take the same attitude to it as you take to other historical narratives!* Make a *quite different* place in your life for it" (CV, p. 32).

Another element is the close connection between religious understanding and religious practice. One aspect of this is the complexity involved in learning religious pictures, including the theology which articulates the grammar implicit in the pictures. "The word 'God' is amongst the earliest learnt – pictures and catechisms, etc. But not the same consequences as with pictures of aunts. I wasn't shown [that which the picture pictured]...."Being shown all these things, did you understand what this word meant?" I'd say: "Yes and no. I did learn what it didn't mean. I made myself understand. I could answer questions, understand questions when they were put in different ways – and in that sense could be said to understand" (LA, p. 59, cf. p. 63). This process is illuminated by Phillips' remark that 'mystery' "... is an integral part of concept-formation in faith and worship" (Phillips, 1988, p. 278).

Given Wittgenstein's general perspective, it is easy to conclude that the most natural way in which people develop the sorts of understanding to which he has been alluding is by being brought up in, and leading, a religious life. This finds some echo in Hamlyn's remark that capability for understanding depends upon how what is being taught fits into the life of the individual (Hamlyn, 1989, p. 221), a remark which, although not originally used in relation to religion, is relevant here.

A number of other elements in Wittgenstein's view lend support to a confessional interpretation of what is required in terms of education in religion. A general theme which can be given application here is the general role of certainty over doubt in upbringing (cf. e.g. C ## 106, 107, 115, 128, 129, 143, 144, 152, 153, 159, 160, 166, 310–317, 476–480; cf. Bambrough, 1993; O'Hear, 1991; Kazepides 1991a).

In his article *Confession and Reason*, Ieuan Lloyd (Lloyd, 1986) develops a case for a confessional approach to education in religion from a broadly Wittgensteinian perspective. Lloyd is suspicious of the claims of 'rationality' in education and bemoans the fact that demands concerning it are often couched: "... in the language of the abstract not tempered by example or an understanding of the past" (ibid., p. 140). In an earlier article, Lloyd develops telling criticisms of John White's aim of maximising the choice of pupils, and accuses him of being in danger of picturing school: "... as being like a sweet shop in which a child has been given money to spend" (Lloyd, 1980, p. 334), and of conceiving the child as: "... without roots, without attachments and without love, concerned only with choosing ... " (ibid., p. 341). In view of this danger, and in the absence of abstract standards of rational judgement in religion, Lloyd holds that it is appropriate, by an extension of the general need for the child to have unshakeable beliefs of a basic sort (Lloyd, 1986, p. 142), to initiate pupils into religion as a precondition of their achievement of understanding in this domain. In arguing for this initiation, Lloyd makes a somewhat un-Wittgensteinian distinction between the 'foundations' of religion and its 'superstructure', (ibid., p. 143), initiation being justified into the former.

It is unclear quite what Lloyd intends in this distinction. His overall philosophical position seems to debar him from referring to a general 'external' foundation for religion (cf. Peters, 1972; cf. Elliott, 1986) and his recognition of the significance of the particular and his concern that a child's 'confession of a faith' might be brought about: "... in an educational institution" (Lloyd, 1986, p. 143) points to his having in mind the confession of a *particular* faith.

In the absence of any indication to the contrary, Lloyd seems to be referring in his argument to education in religion in the common schools of a pluralist demo-cratic society. In this context, however, his view encounters inescapable contem-porary social and cultural obstacles. Although Lloyd makes some reference to the heterogeneity of attitudes to religious belief now prevalent (ibid., pp. 142, 144), he does not address the difficulties that this presents for his advocacy of confessionalism.

There are good Wittgensteinian grounds, in addition to practical ones and those emanating from the LR view, for rejecting a confessional approach in common schools. The most basic Wittgensteinian point here is that the relevant forms of life are not (generally) flourishing in the lives of the pupils and their families in the school. The grounding for the educative task in confessional terms is therefore missing. Such considerations call into question Lloyd's attempt to argue that the need for the child to have unshakeable beliefs can be extended from basic beliefs to religious beliefs in an unproblematic and wide ranging way.[3] Here Hirst's point that religious beliefs have an uncertain epistemological status can be transposed into the point, telling for the Wittgensteinian, that the religious form of life has an uncertain existence.

However, what does emerge from such a line of argument is a more modest and nuanced case for the confessional approach to be acknowledged as having some significance in particular contexts, where the relevant 'forms of life' are in place or under development, as in religious upbringing in the family and reli-gious teaching in religious schools (McLaughlin, 1984, 1992). A form of confes-sional approach in these contexts has certain distinctive benefits (cf. Nichols, 1992) over the LR approach, which has Wittgensteinian overtones (see also Martin, 1987). This does not mean that the form of confessionalism at issue is non-rational or (from an LR perspective) indoctrinatory given that Wittgenstein allows for a kind of assessment of religious beliefs (for Wittgenstein on free will and religious belief see Barrett, 1991, Ch. 11). Although it is likely, however, to lead to charges of indoctrination being seen in a more nuanced way (cf. Thiessen, 1993), Wittgenstein's point of view does not lead to wide ranging rehabilitation of the confessional approach.

The existence of heterogenous moral beliefs and forms of life in common schools also calls into question the view of moral education developed by D.Z. Phillips (Phillips, 1979, 1980), which in its desire to avoid a focus on abstract moral principles stresses the transmission of substantial values which are tacit and implicit in school life and school subjects. This might be thought to presuppose a stability and homogeneity of moral practice which does not exist.

(IV) Advocacy and Elucidation

Can an approach to education in religion based on Wittgensteinian insights be conducted in non-confessional context? A crucial distinction relevant to this possibility is made by Phillips, who distinguishes 'advocacy' from 'elucidation' (Phillips, 1970b, p. 13). Elucidation involves: "... unpacking the significance of values, ideals, different conceptions of worship and love, and the roles they play in people's lives" (ibid., p. 17). Phillips's appeal to Simone Weil's analogy of the display of a thing of beauty underscores the requirement that teachers have a 'sympathetic relation' to religion; they must 'take religion seriously', 'see something in it' and respect it. But, considers Phillips, the teacher need not be a religious believer. An acceptable teacher could: "... include someone who had come to the conclusion that religious beliefs were false in that he had a regard in his own life for conflicting beliefs, but thought a great deal needed to be said to appreciate the nature of religious beliefs" (ibid., p. 17). So the connection that Phillips is making here is not between understanding and belief, but understanding and sympathy. Since Phillips acknowledges that the reactions of children to such elucidation, like that of adults, is likely to be varied, the approach is significantly 'open'.

This is seen in the reaction of Weil to the question: "Is it true?" which Phillips reports as follows: "It is so beautiful that it must certainly contain a lot of truth. As for knowing whether it is, or is not, absolutely true, try to become capable of deciding that for yourselves when you grow up" (ibid., pp. 14–15). Indeed, an attitude of significant neutrality is explicitly attributed to Weil in her remark that: "It would be strictly forbidden to add, by way of commentary, anything implying either a negation of dogma or an affirmation of it" (ibid., p. 15) and Phillips leaves open whether the child will actually regulate his or her life by this conception of beauty in later years (ibid., p. 15).

These are, however, many complex questions which arise in relation to this notion of 'elucidation'. Wittgenstein's concept of religious belief as a kind of 'tightrope' walk has been alluded to earlier. From such a perspective, a religious educator in a common school must achieve a balance in the understanding of students between a crude realism or literalism about religion on the one hand, and an equally crude reductionism on the other.

The Wittgensteinian conception of the nature of religion is intellectually and spiritually sophisticated. (For an example of a set of considerations from this perspective which might confront students see Moore, 1988, p. 67). But how is an understanding of this kind to be brought about in a common school, in the absence of a stable tradition of religious belief and practice? Such a tradition seems crucial for religious understanding for the reasons already mentioned. These include the need to present religious notions in initially literal and realist terms if they are to be grasped. This is relevant to the presentation of the prophetic demands of the religion which were indicated in the last section. Another problem facing the 'elucidation' is the difficulty of illuminating the nature and force of orthodoxy and orthopraxis in religion, in the face of a temptation to eclecticism on the part of students, without invoking realist considerations.

The notion of elucidation from a Wittgensteinian perspective is therefore underexplored. Another of the underexplored notions is the distinctively Wittgensteinian notion of a 'limit to questioning'.

(V) The Limits to Questioning

The Wittgensteinian approach is suspicious of the corrosive and distortive effect of questioning upon a proper understanding of the religious domain. Too much questioning of the wrong kind could lead to religious beliefs being seen as hypothetical metaphysical beliefs. This point is developed by W.D. Hudson who claims that education in religion is only logically possible if the 'constitutive concept' of the religious form of life (god: a distinctive concept in Hudson's hands) (Hudson, 1973, pp. 169–177) is not called into question. Given that religious education is not merely education *about* religion, but education *in* it, Hudson holds that it requires initiation into 'devotion': "... engaging in those ways of committing oneself in trust and obedience to god, which are characteristic of the expression of religious belief" (ibid., pp. 177–178). Referring to the 'scope for reasoning' in religion he writes: "There is however a limit to this reasoning. Within religious belief ... god's existence cannot be questioned because this whole universe of discourse presupposes it. Therefore, one must not say that religious education is not education unless it allows, as part of the process of such education, for the abandonment of religious belief" (ibid., p. 185). Hudson makes a distinction between independence of mind *about* religion and independence of mind *within* it (ibid., p. 187). Religious education is concerned only with the latter and not the former (since Hudson concedes that education more generally should be concerned with independence *about* religion it is not clear how much his point is a definitional one). Although Hudson makes it clear that the religiously educated person is not necessarily a religious believer (Hudson, 1987, p. 111) a form of religious formation seems to be envisaged. Hudson claims in a rather un-Wittgensteinian way that: "... the object of the exercise is not to get one's pupils to accept any particular content, but to initiate them into theology and devotion as such, the content of these being open to change or development as the pupil begins to think for himself in terms of god" (ibid., p. 191) (for further discussion of this argument see Kazepides, 1982; Hudson, 1982). Regardless of the merits of this argument, it seems to be significantly in tension with a Wittgensteinian perspective.

A second way in which limits to questioning arise on this perspective concerns the philosophical interpretation of religion. It is clear that Phillips brings to bear a particular philosophical theory to his account of religious education, which is, in an important sense, non-negotiable. How would Phillips react to a child in the classroom who advocated a non-Wittgensteinian point of view? Phillips regards, for example, a philosophical defence of immortality in terms of survival after death as 'bad philosophy' (ibid., p. 265) (on the general relationship between faith and philosophy see Phillips, 1970a, Ch. 13; 1993, Ch. 14). Any one claiming, contra Phillips, that foundationalism and evidentialism are appropriate ways in which religion ought to be philosophically discussed would be ruled out of court. Phillips claims that he has reached his conclusion by philosophical reflection: "It is not a presumption with which I begin ... But there is a risk involved in philosophical enquiry. The conclusions I have come to cannot be guaranteed in advance, and one may not arrive at them. But the man who is genuinely philosophically puzzled has no choice. He has to go where the argument takes him" (Phillips, 1993, p. 235. For criticisms of this conception of philosophy see, for example, Nielsen, 1971). Phillips is articulating a notion of philosophy as 'disinterested enquiry', but there is no evidence that he would allow other philosophical views in the classroom as other than mistakes to be corrected. He allows (as in the last section) for religious belief (properly understood) to be rejected as unattractive. But it is important to note the very character of the philosophical understanding of religious belief seems non-negotiable. Those unpersuaded by the Wittgensteinian perspective will find this a troubling aspect of its implications for education in religion. A.C. Grayling holds that, for all its importance and interest, Wittgenstein's general approach to philosophy has generally failed to convince (Grayling, 1991, p. 64). It is an interesting question how far the Wittgensteinian perspective can hold its own philosophical presuppositions open to enquiry in the classroom.

Questioning is a crucial element in any genuinely educative process. Questioning, of course, must be within limits. It might be argued, however, that the limits drawn by the Wittgenstein perspective are too tight.

Such an argument, however, leaves open the issue of how questioning, and the 'elucidation' to which it is related, is properly to be conceived and conducted in education in religion in common schools.

CONCLUSION

Wittgenstein's approach to religion is an important part of any assessment of the significance of his thought as a whole for educational thinking and practice. As we have seen, although his view of religion is elusive and stands in need of definitive evaluation, it offers a number of insights and challenges.

Whilst Wittgenstein's approach conflicts in important respects with the LR view of education in religion, because that view is based on important social and cultural realities which are significant for Wittgensteinian principles, it is not supplanted. The Wittgensteinian approach both supplies important perspectives which will enrich the LR view, whilst giving support to a greater pluralism in the way in which education in religion is conceived, including forms of substantial religious upbringing and schooling.

ACKNOWLEDGEMENTS

An earlier version of this paper was presented to a meeting at the Faculty of Psychology and Educational Sciences, Catholic University of Leuven, Belgium, in November 1992. I am very grateful to Professor Dr. Paul Smeyers for the invitation to present the paper, and to him and the participants in the discussion for their helpful comments. I am also grateful to Dr Jeff Astley for allowing me to see unpublished material of his relevant to the matters raised in the paper.

NOTES

[1] cf. Wittgenstein's remarks about Father O'Hara, who claimed that religious beliefs could be made reasonable: LA, pp. 58–59. See also LA, pp. 60–63.

[2] For assessment and criticism of non-realism and religion and some of its proponents see Cowdell, 1988; Hebblethwaithe, 1988; Runzo, 1993; Ward, 1982; White, 1994. For Phillips' reaction to this general position see his papers in Runzo, 1993.

[3] On such basic beliefs see Gardner, 1988; McLaughlin, 1990. For arguments that religious doctrines are not on the same level as 'epistemically primordial' or 'river-bed' propositions see Kazepides, 1991b.

Philosophy and Education: 'After' Wittgenstein

MICHAEL PETERS

University of Auckland, New Zealand

"The truly apocalyptic view of the world is that things do *not* repeat themselves. It isn't absurd, e.g., to believe that the age of science and technology is the beginning of the end for humanity; that the idea of great progress is a delusion, along with the idea that the truth will ultimately be known; that there is nothing good or desirable about scientific knowledge and that mankind, in seeking it, is falling into a trap. It is by no means obvious that this is not how things are."

Ludwig Wittgenstein, *Culture and Value*

"Wittgenstein est un penseur solitaire. Il pense certes 'après' Frege, Russell, le positivisme logique, et sans doute Schopenhauer et Spengler. Mais sa solitude se marque en ceci, qu'il pense aussi 'après' lui-même."

Jean-François Lyotard, *Wittgenstein*, 'Après'

INTRODUCTION

This essay is oriented to the future of philosophy of education rather than its past. My primary intention in this chapter is to propose a reading of the work of the later Wittgenstein which both unsettles the view of Wittgenstein as a place-holder in the analytic tradition and provides interpretative grounds for viewing him within the tradition of continental philosophy. In this context of interpretation, Wittgenstein can be seen as embracing a Spenglerian view of philosophy as a form of cultural criticism and as exhibiting important precursor elements in his thinking which mark him out as a philosopher who anticipated central aspects of the current debate surrounding the re-evaluation of the culture of modernity. These elements are emphasised in the work of Richard Rorty, and in commentaries which explore the parallels between the thought of the later Wittgenstein and various French 'post-structuralist' thinkers. They are also emphasised directly in the creative appropriation of his work by Jean-François Lyotard, who explicitly draws upon Wittgensteinian themes, notions and motifs to argue the case for the 'postmodern condition'. Lyotard's self-consciously sites his work as taking place 'after' Wittgenstein – a leitmotif which forms, in part, the title of this chapter. His creative appropriation of Wittgenstein, I argue, provides the starting-point for a philosophy of education which can seriously engage the issues and problems of what is known as the modernity-postmodernity debate.

In the first section I provide a brief discussion of the later Wittgenstein's view of philosophy and language as a preliminary to establishing an interpretation which recognises the continental influences on his thinking. On the basis of this interpretation, I argue, Wittgenstein can be seen as being heavily influenced by Spengler, and as much closer to the concerns of certain strands of continental thought emphasising the role of philosophy as a form of cultural criticism

189

Studies in Philosophy and Education **14**: 313–328, 1995.
© 1995 *Kluwer Academic Publishers. Printed in the Netherlands.*

(*Kulturkritik*). This anti-foundationalist view of philosophy has been developed most clearly in the English-speaking world by Richard Rorty who argues for a 'post-modernist' philosophy. Yet, Rorty's formulation, which takes its inspiration from the later Wittgenstein, I wish to argue, is not the only form 'post-analytic' philosophy might take. The 'culturalist' interpretation of the later Wittgenstein becomes the sympathetic basis for an alternative reading: what might be called a 'post-structuralist' appropriation of the later Wittgenstein, which, I argue, constitutes a creative and useful reading from which a 'post-analytic' philosophy of education might benefit.

In the second section I examine the direct appropriation of the later Wittgenstein by the French philosopher, Jean-François Lyotard (1984a), who defines the 'postmodern' as an "incredulity towards metanarratives", a scepticism and distrust of those legitimating, philosophical narratives which purport to justify certain practices and institutions by grounding then upon transcendental principles. It is in this context that the combined problems of the legitimation of knowledge and education come to the fore.

Finally, in the third section, I examine the possibility of a 'post-structuralist' philosophy of education, based on these insights.

PHILOSOPHY 'AFTER' WITTGENSTEIN

In the *Philosophical Investigations* Wittgenstein (1953) rejected the essentialism of the *Tractatus* and instead came to embrace a much wider view of language holding, in general terms, that the meaning of a word is its use within a 'language-game' (PI, I, ## 23, 43). The game analogy provides Wittgenstein with the means to emphasize, among other things, the diversity of linguistic usage. Considering the use of the notion 'game' he writes in a now famous passage:

> "We see a complicated network of similarities overlapping and criss-crossing: sometimes overall similarities; sometimes similarities of detail" (PI, I, # 66).

and he adds in the next paragraph:

> "I can think of no better expression to characterize these similarities than 'family resemblances' ... And I shall say: 'games form a family'".

Misconceptions about language arise when in our craving for unity and generality (BB, p. 19f.), from the uniform appearance of words we mistakenly assume their uniform application, insisting that every word can be given a precise or strict definition. Wittgenstein informs us in a preliminary study to the *Investigations*:

> "what causes most trouble in philosophy is that we are tempted to describe the use of important 'odd-job' words as though they were words with regular functions" (BB, p. 41).

He admonishes us, in considering the meaning of a word, not to guess or think but to *look* at how the word is used in various contexts (PI, I, # 66), and he stresses the multiplicity of these contexts or language-games (PI, I, # 23). Wittgenstein's own investigations are not meant as classifications, but rather "to enable the reader to shift for himself [sic] when he encounters conceptual difficulties" (PI, I, # 92); "a picture holds us captive" (PI, I, # 115); or "we do not *command a clear view* of the use of our words" (PI, I, # 122). Thus, "philosophy is the battle against the bewitchment of our intelligence by means of language" (PI, I, # 109) and it is the business of philosophy, by attending to the way words and sentences are used in actual contexts, to command a clear view of a segment of our language – to assemble reminders (PI, I, # 127) of what already lies in plain view.

Clearly, Wittgenstein is repudiating the notion of foundations of language (and of knowledge), and, thereby, also the idea of a linguistic-oriented first philosophy whose central concern is the search for criteria which define, in the form of necessary conditions, our most fundamental concepts and beliefs. Although he still wants to distinguish philosophy from science, Wittgenstein does not hold to its status as a second order or foundational discipline.

Wittgenstein's semantic holism is given in the statement "To understand a sentence means to understand a language. To understand a language means to be master of a technique" (PI, I, # 199). The point here is that no sentence has meaning in isolation. The understanding of one sentence is not independent of other sentences. Wittgenstein's holism has its ultimate expression in the concept of a 'form of life', comprising the various overlapping language-games, themselves "consisting of language and the actions into which it is woven" (PI, I, # 7). Later, in *On Certainty* (1969), Wittgenstein spells out the epistemological implications of his holistic theory of meaning. In that work he claims that our beliefs (C, # 141) and our doubts (C, # 126) form a system and he stresses how a certain framework provides the axis (C, # 152), scaffolding (C, # 211), or hinges (C, # 341), of our thoughts and actions: what we hold fast to is "a nest of propositions" (C, # 225). "All testing, all confirmation and disconfirmation of a hypothesis", Wittgenstein writes, "takes place already within the system . . . The system is . . . the element within which arguments have their life" (C, # 105). It is a claim that Wittgenstein repeats a number of times in various ways (C, ## 166, 248, 253, 274, 410). The epistemological consequences of a holistic theory of meaning have already been foreshadowed in the *Philosophical Grammar* (1974), where Wittgenstein asserts that the calculus itself has no ground (p. 110), and that grammar is not accountable to any reality (p. 185); and in the *Investigations*, where Wittgenstein talks of justification – of the chain of reasons coming to an end (PI, ## 326, 482, 485).

Wittgenstein's assertion of the liberation of grammar from the bounds of logic, and his consequent rejection of any extra-linguistic justification for language and knowledge is taken by some commentators as amounting to a radical anthropocentrism (Pears, 1971, p. 179). For the later Wittgenstein there is no transcendental source for the way in which we speak, think and act; there is no transcendental standard which forms the basis and foundation of our language-use and our thinking in language. There is only some precipitate of common judgements and culturally shared agreements (made in practice) which stand fast for us.

Thus Wittgenstein does not present a simple coherentist account of knowledge. Even the idea of justification coming to an end implies a foundation of sorts or a 'given'. The notion of foundations is introduced explicitly in *On Certainty*: "Something must be taught us as a foundation" (C, # 449). But the foundation is not a set of ungrounded propositions: "it is an ungrounded way of acting" (C, # 110). Wittgenstein appeals to the fact that we simply *do* certain things, we *act* in particular ways, but this appeal is not made to human acting in isolation. It is made to acting as a precondition of the use of language – "our talk gets its meaning from the rest of our proceedings" (C, # 229) – and as part of an interconnected whole; our form of life. The system, then, is our foundation; the form of life is the given.

While Wittgenstein's early work emphasised the logicality of language (and rationality) in the development of a logically perspicuous language, his later work specifically emphasised the liberation of language, and particularly 'grammar' from the bounds of strict logic. His influence in this regard can be clearly seen in both the 'historical' turn taken in philosophy of science – in the work of Kuhn, Toulmin, Feyerabend, Hesse and Rorty – and in the sociology of knowledge (e.g., Bloor, 1983). In an important sense Wittgenstein's influence here can be broadly described as constituting a 'movement' characterised in historical terms as the shift away from a single, universal and formal model of rationality motivated by considerations of logic, to informal, historical and sociological models that more closely approximate the 'rationalities' employed by agents in their practices and in their active construction of social reality. In general terms, this movement can be considered at one level a reaction against the 'positivist' formalist interpretation of *one* paradigm of knowledge (i.e. science) and the treatment and elevation of it to stand as *the* exemplification of rationality – as embodying *the* standards that must be applied to the interpretation of all social practice irrespective of time and place.

In the *Philosophical Investigations*, Wittgenstein forcefully attacks the Cartesian view that philosophy is a foundational discipline – a metadiscipline which provides foundations for first order disciplines. Wittgenstein expends great effort in ridding us of this 'picture which has held us captive'. Philosophy is *not* something that one needs to do before doing anything else. Above all philosophy is not a meta-activity. It is not a science which studies a discipline as a whole to give it a foundation.

At one point in the *Investigations* Wittgenstein (PI, I, # 121) writes:

"One might think: if philosophy speaks of the word 'philosophy' there must be a second-order philosophy".

At another, he asserts plainly,

"The philosophy of logic speaks of sentences and words in exactly the same sense in which we speak of them in ordinary life ... " (PI, I, # 108).

These philosophical remarks in context with the whole tenor of the *Investigations*, show that Wittgenstein, among other things, was concerned to disassemble the *modern* view of philosophy as the meta-activity ('metanarrative') which provides foundations for knowledge.

Janik and Toulmin (1973) in a path-breaking book emphasized Wittgenstein's Viennese origins and the general continental milieu which constituted his immediate intellectual and cultural background (see also Janik, 1985, 1989). In this context we are, perhaps, ready to more openly acknowledge the continental influences on Wittgenstein's thinking and to recognise, for instance, the influence of Oswald Spengler. G. H. von Wright (1982, p. 118), more recently, has given considerable weight to Wittgenstein's Spenglarian 'rejection of the scientific-technological civilization of industrialized societies, which he regarded as the decay of a culture'. Drawing on *Culture and Value* (Wittgenstein, 1980), von Wright remarks upon how Wittgenstein found the spirit of European and American civilization both alien and distasteful and how Wittgenstein 'deeply distrusted' its hallmark belief in progress based on the technological harnessing of science, with its inherent dangers of self-destruction and its capacity to cause 'infinite misery'. Von Wright (1982, p. 118) suggests that it is this aspect of Wittgenstein's thinking which constitutes a link between 'the view that the individual's beliefs, judgements, and thoughts are entrenched in unquestioningly accepted language-games' and 'the view that philosophical problems are disquietudes of the mind caused by some malfunctioning in the language-games and hence in the life of the community'.

Rudolf Haller (1988, p. 76) also clearly demonstrates his sympathy for such a view when he remarks that Wittgenstein, in the sketch of a preface to the *Philosophical Remarks*, saw himself as a critic of Western culture in Spengler's sense. Stanley Cavell (1988) also views Wittgenstein as a "philosopher of culture" and provides a reading of the *Investigations* as a depiction of our times, agreeing with von Wright's assessment of Wittgenstein's attitude as Spenglarian suggesting that Spengler's vision of culture as a kind of Nature is shared in a modified form in the *Investigations*.

Cavell (1988, pp. 261–262) argues that the *Investigations* "diurnalizes Spengler's vision of the destiny toward exhausted forms", toward the loss of culture and community and he draws our attention to the way Wittgenstein's uniqueness as a philosopher of culture comes from "the sense that he is joining the fate of philosophy as such with that of the philosophy of culture or criticism of culture". By doing so, Cavell argues, Wittgenstein is thereby calling into question philosophy's claim to a privileged perspective on culture which could be called the perspective of reason.

Philosophy as criticism of culture, which in denying its historical privilege based on traditional claims for its status as a meta-language, places the activity of philosophy on a par with other activities of criticism. This interpretation would provide strong grounds to regard the philosophy of the later Wittgenstein as much closer to the philosophical themes and interests which motivate the variety of strains of thought called 'post-structuralism' than many would care to admit.

In the same year as Lyotard's (1984a, orig. 1979) *The Postmodern Condition* was first published, Richard Rorty (1979, p. 10) celebrated Wittgenstein as one of the three twentieth-century philosophers, along with Dewey and Heidegger, who attempted to remind us that:

"investigations of the foundations of knowledge or morality or language or society may be simply apologetics, attempts to eternalize a certain contemporary language-game, social practice or image".

Rorty's (1979) *Philosophy and the Mirror of Nature*, which became an instant philosophical *cause célèbre* made central use of Wittgensteinian 'arguments' to demonstrate the destruction and exhaustion of the Cartesian-Kantian tradition, with the aim of showing the pointlessness of talk of foundations.

Beginning his interpretation with a quotation from Wittgenstein's *Vermischte Bemerkungen*, which likens progress in philosophy to the finding of a remedy for itching, a physician-like Rorty diagnoses modern analytic philosophy as simply one more variant of Kantian philosophy – its true heir – which is to be distinguished from its parent predecessor by thinking of representation in linguistic terms and of philosophy of language as exhibiting foundations of knowledge.

Rorty claims that analytic philosophy is an exhausted enterprise. It is to be replaced by 'post-analytical philosophy' which unlike its forebear, no longer conceives of philosophical inquiry as one about the nature of Truth, Reality, Knowledge or Goodness. Such a 'post-analytical philosophy' (with a small rather than capital 'p') is a much more modest affair. As Pascal Engel (1987, p. 15) comments, Rorty's reasoning here "about the coming of a new age... looks very much like the reasoning of philosophers like Derrida...".

For Rorty, as Guigon (1990) explains, Wittgenstein and Heidegger are master diagnosticians whose 'therapies' and 'de-structions' have enabled us to stop doing philosophy. Their similarities are to be found in German philosophies of life which are holistic, anti-dualist and non-foundationalist. By 'holistic' Guigon (1990, p. 666) means "understanding always operates within a hermeneutic circle" where the "world is constituted by a background understanding embodied in practices and shaped by language". Guigon's purpose is not, however, to compare Wittgenstein to Heidegger (although the comparison is explicit); rather it is to inquire of philosophy *after* Wittgenstein and Heidegger, which he construes as a choice between Richard Rorty and Charles Taylor. In contradistinction to Rorty, Taylor (1987, pp. 182–183) argues that Wittgenstein and Heidegger offer us:

"a critique of epistemology in which we discover something deeper and more valid about ourselves [as agents]... something of our deep or authentic nature as selves".

Guigon supports Taylor over Rorty's 'epistemological behaviourism', arguing that not all language-games are optional.

Rorty's picture of all vocabularies as optional makes sense, Guigon (1990, p. 671) maintains, only if we can think of ourselves as "in fact at home nowhere" and this assumption seems to rely on a "notion of the subject as disengaged" which is of itself generated by the very epistemological tradition Rorty seeks to overcome.

Rorty's (1989a) recent contribution, along with past publications, certainly is the most sustained effort to link his kind of 'postmodernism' to the project of a liberal politics. His recent collection of essays is a further defence of what he (Rorty, 1983) elsewhere calls "liberal bourgeois postmodernism" – that is a defence of liberal individualism and 'irony'. In other words, Rorty thinks that we already have the right ideas and institutions in place (McCarthy, 1990, p. 649). The now familiar critique of foundationalism provides the basis for Rorty to argue that there is no ultimate justification for the good society. The best the 'liberal ironist' can do, it seems, is to make the injunction 'Don't be cruel!'

Rorty's (1989a) recent work has been subjected to searching criticism. It has been argued, for instance, that Rorty's picture of society is just as abstract and rarefied as any metaphysician's, even given his small-r realism and large-P Pragmatism (Ball, 1990, p. 103). Further, critics have complained that Rorty's universalisation of 'contingency' results in a political fatalism which finally rests on an ethnocentrism that functions to protect rich, liberal states from criticism (Connolly, 1990).

Rorty's position, which emphasises the general turn against theory and toward narrative to announce the end of metaphysics is not the only Wittgensteinian-inspired appropriation and construction of 'postmodernist philosophy' that can be made. No reading in the spirit of Wittgenstein vindicates Rorty's position and, in any case, we are not restricted in philosophy *after* Wittgenstein to a choice of Rorty or Taylor. One possibility, which ought not to be dismissed out of hand, is to regard 'post-structuralism' in its diverse incarnations, as providing the basis for an alternative reading.

Lecercle (1989, p. 223) has observed that where contemporary French philosophers, whose practice is far from analytic, have imported certain Anglo-Saxon concepts both selectively and indirectly, the process of importation is one of "reappropriation, betrayal and creative misinterpretation". Terry Eagleton (1982, pp. 64–65) has observed that the influence of Wittgenstein's work on Anglo-Saxon linguistic philosophy has "served partly to obscure its deep-seated affinities with a body of thought which has also shaped post-structuralism, that of Martin Heidegger". He complains that the Anglo-Saxon 'Wittgenstein' has sacrificed that "distinctively European timbre" and proceeds to make an explicit comparison between Wittgenstein and Derrida.

Others have noted the relation of the later Wittgenstein to French poststructuralism and Derrida in particular. Marjorie Grene (1976, pp. 265–266) notes that both agree on their starting point – "the traditional conception of language ... immobilizes thought" – but they "differ both in their diagnosis of the pathology and their prescription for treatment". David Allison (1978, pp. 108–109), beginning his account at the same point as Grene, finds a "profoundly positive affinity" between Wittgenstein and Derrida, and he maintains that the difference in their formulations is "rather one of style than substance". For Eagleton (1982, p. 66) "Wittgenstein and Derrida are alike in suspecting all philosophy of immediacy, all grounding of discourse in the experience of the subject". Eagleton notes that for Wittgenstein, as for post-structuralism, "the subject is 'written' from the outset, an effect of the play of the signifier: 'difference' and identity are equally effects of discourse".

Gregory Ulmer (1985, p. 94), in an important essay, discusses the import of Derrida's grammatology to the object of 'post-criticism' in relation to Wittgenstein's dictum 'the meaning is the use'. He writes at one point:

> "Post-criticism, then, functions with an 'epistemology' of performance – knowing as making, producing, doing, acting, as in Wittgenstein's account of the relation of knowing to the 'mastery of a technique'. Thus post-criticism writes 'on' its object in the way that Wittgenstein's knower exclaims, 'Now I know how to go on!'".

Hans Sluga (1989) begins an article with a quotation from *The Blue Book*: "We may say that thinking is essentially the activity of operating with signs"; and he views writing in Wittgenstein's philosophy as an embodiment of thinking, comparing it to Derrida's grammatology. In a footnote he acknowledges the way Wittgenstein's remark reveals an affinity between his thought and French post-structuralism, commenting on Wittgenstein's critique of mental agency by comparing it with the critique mounted by Lacan, Foucault and Derrida of both the empirical and transcendental subject.

In this regard, Robert Goff's (1969) early essay which treats aphorism as *Lebensform* in Wittgenstein's *Investigations* is particularly noteworthy. While Goff does not attempt to draw parallels between Wittgenstein and Derrida, he does situate himself in relation to Erich Heller (1959, p. 217) who treats Wittgenstein within the same cultural context as Nietzsche: both Wittgenstein and Heidegger are seen as fulfilling the same Nietzschean intention of tracking down to their source in language "the absurdities resulting from the human endeavour to speak the truth". For Goff (1969, p. 70) "It is not philosophically appropriate to distinguish his (Wittgenstein's) style from his meaning, nor the use of language from theories he is alleged to have about language".

More recently, there has been a tendency to recognise the two elements in his thought: the analytic and the Continental. Thus, for instance, Churchill (1989) distinguishes both a romantic and a prosaic side, where the latter deals with problems of logic which are resolved by *ad hoc* strategies; and the former deals with deep existential issues and regards philosophical inquiry as a process of struggle between doubt and certainty which *is* capable of ultimately resolving philosophical problems. McDonald (1990) detects a similar co-existence of different elements: the 'analytic' he represents in terms of the Humean scepticism advanced by Kripke; the 'Continental', by Staten's Wittgenstein as a Derridean sceptic. While clearly at odds with one another, McDonald indicates that Kripke's and Staten's views are, nevertheless, similar in certain ways: both characterise Wittgenstein as a sceptic reacting against his earlier work. At bottom McDonald (1990, pp. 271–272) tends to agree with Staten that Wittgenstein was offering a non-transcendental conception of rules (see also Diamond, 1989).

> "Staten's Derridean perspective has made him acutely sensitive to what in my view is an important element of Wittgenstein's work: the latter's treatment of language as a form of action in which there is no *boundary of essence* between what we call language and what we think of as non-language ... ' There is, in this regard, a very real analogy between Derrida's concept of *difference*

and Wittgenstein's contention that 'there is no code – an organon of iterability – that is structurally secret' . . . and Wittgenstein's argument against the possibility of a private language".

He indicates, however, that there is also another thrust of Derrida's deconstruction that is less congenial to Wittgenstein's project (and Staten's basic argument). Derrida's tactic is to undermine the basic binary oppositions that philosophy sets up by reversing the terms of the hierarchy. This, McDonald (1990, p. 272) suggests, "makes Derrida's method at once *more sceptical* and *less radical* than Wittgenstein's". Wittgenstein's is more radical, we are told, because he wants us to give up the philosophical pursuit altogether.

Staten's (1985, p. 157–158) purpose is to bring "Derrida's project into relation with Wittgenstein's in order to suggest an Anglo-American context within which deconstruction makes sense". In Wittgenstein's later philosophy, Staten (1990, p. 14) maintains, the "critique of the concept of a rule is aimed at showing that the form of a rule is essentially multiple". Staten also emphasises the kinship in the way that both Wittgenstein and Derrida approach the language of philosophy in terms of a deconstructive style, emphasising the importance of the phenomenality of language and the relation of style to the discourse on truth. Wittgenstein's style of philosophy, then in Staten's terms, is a form of 'lateral displacement', a practice of deconstruction which uses satire and figures to picture mental activities. It is also ironic and has a 'scenic' character. Philosophy is to Wittgenstein above all *not* a doctrine; it is rather 'a skill, a method, a strategy'. Wittgenstein's method is connected with

"Saussure's point . . . that the sign has no 'positive content', only a relational value arising from reciprocal demarcations among an entire system of forms" (Staten, 1990, p. 79; see also Harris, 1988).

Lawson (1989), more generally, draws the link between Wittgenstein's later work and postmodernism. She identifies two strains of attack on truth: relativism and postmodernism. The former tradition, she suggests, stems predominately from the social sciences in the work of Mannheim, Frazer and Malinowski and later in the thought of Winch, Kuhn and Feyerabend. The latter, she asserts, originates with Nietzsche and is characterized in more recent times by Lyotard, Foucault and Derrida. She writes:

"While relativism can be described as the view that truth is paradigm-dependent, postmodernism might be described as the view that meaning is undecidable and therefore, truth is unattainable. Relativism combined with its self-reflexive consequences yields an outlook with many points of contact with continental postmodernism. As a consequence a major figure like Wittgenstein is probably better understood with a postmodernism label rather than a relativist one (Lawson, 1989, p. xii).

Her major point is that there is a reflexivity in Wittgenstein's work (his attack on the correspondence theory of truth) such that "we need an implicit understanding of his position in order to make any sense of his writing at all" (Lawson, 1989, p. xxiv) and that the addition of this reflexive concern to Wittgenstein provides a link with the Continental tradition.

LYOTARD, WITTGENSTEIN AND THE CRITIQUE OF MODERNITY

Lyotard's (1984a) *The Postmodern Condition* does not set out to propose a scholastic interpretation of the later Wittgenstein in the way his countryman Jacques Bouveresse (1976) has done: rather Lyotard has made creative use of Wittgensteinian themes, motifs and arguments in order to pursue a particular line of thinking. Yet Lyotard (1984b, p. 61) acknowledges a clear sense in which his own work takes place 'after' Wittgenstein. 'After' Wittgenstein,

> "Il n'y a pas d'unité du langage, mais des îlots de langage, chacun d'eux régi par un regime différent, intraduisible dans les autres".

Lyotard refers to Wittgenstein in the *Investigations*, quoting the proposition at 110 with approval:

> "'Language (or thought) is something unique' – this proves to be a superstition (*not* a mistake!), itself produced by grammatical illusions".

Lyotard (1984b, pp. 61–62) continues:

> "Cette superstition, que Kant appelait illusion transcendentale, n'empêchait par l'Aufklärer d'espérer pour l'histoire humaine une finalité d'émancipation universelle, à laquelle la philosophie contribue. La maladie est pour Wittgenstein sans remède prévisible. Elle est liée à l'hégémonie de la techno-science industrielle, dont l'âge est peut-être 'le commencement de la fin de l'humanité' (*Culture and Value*, p. 56), et qui a pour 'expressions "culturelle" des assommoirs comme la théorie des ensembles et la psychologie behaviouriste. La philosophie n'y peut rien par elle-même, la maladie qui suscite ses problèmes ne peut être guérie que par un changement dans les manières de vivre et de penser' (*Foundations of Mathematics*, II, p. 23)".

Clearly, Lyotard aligns himself with Wittgenstein's Spenglarian attitude to the present age, dominated by an industrial 'techno-science'.

The debate over the question and status of modernity is exemplified best in the series of international exchanges between the French 'post-structuralist' thinker, Jean François Lyotard, and Jürgen Habermas, the leading representative of the Frankfurt School. It was Lyotard who first captured and crystallised the debate in global terms with the publication of *La Condition Postmoderne* in 1979. He defines *postmodern* as "incredulity towards metanarratives", a distrust of 'stories' which purport to justify certain practices or institutions by grounding them upon a set of transcendental, ahistorical or universal principles. In contradistinction, Lyotard (1984a, p. xxii) uses the term *modern*

> "to designate any science that legitimates itself with reference to a metadiscourse ... making an explicit appeal to some grand narrative, such as the dialectics of the spirit, the hermeneutics of meaning, the emancipation of the rational or working subject, or the creation of wealth."

As Jameson (1984, p. vii) notes Lyotard's *The Postmodern Condition* is a "thinly veiled polemic" against Habermas' concept of a 'legitimation crisis' and vision of a fully transparent communicational society. Lyotard is certainly suspicious of Habermas' quasi-transcendentalism, of Habermas' project of attempting to save the emancipatory impulse of the Enlightenment by offering universalistic principles to ground and provide foundations for his reconstructive theory of communicative action. Habermas (1981, p. 13), for his part, christens the French post-structuralists 'conservatives' comparing them to the *Young Conservatives* of the Weimar Republic. To Habermas, the post-structuralists have simply "recapitulated the basic experience of aesthetic modernity" and in their critique of reason, he claims, they have fashioned a principle "only accessible through evocation, be it the will to power or sovereignty, Being or the dionysiac force of the poetical". Rorty (1985, p. 161) explains the difference between them in the following terms:

> "From Lyotard's point of view, Habermas is offering one more metanarrative, a more general and abstract 'narrative of emancipation' than the Freudian and Marxian metanarratives. For Habermas, the problem posed by 'incredulity towards metanarratives' is that unmasking only makes sense if we 'preserve at least one standard for the explanation of the corruption of *all* reasonable standards'. If we have no such standard, one which escapes a 'totalising self-referential critique', then distinctions between the naked and the masked, or between theory and ideology, lose their force".

Yet both appropriate Wittgenstein to argue their case. Habermas applauds the later Wittgenstein's refusal to grant philosophy a distinctive status or the constantive use of language a privileged position. He notes that similar considerations to those which motivated Heidegger to write a series of lectures on Nietzsche in 1939 – emphasizing, in particular, the "mutuality of understanding" – are the starting point for not only the linguistic philosophy of Wittgenstein, but also for the methodology of the interpretive *Geisteswissenschaften*, the pragmatism of Pierce and Mead, and the philosophical hermeneutics of Gadamer. The intersubjectivity of language is seen to be fertile ground for finding a path leading out of the philosophy of consciousness, of subject-centred reason, but for Habermas (1990, p. 138), Heidegger "remains attached, in a negative way, to the *foundationalism* of the philosophy of consciousness". Habermas (1990, p. 74), here is bent on demonstrating how all paths which seriously purport to lead beyond the philosophy of the subject – Heidegger's and Derrida's, Bataille's and Foucault's – have failed and that we should return "to the alternative that Hegel left in the lurch back in Jena – to a concept of communicative reason . . . ".

Lyotard also acknowledges his intellectual debt to the later Wittgenstein. Taking his cue from Adorno, he champions the 'micrologic' in opposition to the speculative – the grand narrative of Hegelian philosophy – and asserts that

> "another perspective has been opened up through which it may be possible to measure up to the crisis [of metaphysics] and the reflective response it demands. This perspective is pointed to notably in the *Philosophische Untersuchungen* and *Zettel*, under the name of *Sprachspielen* (Lyotard, 1983, p. 122).

In *The Postmodern Condition*, Lyotard (1984a, pp. 9–10) claims that the great legitimating myths or metanarratives are being dispersed in "clouds of . . . language elements", each with "pragmatic valencies specific to its kind". His claim is squarely based on the Wittgensteinian "method of language-games". It is equally clear that Lyotard has taken on board a number of central themes from Wittgenstein, yet his 'reading' is both playful and innovative rather than simply exegetical. He emphasises the pluralistic nature of language games to advance an attack on the conception of a universal reason. Each of the various types of utterance – denotative, prescriptive, performative etc – comprises a language-game, with its own body of rules defining its properties and uses. The rules are irreducible and there exists an incommensurability among different games. Further, he argues in true Wittgensteinian fashion that the rules do not have a bedrock justification, nor do they carry with themselves their own legitimation. Where Wittgenstein might say they are constituted in practice, Lyotard claims they are the object of a contract, explicit or not, between players. He adds, "if there are no rules there is no game" and "every utterance should be thought of as a 'move' in a game".

This is Lyotard's 'innovation' for he emphasises a notion of 'language-games' which is based on the idea of struggle and conflict. Two principles underlie Lyotard's (1984a, p. 10) adopted method as a whole: "To speak is to fight, in the sense of playing, and speech acts fall within the domain of a general agonistics". As Jameson (1984, p. xi) explains, utterances are not conceived of either as a process of the transmission of information or messages, or a network of signs, or even in terms of a semiotics as a signifying system: rather they are seen as an *agonistics of language*, as "an unstable exchange between communicational adversaries". This elevates the conflictual view of language – a view which is to be considered 'political' in the widest sense of the term – as a model for understanding the nature of the social bond (and even science itself). For Lyotard there is no principle of unitotality; there is no universal meta-language. The reality is that there are many languages and, as Wittgenstein argued (Lyotard notes), new languages are added to the old ones, like suburbs to an old town. Lyotard mentions Wittgenstein's examples of the symbolism of chemistry and the notation of infinitesimal calculus. Less than fifty years on, he argues, we can substantially add to the list and he mentions: the growth of machine languages, the matrices of game theory, new systems of musical notation, systems of notation for nondenotative forms of logic, the language of the genetic code, graphs of phonological structures, and so on.

The proliferation and splintering of language games, which prevents an overall mastery, allows Lyotard (1984a, p. 41) to claim that

"speculative or humanistic philosophy is forced to relinquish its legitimation duties, which explains why philosophy is facing a crisis wherever it persists in arrogating such functions and is reduced to the study of systems of logic or the history of ideas where it has been realistic enough to surrender them".

Lyotard's (1984a, p. 3) *The Postmodern Condition* is centrally concerned with notions of 'education' and 'knowledge': his working hypothesis is that "the status of knowledge is altered as societies enter what is known as the postindustrial age and cultures enter what is known as the postmodern age". The central problem addressed by Lyotard is the legitimation of knowledge and education after the collapse of the grand narratives:

"the progressive emancipation of reason and freedom, the progressive or catastrophic emancipation of labour..., the enrichment of all humanity through the progress of capitalist technoscience" (Lyotard, 1992, p. 29).

In a recent interview with William van Reijen and Dick Veerman, Lyotard seeks to defend the position he has adopted in *The Postmodern Condition* against his 'rationalist' American and German critics by following a line of Kantian and Wittgensteinian thought. He says, quite simply: "there is no reason, only reasons". Later in the interview Lyotard (1988, p. 279) expands this statement by arguing:

> "As we think through this side of Kant's thought (and it is also possible to find an analogue in the late work of Wittgenstein), it is easy to show that it is never a question of *one* massive and unique reason – that is nothing but an ideology. On the contrary, it is a question of *plural* rationalities, which are, at the least, theoretical, practical, aesthetic".

This statement by Lyotard is an elaboration of the position he originally adopted in *The Postmodern Condition* based on the incommensurability of language-games – what Gérard Roulet (1983, p. 205) has described in reference to Lyotard's description of postmodernity as "a breaking apart of reason; Deleuzian schizophrenia". It can be taken in one sense as an extension of the Frankfurt School's critique of instrumental reason, as Michel Foucault (1989, p. 243) explained in an interview with Gérard Raulet in 1983. Raulet first discusses the "bifurcation of reason", its division into two realms, 'technical' and 'moral' reason, as a one-time historical split. The analysis of this bifurcation is Kantian in its origin and the division between technical and practical reason, he maintains, "governs all of the history of thought in Germany". Foucault responds in a manner close to Lyotard's Wittgensteinian-inspired position:

> "In fact, I do not speak of a bifurcation of reason. Rather I speak of multiple bifurcations. I speak of an endless prolific division".

In a highly original and instructive essay Plinio Prado (1991, p. 93) "shows how and why Wittgenstein comes to form an unavoidable passage for Lyotard's thinking on the different". Prado clarifies the ethico-political background and the stakes of the linkage between Lyotard and Wittgenstein. As Kauffman (1991, p. 10) comments:

> "Wittgenstein's insistence upon the diversity and incommensurability of language games, the paradox of the rule, and the rejection of metalanguage are presented as his philosophical response to the uprootedness and contingency, to the general nihilism and sense of 'delegitimation' which profoundly affected mid-century European life and culture – forming the context for Lyotard's 'politics of the different' as well. Prado's essay evokes the 'reflective', analogical power of Wittgenstein's late thinking, arguing that his view of langauge was less 'humanist' and 'anthropological' than Lyotard claimed in the Differend. The Aristotelian wisdom (*eustochia*) – precursor to the Kantian reflective judgement – which Prado sees at play in Wittgenstein and in Lyotard is yet another sense in which Lyotard's work takes place (as Lyotard has acknowledged) 'after' Wittgenstein".

Prado (1991) traces the development of Lyotard's thought from the early days of the group *Socialisme ou Barbarie* with its commitment to the Marxist metalanguage of 'critique of ideology' through to the point where Lyotard began a withdrawal from Marxist dialectics and from the universalist pretensions which accompanied it. Lyotard's reading of Wittgenstein, Prado maintains, was the determining point for the direction Lyotard's work henceforth was to take. Prado (1991, p. 96) writes:

"If Lyotard welcomes Wittgensteinian thinking, it is rather as a result of ethical and political questions concerning 'delegitimation': that is, on the basis of the crisis 'which resides in any attempt to moralise politics' ... and that of the difficulty of speaking about it in the 'right' terms".

PHILOSOPHY OF EDUCATION 'AFTER' WITTGENSTEIN

"After philosophy comes philosophy. But it is altered by the after. After the *Tractatus* come the *Philosophische Untersuchungen* and the unpublished works. After the coveting of an absolute and pure language that speaks of the world comes the deceptive discovery of the plurality of tongues entangled in the world".

Jean-François Lyotard, *Foreword: After the Words*

It is not surprising to find that analytic philosophers of education in the English-speaking world have given an 'analytic' reading of the later Wittgenstein for such a reading follows the more general tendency for analytic philosophers to view Wittgenstein as a place-holder in the analytic tradition, following in the tradition of Russell in his early work and helping to inaugurate 'ordinary language' philosophy revolution in his later work. Such an interpretation of the later Wittgenstein, as I have shown, is entirely one-sided: in one sense it indicates the problems of interpretation in philosophy, the force of parochial traditions – the lack of their interpenetration until quite recently – and the consequent ahistorical insensitivity of analytic philosophy to questions of influence outside its own cultural context. In another sense it has indirectly raised the question of interpretation and readings of philosophical texts as explicit philosophical issues. Derrida's notion of philosophy as a kind of writing becomes an important consideration with a philosopher like Wittgenstein, where the question of style cannot be easily divorced from that of content.

To make matters more complex, an historical reading of analytic philosophy of education may well reveal that it was deeply ambivalent in its approach to Wittgenstein, fusing aspects of the early Wittgenstein of the *Tractatus* and Russellian search for a logical perspicuous language with the Wittgenstein of the *Investigations*. This is not to argue that there are no important continuities in Wittgenstein's thinking. The doctrine of saying and showing provides a bridge between the early and the later work, as does the very conception of philosophy that Wittgenstein embraced. It is to argue, however, that analytic philosophy of education in its own self-understanding took place, so to speak, 'before' rather than 'after' the later Wittgenstein.

The possibility of 'post-analytic' philosophy of education takes place, self-consciously, 'after' Wittgenstein in the ethical and political sense given to this phrase by Lyotard. An important variant of 'post-analytic' philosophy of education is that based on the direct and creative appropriation of Wittgenstein's work by Lyotard and by the similarities between the work of the later Wittgenstein and that of French post-structuralist philosophers. Such a 'post-structuralist' philosophy of education, as a starting point, might regard as central an examination of the legitimation and status of knowledge and education in the 'postmodern condition' (see Peters, 1989, 1992, 1995; Marshall & Peters, 1994). As part of the 'philosophy of culture', in the broadest sense, it would be directed at the understanding and critique of education as one of the primary institutions of the culture of modernity, which is increasingly 'techno-scientific'. One of the most important tasks for contemporary philosophers of education in accepting the challenge of Wittgenstein's later philosophy is to develop positive characterisations of education in the 'postmodern age', in an age at the 'end of modernity' when the ruling liberal and marxist meta-narratives of education have become exhausted.

A 'post-analytic' philosophy of education which adopts the themes and motifs of 'postmodernism' can be seen to offer a problematic comprising, at least, the following elements. First and foremost, such a philosophy would involve a serious engagement and re-evaluation of modernity. From this point of view it is useful to distinguish between different modes of 'postmodern' thought and action: a postmodernism of resistance versus a postmodernism of reaction, where the former represents a deep ethical and political questioning of modern institutions and the legitimations of them that have been made and the latter, a simple, ahistorical and neo-conservative repudiation of modernism (Foster, 1985). The former arises as a counter-practice to the culture of modernity and to reactionary postmodernism. It concerns itself with deconstructing and providing a genealogical critique of the foundational interpretive frameworks which have served to legitimate techno-scientific and political projects in the modern world. Its spirit of resistance is tied to what Lyotard has called "incredulity toward meta-narratives".

Second, such a philosophy would involve a better understanding and critique of the costs and dangers of the increasing rationalisation of modern society and of the general role that education plays in this process of modernisation. For philosophy of education this must represent a 'return' to political and economic questions, and to theories which construe education no longer as a universal welfare right but rather as the means of 'human capital' development required for increasing the global competiveness of the modern nation-state. In conjunction with this philosophers of education, on this view, need to confront more critically the rise of the new information technologies, their place in the on-going process of societal modernisation and the ways in which they affect education. Inevitably, this kind of philosophising will mean a new appreciation and confrontation with the nature and logic of multi-national corporate capitalism.

Third, such a philosophy of education will involve, most importantly, a re-assessment of the 'philosophy of the subject', of subject-centred reason, as part of the project of modernity underpinning modern educational theory and the project of liberal mass schooling (Peters and Marshall, 1993). This line of philosophical investigation might question the way the modern 'subject of education' has been grounded in a European universalism and rationalism heavily buttressed by highly individualist assumptions inherited from Enlightenment grand narratives. Informed by a new awareness of the dangers of Western ethnocentrism and a critical understanding of difference and 'otherness' it would provide approaches to the constitution of subjectivity which recognise and redefine the relationship between representation and power at the levels of discourse and practice.

Wittgenstein and Foucault: Resolving Philosophical Puzzles

JAMES D. MARSHALL

University of Auckland, New Zealand

In this chapter I wish to look first at two potential ways of asking philosophical questions about education, or of doing philosophy of education. It is argued that when framed around punishment these philosophical approaches generate conflicting answers and thereby pose several puzzles for educators trying to talk about the punishment of children. Then I wish to use an interpretation of Wittgenstein to show how these puzzles might be resolved. It will be argued that the insights offered by Foucault in the second approach have similarities to Wittgenstein's approach to doing philosophy.

Punishment is an appropriate topic as it involves both educational issues and philosophical issues, and has been a recurring topic in philosophy of education. There is both an educational literature and a philosophical literature, and identifiable recent debates in journals such as *Philosophy of Education* (1984) and *The Journal of Moral Education* (1984–6–9).

The first approach, the analytic, dominated philosophy of education in the Anglo-Saxon 'world' for nearly two decades. The second is that offered by the French philosopher historian Michel Foucault. These approaches will be *illustrated* by reference to the account of punishment by R.S. Peters in *Ethics and Education* (1966), on the one hand, and Foucault's account in *Discipline and Punishment* (1979a) on the other hand. Philosophical puzzles for talk of the punishment of children vis-a-vis the punishment of adults are raised by different answers given by these accounts. Peters' work is used only to illustrate a general analytic position on punishment, which is readily available, and which has set the grounds for debate on the meaning of 'punishment' and its legitimation in philosophy of education.

A solution to these puzzles, it will be argued, is to use the insights of Wittgenstein. In particular his views on concepts, following a rule, and how concepts are learned. The solution, derived from Wittgenstein, will be closer to the position of Foucault than to Peters and analytic philosophy which, from a Wittgensteinian point of view, was mired in a mistaken search for necessary and sufficient conditions for the concept 'punishment' and a mistaken interpretation of Wittgenstein's notion of a rule. Such an approach would be incompatible with the later Wittgenstein. One need not follow Foucault then but, instead, accept the challenge offered by Wittgenstein.

The chapter is divided into four parts. I look in Part I at the traditional legalistic model of punishment, normally known as the Hart-Flew-Benn model and as exemplified in Richard Peters' *Ethics and Education*, and where there are refer-

Studies in Philosophy and Education **14**: 329–344, 1995.
© 1995 *Kluwer Academic Publishers. Printed in the Netherlands.*

ences to the authority of Wittgenstein to claim justification for this approach to punishment. This account, insofar as it involves Wittgenstein, not only involves a misuse of Wittgenstein but it also generates philosophical puzzles about talk of the punishment of children. Part II looks at Foucault's approach to the concept of punishment in *Discipline and Punish*. But Foucault's account also generates puzzles for talk of punishment. In Part III I try to show that Wittgenstein may be closer to Foucault, at least on this issue, than at first sight may have seemed possible. The conclusion resolves the puzzles through arguments derived from Wittgenstein but which may incline us to follow Foucault in approaching the discussion of punishment in education, rather than seeking 'insight' from analytic philosophy of education.

I PETERS AND WITTGENSTEIN

Those philosophers who have been interested in punishment have tended to concentrate upon two major questions. These are concerned with *meaning* and *justification*. The questions, What is the meaning of 'punishment'?, and, How is punishment to be justified?, have almost come to dominate philosophical literature. The selection of papers edited by H.B. Acton (*The Philosophy of Punishment*, 1963), illustrates this point.

The philosophical literature concerns itself with a particular model of punishment. This (legal) model is presented by H.L.A. Hart in *Punishment and Responsibility* (1968), as an answer to these questions. As Hart's work draws upon earlier work of Antony Flew and Stanley Benn, the model is sometimes referred to as the Flew, Benn, Hart model of punishment. And it was to be adopted by R.S. Peters in his enormously influential writings on philosophy of education (*Ethics and Education*, 1966).

Hart says that he is merely drawing upon "recent admirable work scattered through . . . philosophical journals". That Hart specifically added the qualifier 'English' to his list of journals need not be of too much concern. If this does represent a certain insularity or philosophical myopia, Hart was probably correct at that time that there was little need to go beyond this literature in English speaking philosophy (see, in particular, the edited collection by Acton). However, it should be added that he is also writing from within an established legal tradition and with more than merely an analytic methodology as he relates his approach to that of Locke's discussion of property.

Along with Flew (1954) and Benn (1958) he says that he will define the standard case of the concept of punishment as containing five elements. These were said to be (Hart, 1968, p. 4f.):

 (i) it must involve pain or other consequences normally considered unpleasant;
 (ii) it must be for an offence against legal rules;
(iii) it must be of an actual or supposed offender for his offence;

(iv) it must be intentionally administered by human beings other than the offender;

(v) it must be imposed and administered by an authority constituted by a legal system against which the offence is committed.

Hart immediately excludes from the standard or central uses, by relegating them to the position of *sub-standard or secondary cases*, the following possibilities: pain or consequences for breaching other than legal rules – here he gives as specific examples, the family and the school; by other than authoritative officials; and unpleasantness or pain imposed deliberately by authorities but upon non-offenders. Hence these philosophical puzzles are posed for educators. How can we talk meaningfully, in more than a sub-standard sense of the term 'punishment', and more than metaphorically, about the punishment of children?

This standard account is to be found, essentially, in R.S. Peters' *Ethics and Education* (1966). Peters also adopts Hart's fourfold division of meaningful questions about punishment. These are said to be (Hart, 1968, p. 4) questions of *definition, justification* and *distribution*, with the latter divided into questions of *who* should be punished, i.e., *entitlement*, and the *form* and severity. Peters, however, sees the first two questions only as being philosophical questions, with the remaining two being the province of jurists and administrators. In effect then we have a philosophical division of labour, with the efforts of philosophers directed at the first two questions about punishment and the relegation of the last two questions to the status of administrative, juridical or, in Peters' case, educational questions. We will return to these questions below.

If Peters' particular account of punishment did not meet with universal approval (see, e.g. P.S. Wilson, 1971; John Wilson, 1977), nevertheless the model set the form of the debates that ensued in philosophy of education.

According to Peters "the most crucial concept for discussing social control in the school is that of authority" (Peters, 1966, p. 237). Peters discusses several closely related concepts, namely 'discipline', 'authority' and 'punishment'. But in his account of authority he is clearly drawing upon a reading of Wittgenstein, conceding to Winch (Peters, 1966, p. 246) that authority is necessarily linked with rule governed behaviour in Wittgenstein's sense, which is stronger than his earlier announcement (op. cit., p. 238) that "the concept of authority is inseparably connected with a rule governed form of life". It (loc.cit.):

"presupposes some sort of normative order that has to be promulgated, maintained and perpetuated ... (by) ... procedural rules which give such people the right to decide, promulgate, judge, order and pronounce ... (it) would be unintelligible unless we first had the concept of following rules with the built in notion that there are incorrect and correct ways of doing things".

It is not at all clear that Peters has read Wittgenstein correctly on rules. There is too much of the command sense of a rule here – see below.

In the school then authorities pronounce upon the rules, which are themselves related to Wittgenstein's notion of rule following behaviour by Peters, and are the authorities which in turn administer discipline and punishment (though for

Peters punishment is a necessary evil – in contrast to John Wilson who holds
that it is in some sense logically necessary – see Marshall, 1984b).

But Peters has smudged the notion of a rule, from its legal sense in the Flew-
Hart-Benn model, because it is no longer a legal rule, but a school rule, or
family rule or any old rule. The philosophical puzzles remain.

Punishment in this account is for the breaking of a rule, it is intentionally
given by an authority, and the rules depend upon Wittgenstein's notion of rule
following behaviour. Here Peters seems to interpret Wittgenstein as seeing rule
following behaviour, as requiring submission to rules, as if rules were commands from authorities, or as if perhaps they are reasons for action. A similar
interpretation is made by John Wilson (1977).

II FOUCAULT ON PUNISHMENT

Hart assumes that analysis and considerations of penal theory alone will set the
framework for the discussion of the mounting complexity surrounding the institution of criminal punishment as if, apriori, history and sociology, for example,
have no contribution to make to these framework questions. By 'settling' framework questions in this manner, the alleged punishment of children in family and
school is relegated to the position of sub-standard or secondary cases (Hart,
1968, p. 5). Almost by definition the history of the punishment of children has
nothing important to offer to the resolution of the complexity of this area of per-
plexity and debate in education.

It will be argued that in fact historical and sociological issues arising from a
consideration of the second two questions – entitlement and amount (form and
severity) – are germane to answering questions about the meaning and justification of punishment in general, and the punishment of children in particular. The
thinker who has turned these questions on their head, so to say, is Michel
Foucault. Foucault (1979a) starts with questions of entitlement and amount and
ends, albeit perhaps implicitly, with questions about meaning and justification.
Also, whilst sensitive to language, he turns to *practices* and accounts of what
was done to people in the name of punishment.

Foucault is one of the more interesting and controversial thinkers to have
emerged in the Western World in the twentieth century. Yet it is not easy to say
exactly how he impinges upon traditional mainstream philosophy and upon education. If he has influenced the philosophical mainstream, it might be thought
that it was at the periphery, perhaps heralding the end of philosophy in the
company of Jacques Derrida. If he has been seen as a visiting European scholar
at North American Universities he is not to be taken as a serious philosopher
but, rather as a *visitor* to established intellectual fortresses, or as a vagabond
outside the gates demanding entrance. If he has influenced education, it can be
claimed, it is at best indirectly. How can one who says this be taken seriously by
academics (Foucault, 1984, p. 343)?:

"I think I have in fact been situated in most of the squares on the political checkerboard, one after another and sometimes simultaneously: as anarchist, leftist, ostentatious or disguised marxist, nihilist, explicit or secret anti-marxist, technocrat in the service of Guallism, new liberal etc. An American professor complained that a crypto-marxist like me was invited to the U.S.A., and I was denounced by the press in Eastern Europe for being an accomplice of the dissidents. None of these descriptions is important by itself; taken together, on the other hand, they mean something. And I must admit that I rather like what they mean".

Foucault should be taken for himself and not as some other person neatly classified into recognisable categories.

At the time when he was at the height of his influence upon French intellectual life, when he had begun to occupy the position held formerly by Jean Paul Sartre, Michel Foucault died at the untimely age of 57. Paul Veyne, a distinguished classical historian and former colleague at the College de France, was to declare in an obituary in *Le Monde* that Foucault's work was "the most important event in thought of our century". Although Veyne cannot be considered as impartial towards Foucault, this is a claim worthy of consideration. What grounds are there for judgments such as that made by Veyne? Why might philosophers and philosophers of education be interested in Foucault?

It will be argued that whereas Foucault bypasses the traditional questions asked by philosophers on this topic, they are not excluded. What he says on the methods and techniques of punishment impinges explicitly and implicitly upon traditional philosophical concerns with questions of the meaning and the justification of punishment. Insofar as these traditional concerns have impinged upon education and philosophy of education he has something to say to us as philosophers of education. If his approach is different its worth must be assessed ultimately by its fruitfulness. It will be argued that, on this topic at least, Foucault brings to us as philosophers of education important *philosophical* insights. We will see below how he confronts the Hart-Flew-Benn model of punishment, and the extent to which Wittgenstein can be seen to hold a similar position.

According to Foucault (1979a) the modern prison dates from the end of the 18th century. Of course the prison had existed before then, but imprisonment as a major form of punishment had not. The prison had been a place for holding prisoners awaiting other punishments such as death or torture, or banishment, and was not listed in France as a serious penalty except, for example, as a substitute for those women, children and infants who could not serve in the galleys (Foucault, 1979a, p. 118). Foucault's central thesis is that the modern prison was from the outset concerned with techniques of transformation based upon individualisation and normalisation which were directed at the criminal and not at the act. Imprisonment then, as a form of punishment, marked a change in the *target* of punishment, according to Foucault.

The key events for Foucault's account of the modern prison were the reorganisation of the Maison De Force at Ghent in Belgium in 1775, the building of the Gloucester Penitentiary in 1779, and the reorganisation of Philadelphia's Walnut Street Prison in 1790. Exhibited in each of these new prisons were disciplinary techniques associated with individualisation and normalisation: the work ethic with strict timetabling; solitary confinement (though not total); surveillance (Ghent was built on Bentham's panopticon as model); and individualisation. The question "Who are you?" became important because the knowledge obtained from surveillance and careful documentation was a prerequisite for transforming the individual. If such knowledge was seen as necessary for the control of inmates within the prison it was also necessary for their transformation. This knowledge permitted the classification and distribution of dispositions of vice within the prison for both control and transformation. This new knowledge was not directed towards the acts which the prisoners had performed but towards "the potentially of danger that lies hidden in an individual and which is observed in his observed everyday conduct" (Foucault, 1979a, p. 126).

Foucault claims that this transformation in the form of punishment is not to be treated as a mere rearrangement of penalties. If the new form was also future directed "not to efface a crime, but to prevent its repetition" (Foucault, 1979a, p. 126), the major difference is to be found in the techniques (ibid., p. 127):

> "in the procedure of access to the individual, the way in which the punishing power gets control over him, the instruments that it uses in odder to achieve this transformation".

These new techniques are applied to the body, time, everyday gestures and activities. Forms of coercion are applied to the body to produce the obedient subject who, by subjection to rules, orders, imposed habits and authority continually exercised around him and upon him, "must allow (these) to function automatically in him" (ibid., p. 129). This represents a move from reacting to an offence in terms of a judicial subject willingly breaking a social pact, to that of shaping an obedient subject through a form of power based upon knowledge of that subject. It is not just a question of coercion, for that applies in both cases but, rather, that the new forms bring with them different consequences, namely individuals "corrected" by the power matrix that in enveloping individuals comes to function automatically within them.

Foucault claims that this coercive, corporeal, solitary and secret model of power was not to be confused with the punitive models thought up by earlier reformers. Here he cites the Rasphius of Amsterdam and the Maison de Force at Ghent (prior to its transformation). In these earlier institutions the spiritual transformation of inmates was sought by extolling a work ethic, continuous exercise, continuous exhortation and religious readings. But the major difference was that in the later institutions this transformation required as a condition of application of coercive techniques, knowledge of the individual. Through observation, surveillance and classification, knowledge of the individual was obtained, and through the continuous application of these techniques further knowledge of the normalised individual was compiled. In other words knowledge was both a condition and a consequence of this transformation of behaviour. It was this feature which distinguished the new forms of punishment both from those of the Ancien Régime and the ideas of the reformers.

In considerable gruesome detail Foucault discusses the changes that took place in the forms and techniques of punishment. The opening harrowing pages of *Discipline and Punish* are not there to shock or titillate but, rather, to draw a sharp contrast with the timetable of activities drawn up for offenders in the house of young offenders" in Paris. This timetable was devised by the criminologist Faucher in 1838, some 80 years after the earlier example of the harrowing execution of the regicide Damiens.

First, it can be noted that punishment is no longer a spectacle. The ceremony, theatre and public participation that accompanied Damiens' execution are to be eliminated. Far from the public spectacle of the scaffold, punishment is instead to be private, secluded behind walls, and "behind" legal and human science knowledge. The public spectacle was needed so that people could see the Sovereign reassert his power on the body of the condemned. As Foucault says (ibid., p. 5):

> "It brought to a solemn end a war, the outcome of which was decided in advance, between the criminal and the sovereign... A body effaced, reduced to dust and thrown to the winds, a body destroyed piece by piece by the infinite power of the sovereign constituted not only the ideal, but the real limit of punishment."

But this physical confrontation had to end. If it was revolting and cruel it was also dangerous, because it threw down a further challenge to the people. If reformers such as Beccaria (1764) influenced change nevertheless, Foucault argues, there was a legal and bureaucratic thrust towards the control of populations in a more regular and efficient manner. Power was to be exerted more efficiently by separating the right to punish from the personal power of the sovereign and by setting up a new 'economy' of power. The reform of criminal law can be seen as a strategy for reorganising the power to punish so as to make it more effective and at less economic and political cost. In this strategy of "reform" the spectacle of the scaffold had no place. As the new established form of punishment, imprisonment makes the punishment private.

The second aspect to be noted is a shift in the target of punishment away from the body per se. The account of Damiens' execution identifies the target of punishment as being the physical body – unbearable pains are inflicted upon the body for the purpose only of pain. By contrast, later, the guillotine is to administer a quick and sudden death to the body but not attack those parts of the body where 'exquisite' and unbearable pain could be produced. In the new form of punishment there is a new relation between the body of the condemned and punishment.

The target shifts to the 'soul' of the offender. Punishment is directed at the 'soul' but 'through' the body, not so that power produces unbearable pain, but so that power envelopes individuals to the extent that they function automatically within certain norms. The 'soul' then is sited within a wider target area that includes the body, but it is a body so timetabled that everyday gestures and all activities are minutely observed and controlled. It is this matrix that is the new target of power.

If punishment is not to be misunderstood, Foucault argues, it must be analyzed so as to be part of a general network of power relations that extends beyond the penal regime, for the techniques that he discusses are to be found also in the hospital, the workplace, the military, the asylum and the school. In many of these areas, where power of the same form is exerted, the law has little or no application.

In widening the scope of the application of such techniques to both the law breaker and the law abider, Foucault is able to show that punishment serves certain ritual functions associated with sovereignty and the functions of correction and reform. Punishment as an exercise of power is not merely repressive then, and is not merely directed at the breaking of law, but it can have positive effects, normalising people to take an effective (if docile) place in society, in forming the 'self', and in promoting pleasure.

In *Discipline and Punish* Foucault identifies a penal theory of punishment as exemplified in and developed from the writings of Thomas Hobbes (*Leviathan*, 1564). This he calls 'juridico-legal punishment' and is to be sharply distinguished from those modern forms of punishment which he calls 'disciplinary punishment'. It is to be distinguished by such notions as the target of punishment and the forms that the punishment takes. In his view modern penal theories essentially exemplify the juridico-legal and thereby obscure the exercise of modern power (see Foucault, 1979b). To this extent they are mystifying he believes because, whilst they talk of acts against the law and of the repressive nature of punishments which uphold the law (and thereby property in a wide Lockean sense), in fact, modern disciplinary punishment is concerned with the individual, the character of the individual, and the normalising of behaviour so that the individual can take a "responsible" place in society. In disciplinary punishment power is exerted not in a repressive but in a positive way (Foucault, 1977). Foucault's account, which analyses punishment independently of criminal illegalities, is possibly the first major attempt to do so since Rusche and Kirchheimer in *Punishment and Structure* (1939).

From Foucault's position and in reference to Hart's model and his five necessary and sufficient conditions (section I), we can now say this:

   (i)   punishment need not involve unpleasant consequences;
   (ii) punishment is not for an offence but for the good (the 'soul') of the individual;
   (iii) it is of an offender, not for an offence but for the offender's sake;
   (iv) given that the ultimate aim is self-surveillance and self-domination punishment can be given by the self;
   (v)   as power can be exercised by anyone, and a punishment is an exercise of power, there need not be an authority for punishment to occur.

The legal model (the Flew, Benn, Hart model) is taken as a major answer to the question of the meaning of punishment. It is of course correct that these conditions for the correct application of the concept have not met with universal agreement yet, in the literature, they have been the major contenders, with debate blossoming on particular conditions, e.g. authority, as to whether it must necessarily or only usually be present. But Foucault's 'historical' examination of the forms and techniques of punishment common to a wide variety of human institutions and practices has severe implications for any claims about the meaning of punishment. There is disagreement with the Flew, Benn, Hart model on all five conditions. The punishment of children is not a non standard case. Now the puzzles are:

(i)   is legal punishment the appropriate model for determining standard or non-standard uses of the concept of punishment?;
(ii) has the concept of punishment changed its meaning?;
(iii) if so is talk of rules discipline, etc. in schools anything much to do with this "new" concept of punishment?;
(iv) what happens to the traditional justifications of punishment?

These issues have been addressed elsewhere (see e.g., Marshall, 1975).

III WITTGENSTEIN AND FOUCAULT

In this section we will look at various similarities between Wittgenstein and Foucault. As indicated above the Peters' interpretation of Wittgenstein's notion of rule following activity is, I believe, mistaken (Marshall, 1985). What also seems to be the case is that Peters account of punishment is firmly within the juridico-legal model of punishment which was one of Foucault's targets in *Discipline and Punish*. Another of Foucault's targets was the notion of the autonomous person, with its associated notions of choice and free will. This is to be found in his attack upon Man/human sciences.

Wittgenstein, like Foucault, seems to be attacking the notion of the autonomous person. Reason giving has to come to an end according to Wittgenstein so that the notion of acting for a reason, explicit or implicit, has limits. Of course we can act in accordance with reasons but reason giving has to come to an end. Reason giving has to stop, I can only show, or say "This is how I/we do it", and if I follow the rule then in some way I must be *moved* to follow the rule. A dark conservative interpretation of Wittgenstein on these problems (e.g., Nyíri, 1982; von Wright, 1982) is that ultimately the self is constituted by obedience and appropriate reactions within a form of life, rather than the independence and emancipation offered by the adoption by an autos of a nomos, as in the notion of personal autonomy. Wittgenstein then, like Foucault, has a critique of the Enlightenment notion of the self (Janik & Toulmin, 1973). For both Foucault and Wittgenstein, on the notion of the self, there is a dark face to the Enlightenment message of emancipation.

Foucault also argued that reason giving had limitations, that not everything could be explained. In particular he argued that there were gaps in our accounts of history, and that not all of individual human behaviour could be explained. The notion that it could had resulted, for example, in the absurd notion of monomania (Foucault, 1978). In both Wittgenstein and Foucault there are 'ends' to reason, but the ends are different. For Wittgenstein the ends are the limits of language where language 'butts' onto forms of life, whereas for Foucault the limits arise in his explorations of political rationality (Foucault, 1979b). But in another sense there are similarities. Wittgenstein tells us that a rule is made in practice through time: what Foucault describes in *Discipline and Punish* are the practices through time that have come to constitute modern concepts in the human sciences, showing us how the practices and hence the 'rules' have arisen, and that where the 'rules' have not fulfilled their purposes they have been changed.

Both Wittgenstein and Foucault offer explanations as to how and why concepts change their meaning. In order to see this something needs to be said about Wittgenstein's notion of the use of a sign. Wittgenstein says (PI, I, # 87): "the sign is in order – if, under normal circumstances, it fulfils its purposes". The qualifying clause here is important because it points to the purposes, aims and practices of human beings. Much of what human beings do and say is habitual though this *need* not be to say that it is *merely* habitual or that there is no intelligence associated with these actions (see Dewey's sense of 'habitual', 1938). In these cases actions are mainly predictable as no other alternative is needed or even occurs to human beings. However, as Dewey points out, the regularities in our experience are the results of our orderings of experience and our habitual actions are intelligent responses to our perceived regularities. Similarly, for Wittgenstein, where regularity is perceived, the rule is already "laid down"; if the present situation is sufficiently like previous situations, then there is warrant for following the rule. Nevertheless, even in the dullest and most repetitious action which accords to a rule, there is a creative 'act' so that the rule is both made and remade by this creative practice. In more complex situations vigilance and flexibility will be required so that the rules, if followed, will not be followed in a merely habitual manner with little or no associated consciousness. In such situations rules may need to be adapted or refined.

The 'reason' then for following a rule is that regularities are perceived in the world. But this is not to offer an explanation of following a rule *in terms of* the perception of regularities in the world. Following a rule and perceiving regularities are essentially the same thing (Bolton, 1979, p. 142). Indeed no reason can be given for following a rule in the sense of providing a reason as *support* for following the rule. Although reasons can be given for following a rule in such-and-such a way, e.g. from past experience, teaching, past practice, etc., these can be given only on the condition that this way *is* the way to follow the rule – whether it is *the* way will be judged from practice. As Bolton (1979, p. 143) says: "reason is not a 'super-cause' responsible for our following the rule". At PI I, 211, Wittgenstein says:

> "How can he *know* how he is to continue a pattern by himself – whatever instruction you give him? – Well, how do *I* know – if that means 'Have I reasons?' the answer is: my reasons will soon give out. And then I shall act, without reasons".

The sceptical argument in the *Philosophical Investigations* (pp. 143–242) and the use of such things as sign posts and tables as expressions of rules, are meant to establish that the expression of the rule cannot carry with it an interpretation *which is not potentially equivocal*. The interpretation of the expression of the rule comes from practice; we follow the direction of the finger in the sign post example; we have been taught this practice by people who also followed the direction of the finger, and who, after letting us try it on our own, offered us guidance until the practice was 'grasped'. A limited (i.e., finite) number of examples are offered of the use of the sign post; what the learner must acquire is the ability to make a potentially unlimited number of judgements. But the future path to be followed is left unsaid; it cannot be grasped in this sense. We can grasp it *now* but this does not guarantee that this is how the sign post is to be interpreted in the future. Furthermore the rule is grasped in conjunction with other rules in an interlocking web of human practices.

The rule then is made in practice through time and this practice is not merely habitual but, rather, is *creative*. This is not too far from Foucault's notion of the other and his notion of transcendence. Built into the notion of the other is the fundamental notion of *difference* which arises in turn in logic and the interpretation of the copula 'is'. When the copula is interpreted *not* as the is of identity, but instead as involving a certain non-being, then a notion of difference is always included in the application of a concept, as opposed to being excluded. Every application of a concept then for Foucault involves a potentially equivocal situation in which the other may surface or predominate.

Where the application of concepts do not fulfil their purpose then either the rules must change or different concepts be adopted. In relation to the self freedom is to be obtained for Foucault by transcending the rule, by attempting to change agreements. Every application then of a concept for Foucault involves an equivocal situation – as in the Wittgensteinian paradox developed in Kripke's (1982) reading of Foucault, where it appears that any new practice at all can be in accord with the rule. Whereas Wittgenstein says I must feel moved to follow the rule, because they are no longer rational criteria which compel us to follow the rule, Foucault says that we just 'know' when to reject the rule, and that this may not involve the use of reason.

Foucault is talking amongst other things of the use of concepts to describe oneself, and how classifications such as being a homosexual can describe, objectify and subject the self. But for Foucault the applications of concepts is not an all or nothing affair, as included in the concept 'X' are notions of 'not-x'. So the very use of 'X' to describe carries within it notions of otherness. The political problem is to resist these classifications which constitute the self, by turning them back into the other, and through an ethics of the self, constituting the self differently. But how is one to know when to resist or when to reject such classifications? Foucault is criticised for failing to provide criteria either for resistance to following rules (to accepting the description of oneself as an X say), or for following rules, principles or practices. For Foucault the sign is not in order but it is unclear how this is known.

Much of Foucault's insight into psychology and psycho-analytic theory was gained from his early study of Freud. Foucault talks a lot about the clinical examination underlying psychoanalytic theory and the ways in which, said to the 'right' professionals, one's identity could be constituted in certain ways that left one subjected (Foucault, 1980). Wittgenstein has a similar insight:

"Analysis is likely to do harm. Because although one may discover in the course of it various things about oneself, one must have a very strong and keen and persistent criticism in order to recognise and see through the mythology that is offered or imposed on one. There is an inducement to say, 'Yes, of course, it must be like that'. A powerful mythology" (LA, 52).

It lacks Foucault's dazzling style but it might have been said by him, especially in his later writing. (Nor, like Wittgenstein, was he totally averse to Freud – Miller, 1993, p. 282).

Wittgenstein has a prolonged attack upon psychological theory. His major point was that causal *explanations* did not provide understanding of human 'behaviour'/action. Instead of turning to psychological theory then we must come to *understand* puzzling behaviour by seeing what is distinctively human about that behaviour. We must find connecting links between that puzzling behaviour and other non-puzzling behaviour. So we must lay out the facts, 'placing things side by side', only placing together what one knows, and see the *connections*. In commenting on Frazer's *Golden Bough* he says:

"I think one reason why the attempt to find an explanation is wrong, is that we have only to put together in the right way what we know, without adding anything, and the satisfaction we are trying to get from the explanation comes of itself...and the explanation isn't what satisfies us here anyway" (GB, 2e).
"We can only *describe* and say, human life is like that" (ibid., 3e).

In the *Order of Things* Foucault mounts sustained attacks upon the human sciences. Elsewhere he tracked the 'history' of psychology (Foucault, 1987). It is clear that he has philosophical doubts about the very basis of the human sciences. He sees them as internally incoherent and their explanations as being potentially politically dangerous, because their descriptions and explanations of human beings involve classifications and objectifications which, in turn, lead to treatments. In his early work on psychology (Foucault, 1987) he seeks answers to the questions, "Why did we start to treat madness as *mental illness*?", and, "Why do we assume a unitary pathology in the psychological and pathological domains?" He argues that mental 'pathology' requires methods of analysis different from physical pathology. Here there are close parallels to Wittgenstein's approach to psychology.

But Foucault stands with Wittgenstein not only in the rejection of a psychology based upon the natural sciences but also on the notion of the laying out of facts. On this latter point we need only turn to *Discipline and Punish* to see his clear rejection of former marxist approaches to punishment (e.g., Rushke & Kirchheimer, 1939), of legal/criminology theory (dismissed in his attacks upon the juridico-legal model of punishment) and in his rejection of the humanistic interpretation of changes in the forms of punishment. Instead we have a long protracted attempt to lay out the detail of what we know about the practices of punishment and the detailed daily lives of people suffering punishment. But he lays out the facts also of practices and daily lives in asylums, hospitals, military barracks and schools. He places things side by side and, thereby, we see connections. Punishment is not concerned with laws and offenses as the legal model would have us believe but with the offender and his soul – it is *disciplinary*. In *I*

Pierre Rivierre Foucault lays out the facts (Foucault, 1975). He provides a cacophony of sound where several competing descriptions of the murders by Pierre Rivierre of his mother, his sister and his brother, and of his own life history, occur side by side. His motives in laying out the facts are to question the early psychiatric descriptions and explanations, and to question their truth and ascendency over the other descriptions and stories.

The creative aspect of rule following in Wittgenstein is derived from my reading of Kripke (1982). If this reading of Wittgenstein is correct then there are marked similarities between Foucault and Wittgenstein. If not, but if the creative position on rule following is sustainable independently, then it would have these similarities also to Foucault's thought on the application of concepts.

There have been several other misinterpretations of Wittgenstein's notion of rules. These are that they are like conditional imperatives, commands, and as reasons for acting. These have been exposed by Waismann (1965), Kenny (1973) and Bolton (1979). Whilst it is not certain that all of these apply to Peters' account of authority and rule following behaviour, his use of notions like 'promulgations', 'order', 'decide' and 'judge' to explicate the rules for these concepts, give grounds for believing that they may. In other words Peters' use of Wittgenstein can be further called in question.

Wittgenstein presents us with an anti-foundationalist philosophy. In this respect he can be compared to Dewey as both are anti-foundationalist in their epistemologies (Rorty, 1979) and to Foucault. It should be expected then that Wittgenstein would be anti-foundationalist in the implications of his thought for a social philosophy. Those who interpret Wittgenstein's sense of a rule as presupposing authority impose a foundational aspect upon Wittgenstein that is incompatible with his later general philosophical position. British philosophy of education with its general empiricist and thereby, foundationalist sympathies, would need to interpret Wittgenstein in this manner if it is to appeal to him for support in what they say about discipline, and thereby, social control.

Finally, for here, both Wittgenstein and Foucault see and live the philosophical task as being that of human self understanding. In Wittgenstein's case Janik and Toulmin say (1973, p. 224):

> "So that same humane and cultivated Viennese who had begun, in his youth, by mastering the mechanics of Hertz and the thermodynamics of Boltzmann; whom had gone on, in his thirties, to play a leading part in the development of symbolic logic; who had abandoned philosophy, at the age of thirty, in favour of other, humanly more valuable occupations – that same philosopher found himself, at fifty, urging his hearers to reflect more carefully on the ways in which children do in fact learn (or might alternatively learn) the standard patterns of behaviour within which our language has a practical function, and on the metaphysical confusions that can flow from any failure to keep these practical functions in mind. Yet, for all its seeming changes, his intellectual Odyssey had been directed along a single, constant compass bearing. A man (sic) could obey the Socratic injunction, *Know Thyself*, only if he came to understand the scope and limits of his own understanding: and this meant, first and foremost, recognising the precise scope and limits of language, which is the prime instrument of human understanding".

Wittgenstein is stressing not merely language but language-and-the-world. Foucault talks of discourse but 'discourse' is not merely a linguistic entity either.

Towards the end of his life and perhaps in some difficulty, but with increasing confidence, Foucault attempted to outline the peculiarly personal aspect of his intellectual, scholarly, and public, life and work. There is little doubt that his work had been for him a particular kind of test or 'essay' (to use Miller's (1993) term to describe Foucault's notion of a trial or experiment or *assay*) in which the philosopher changes or transcends the self in the pursuit of 'truth' or understanding. The philosopher must be able to understand oneself and thereby to change oneself in the process of philosophy. Transgression was not merely an exercise in thought for Foucault but, also, a transgression in reality, and a transgression which reconstituted the self. In the insight and understanding of the self brought about by the injunction *Care for Thyself* the self was to be transformed by the central notion of care and secondarily by the notion of knowledge. Foucault argued and claimed that the Delphic maxim had been transformed to *Know Thyself* whereas it should be understood as *Care for Thyself*

Given Wittgenstein's limits to reason Janik and Toulmin may be incorrect in interpreting Wittgenstein in the above paragraph. Certainly when forms of life came to the fore there was an end to reason and understanding – things could only be shown because reason and explanation had limits. But both Wittgenstein and Foucault express the limits to reason concerning the self and therefore other ways to 'care for the self'.

IV RESOLVING THE PUZZLES

The puzzles are generated by the Flew-Hart-Benn model, or juridico-discursive model of punishment. If we adopt this essentially legal model of punishment how can we talk meaningfully about the punishment of children? Hart delegated such uses of the concept to a secondary use – quite correctly if punishment *does* mean what 'the' legal model says. The puzzles which emanate from Foucault's account, if we take the central notion of punishment to be its disciplinary function, centre upon the role of the legal model in education: disciplinary punishment is not about rules, authority and offenses, but about *persons*, about turning people into beings of a certain kind, and not in taking retribution upon wrongdoers, or in deterring potential wrongdoers.

Wittgenstein emphasises the close connections between the meaning of a concept and how it is learned. Luise and David McCarty (above) emphasise this connection, arguing that there is a form of conceptual connection between the two. Whilst they claim that the scheme, " In order to grasp the concept X, one has already to have undergone a process of teaching/learning via p" (where 'X' and 'p' are stand ins for *specific* descriptions) is not a logical truth, nevertheless, there are connections, stronger than mere historical contingency. The connections which they identify might be called therefore 'conceptual'.

If this general point is now applied to punishment we can discern marked similarities between the account of Foucault and Wittgenstein's general position. Foucault asks How questions, inviting us to look at practices of punishment and thereby arrives at a concept of disciplinary punishment. Whilst he does not emphasise learning per se, many of the disciplinary blocks which he writes about, are learning institutions – as well as the school, there is the army, the reformatory and the asylum. He shows how people are not only shaped up in disciplinary blocks but also how concepts fundamental to disciplinary blocks – concepts like 'soldier', 'madness', and 'punishment' – are themselves developed upon learning paths as human beings are shaped up by increasingly sophisticated and refined techniques to function along various parameters according to certain norms. That is the modern concepts of 'madness', 'soldier', ... cannot be understood independently of the learning paths about madness, etc., that have been established and refined in the disciplinary blocks.

If we follow the later Wittgenstein on the notion of understanding and how this is to be achieved by recourse to a laying out of the facts and that there are conceptual connections between the meaning of 'punishment' and how it is learned, then we would tend to follow Foucault's account of punishment as being disciplinary, and that the punishment of children is directed in a disciplinary fashion at their 'souls'.

Foucault, by asking *how* questions about the practices of punishment, by contrasting Damiens' punishment with those of the young offenders in Faucher's reformatory, shows us the concept of punishment has possibly changed – it has different *empirical* content. Certainly there are two concepts of punishment: the juridico-discursive concept and the disciplinary concept. In Wittgensteinian fashion the child must learn the meaning of 'punishment' in child rearing practices, in family and later at school, and these are contexts where clearly the punishment of the child has logical and temporal priority (though Wittgenstein would see this as a logicist distinction). Necessarily the learning of the abstract legal model of punishment must come later as a theoretical abstraction.

Wittgenstein would probably reject approaching the understanding of the punishment of human beings from a form of legal theory, because of his opposition to theory in the understanding of human behaviour. In the understanding of human behaviour he was opposed to theory and, at best, theory must be translated back to forms of life and language-and-the-world. The Hart-Flew-Benn model of punishment, in which the punishment of children is seen as a secondary or peripheral use, would run counter to Wittgenstein's notion of translation back into forms of life and the contexts in which concepts are learned. If the punishment of children is secondary and peripheral then there can be no translation back to a form of life in which punishment in the legal sense is learned. No, the order of learning must be different. From this perspective it would be the legal model concept of punishment, with its derived and abstract character, which is secondary and peripheral, or which needed to be translated back.

What is the resolution of the puzzles? How, as educationalists, are we to talk meaningfully about the punishment of children. At PI, I, # 87 Wittgenstein says that the sign is in order if it fulfils our purposes. Does 'punishment' fulfil our educational purposes in either of its above senses? If not can we be creative about the rules? I believe that both Wittgenstein and Foucault show us that the punishment of children must have priority over the legal model and that punishment, if we follow Foucault's 'creative act', is more like disciplinary punishment than legal juridico punishment.

The solutions to the puzzles are therefore:
  (i) to reject the legal model meaning of 'punishment' because it is disconnected from how the concept is learned (Wittgenstein) and does not reflect how punishment is practised (Foucault);
 (ii) to reassert the punishment of children as being the context for a standard use (Wittgenstein and Foucault);
(iii) to emphasise the disciplinary function of schools in relation to Foucault's disciplinary concept of punishment; and,
(iv) to search for some new justification for disciplinary punishment in relation to child rearing practices (see e.g., Marshall, 1984a).

The conclusion which should be drawn then is that the way to approach philosophical problems is through the facts, by a laying out of the facts. The original puzzles were generated by contrasting analytic approaches to a philosophical issue with the archaeological/genealogical approach of Foucault. What Foucault shows is that a concept of disciplinary punishment has come to replace the legal model. What the first approach shows us is that analysis of 'punishment', whilst (arguably) arriving at a coherent concept has lost touch with the practices of punishment. The second approach asserts the necessity of starting with the practices. Whilst Wittgenstein asserts the importance of laying out the facts he does not provide 'analytic' tools for such a practice whereas Foucault does – see e.g., Foucault (1992).

Finally what recourse to Wittgenstein and Foucault shows us, but from different approaches, is that indeed language went on holiday in the case of the educational discussion of the punishment of children by philosophers of education. By accepting the juridico-legal (Hart-Flew-Benn) model the concept 'punishment' had ceased "to come to where it was meant to be working".

Epilogue

PAUL SMEYERS AND JAMES D. MARSHALL

University of Leuven, Belgium, University of Auckland, New Zealand

Wittgenstein's philosophy has left neither philosophy nor philosophy of education as it was. It has challenged and changed the understanding of some of our basic concepts, including those of 'experience', 'learning' and 'teaching'. In education his philosophy generated typical Wittgensteinian issues and required theory of education to raise particular educational 'questions'. Although some of the philosophical problems were dissolved, others press themselves even more vigorously upon us. And, as is often the case with other *great* philosophers, this was not made easier by the plausibility of different readings of Wittgenstein's writings.

In this epilogue we will not offer a summary of the different chapters, nor will we try to list all of the remaining questions and issues, and new questions and issues posed. Instead we will extract from the contributions *some* possible guidelines for philosophy of education and education resulting from accepting Wittgenstein's challenge.

Stressed in the introduction, and reappearing in a number of chapters, is *a fascination with Wittgenstein's theory of meaning* and the possibilities generated for philosophy in general, and for philosophy of education in particular. But, as has become clear, there is more than one interpretation of his works. These interpretations can be placed on a scale which at one end emphasizes *the importance of an actual (linguistic) community* and, at the other end, a contrasting position of *the possibility of giving personal (and maybe new) meaning to situations and phenomena*. The relevance of this difference is clear: if the touchstone of meaning in the end is the community to which one belongs, there is a threat of conservatism and conformism – as the possible meaning is limited to the hitherto existing meaning; on the other hand if the touchstone is the individual, one has to delineate the boundaries of meaning so that not 'anything goes'. Accepting one arm of this opposition could result in the extremes of only repetitions of meaning on the one hand, or of using concepts arbitrarily on the other hand. Adopting only one arm of this opposition can lead to serious insurmountable difficulties. In the first case one will be left to answer the question of how the world and concepts are related (as our understanding of reality changes on the basis of different experiences); in the second case one is confronted with the possibilities of private languages. Moreover, adopting either position on its own would not be very Wittgensteinian.

Talking about meaning and concepts is not only or merely a technical matter. Schools for instance do not only initiate children into a neutral set of language skills which can be used for any communication whatever, for they also deal

221

with content including matters of considerable substance. Therefore it becomes very important to realise where one stands on 'the scale' from individuality to community, including the importance of how these basic concepts themselves are understood. Discussions of 'justice', 'equality of opportunity', 'quality' and of many other concepts make it clear that not only matters of understanding each other are at stake, but that at the same time moral, social and political priorities may be determined. Not only meaning and understanding, but *significance and relevance*, and therefore how power is distributed and dealt with in society, are at stake. When the significance of these matters is grasped the dilemma posed above, of keeping things as they are or changing them, presses itself upon us even more vigorously. And though Wittgenstein was a rather conservative person, this is not to say that his philosophy – as a number of interpretations have indicated – leads necessarily towards conservative positions.

Wittgenstein has made it overwhelmingly clear that following a rule can never mean just following another rule. Though we follow rules blindly as Wittgenstein states, it is not just a question of making them exhaustively explicit. Here the idea of the 'form of life' elicits that 'what we do' refers to what we have learnt, to the way in which we have learnt it and to how we have grown to find it self-evident. The reference to the 'bedrock', to what was originally learnt, is however the only kind of situation for which it makes sense to ask whether the meaning of a concept is correctly stated. In all the other situations it is a matter of dialogue, conversation, and exchange of ideas. What is 'certain' for Wittgenstein is only that which cannot be proved: the frame of reference itself. It is part of our life as inherited, not the result of (rational) teaching. We do not hold the basic propositions now on rational grounds and we do not change them on rational grounds: to put this differently, the frame of reference is just there and cannot be rationally 'assessed'. These insights gave rise to the criticism that perhaps too often and too quickly a reference is made to "That's just the way it is". And though this is understandable, it seems to be contradictory to Wittgenstein's philosophical intentions. To seek for a justification of how things are (politically or educationally for instance) in the sense of searching for *grounds*, is according to Wittgenstein wrong-headed. Nor is it possible on the basis of Wittgenstein's insights to decide for or against the legalization of euthanasia, or of abortion. But at the same time it is clear that the way things are *now* determines to a large extent what will count as 'normal' (use and situation) and therefore clearly carries conservative tendencies. Second, though Wittgenstein's philosophy does not determine a particular concept of 'education' or of 'community', nevertheless it is not compatible with any or all of the possible concepts to which terms such as 'education' and 'community' might refer.

The challenge of Wittgensteinian philosophy seems to be that of balance, as Wittgenstein himself exhibits between, 'individual' and 'community'. At the pure epistemological level this was expressed by the notion of 'language-and-the-world'. Here the notion of 'individual-in-the-community' may do the same work. This raises again the importance of the concept of the 'form of life' in which, according to Wittgenstein, one is 'embedded', because one is initiated into it by particular practices. Does one have to embrace totally the 'form of life' in order to fully *understand* it? Is it possible to distance oneself from the 'form of life' to which one belongs, conceptually and/or in reality ? Furthermore does the 'form of life', understood as what lies at the bottom of our culture, hold in the more individualistic culture in which we live as it once held (and still holds) for more collectivistic types of culture in which we once lived?[1] The insight of Wittgenstein lies here in holding the balance between the extremes. In this modern age if we can indeed reject our culture in ways that were impossible before, this need not imply a criticism of the necessarily social embeddedness of human life either in terms of the appreciation of others or of the horizons of significance. For Wittgenstein one, perhaps even *the* basic concept to understand human life is 'trust', and not 'having rights' which carries a presupposition of rivalry and opposition.

Wittgenstein's stance that justification comes to an end in our acting, helps to a certain extent to 'dissolve' the justification debate in education. Though it is possible to conceive that things could have been different, they cannot be thought now but with the conceptual 'pieces' of an already existing apparatus, i.e. in terms of 'what is justified for us now'. It exemplifies that there is for Wittgenstein no 'view from nowhere', neither in (philosophy of) education nor in philosophy, that any stance is always 'embedded', interwoven with particular historical, economical, and social conditions. Differently worded, human beings are not invented ex nihilo, as what is typically human belongs to *human* history. That this is so will determine the kind of questions which will be raised, the kind of answers that can be given, and the kind of solutions which will make particular questions disappear for us.

At the anthropological level the concept of 'trust' rather than 'opposition' seems to characterize the relations between human beings. The idea of 'community' as developed within the work of MacIntyre and Taylor seems to be more in the Wittgensteinian line than apparent similarities with analogous ideas in the works of Derrida or Lyotard. At the more individual level 'integrity' and 'authenticity' seem to be the offsprings of the Wittgensteinian stance within the broader idea of the person who is in harmony with her or himself. Indeed, that what people say is not separated from what they do, seems always to be presupposed. Integer persons are truthful to what they essentially stand for, i.e. to those things they have engaged themselves in and which have a privileged status in their life because they reflect what is of the utmost importance to them, what makes their life meaningful. Again, if one tries to avoid the pitfalls of essentialism on the one hand and conformism and arbitrariness on the other, it is not easy to indicate the precise consequences for instance for the content of schooling or education generally. Though Wittgenstein's guidelines do not lead us up a blind-alley, they do not direct us precisely.

The subtitle to the collection is 'accepting the challenge'. We have attempted to throw down a Wittgensteinian gauntlet. There remains much to be done. For example in the area of educational psychology, and the emergence of a descriptive psychology, which is not already theoretically constituted, and in the general area of curriculum. After science Wittgenstein sees our 'theories' very much as human constructions. Mathematics fell into that category for Wittgenstein and his work has been sought as justification by some mathematicians and mathematics educators who might loosely be described as constructivists. In many cases this search seems to be mistaken but these issues need to be pursued. Similarly in the general area of curriculum there is much work to do particularly in the general area of arts education in the face of the march of technocratic rationality, technology and education narrowly construed in vocational terms. These are but some of the challenges left to us as educators by Wittgenstein.

Wittgensteinian philosophy demonstrates overwhelmingly the complexity of understanding 'meaning' and 'human behaviour'. Though stressing the importance of 'who we are' – undoubtedly a naturalistic tendency – it is at the same time anti-metaphysical. It exemplifies the relevance of education for understanding what we do and, thereby, helps to clarify the important educational questions. And though it solves some of our questions by indicating how to understand them correctly, how particular concepts are and have to be used, it is more than anything else a philosophy which offers consolation and evokes a feeling of modesty, of how little there is we can do to change the world. Instead we have to change ourselves. There is therefore the danger of eroding the motivation to change 'how things are'. However this is countered by the importance Wittgenstein gives to each individual's personal stance. Persons must speak for themselves and do what they *can* do. Here the metaphor of the fly-bottle is particularly insightful. There can be at least three reasons why the fly does not want to be shown the way of the fly-bottle. One would be that it's good inside, and another that it is bad (or worse) outside. But there is a third alternative, namely that one can't be sure that there is a place where we will be better off than where we are now.[2] In showing us how to understand, appreciate and enjoy the fly-bottle we are in, we are shown also Wittgenstein's appreciation of the wonderfulness of his own life.

NOTES

[1] We owe this idea to Bas Levering.
[2] We are grateful to J.C.B. Macmillan who developed this thought.

References

ALL REFERENCES TO WORKS OF WITTGENSTEIN ARE TO THE FOLLOWING
PUBLICATIONS AND WITH THE USE OF THE INDICATED ABBREVIATIONS.

Wittgenstein, L.: 1922, *Tractatus logico-philosophicus*, trans. D. Pears & B.F. McGuinness, Routledge and Kegan Paul, London. **TLP**

Wittgenstein, L.: 1953, *Philosophical investigations/Philosophische Untersuchungen*, trans. G.E.M. Anscombe, Basil Blackwell, Oxford. **PI**

Wittgenstein, L.: 1961, in G.H. von Wright & G.E.M. Anscombe (eds.), *Notebooks, 1914–1916*, trans. G.E.M. Anscombe, Basil Blackwell, Oxford. **NB**

Wittgenstein, L.: 1964, in G.H. von Wright, R. Rhees, & G.E.M. Anscombe (eds.), *Remarks on the foundations of mathematics/Bemerkungen über die Grundlagen der Mathematik*, trans. G.E.M. Anscombe, Basil Blackwell, Oxford. **RFM**

Wittgenstein, L.: 1965, A lecture on ethics, *Philosophical Review* 74, 3–12. **LE**

Wittgenstein, L.: 1966, in C. Barrett (ed.), *Lectures and conversations on aesthetics, psychology and religious belief*, Basil Blackwell, Oxford. **LA**

Wittgenstein, L.: 1967, in G.E.M. Anscombe & G.H. von Wright (eds.), *Zettel*, trans. G.E.M. Anscombe, Basil Blackwell, Oxford. **Z**

Wittgenstein, L.: 1968, *The blue and brown books*, Basil Blackwell, Oxford. **BB**

Wittgenstein, L.: 1969, in G.E.M. Anscombe & G. H. von Wright (eds.), *On certainty/Über Gewissheit*, trans. D. Paul & G.E.M. Anscombe, Basil Blackwell, Oxford. **C**

Wittgenstein, L.: 1974, in R. Rhees & A. Kenny (eds.), *Philosophical grammar*, Basil Blackwell, Oxford. **PG**

Wittgenstein, L.: 1977, in G.E.M. Anscombe (ed.), *Remarks on colour/Bemerkungen über die Farben*, trans. L.L. MacAlister, Basil Blackwell, Oxford. **ROC**

Wittgenstein, L.: 1979, 'Remarks on Frazer's Golden Bough', in C. Luckhardt (ed.), *Wittgenstein: Sources and perspectives*, pp. 61–81, The Harvester Press, Hassocks, Sussex. **GB**

Wittgenstein, L.: 1980, in G.H. von Wright & H. Nyman (eds.), *Remarks on the philosophy of psychology/Bemerkungen über die Philosophie der Psychologie*, vol. 1, trans. C.G. Luckhardt & M. Aue, Basil Blackwell, Oxford. **RPP I**

Wittgenstein, L.: 1980, in G.H. von Wright & H. Nyman (eds.), *Remarks on the philosophy of psychology/Bemerkungen über die Philosophie der Psychologie*, vol. 2, trans. C.G. Luckhardt & M. Aue, Basil Blackwell, Oxford. **RPP II**

Wittgenstein, L.: 1980, in G.H. von Wright (ed.), *Culture and value/Vermischte Bemerkungen*, trans. P. Winch, Basil Blackwell, Oxford. **CV**

Studies in Philosophy and Education **14**: 349–360, 1995.

REFERENCES

Acton, H.B.: (ed.): 1963, *The philosophy of punishment*, Macmillan, London.
Allen, R.T.: 1989, 'Metaphysics in education', *Journal of Philosophy of Education* **23**, 159–169.
Allison, D.: 1978, 'Derrida and Wittgenstein: Playing the game', *Research in Phenomenology* **8**, 93–109.
Anderson, J.: 1962, 'Classicism', in *Studies in empirical philosophy*, pp. 189–202, Angus and Robertson, Sydney.
Anscombe, G.E.M., and Geach, P.T.: 1961, *Three Philosophers*, Basil Blackwell, Oxford.
Archambault, R.D.: (ed.): 1965, *Philosophical analysis in education*, Routledge and Kegan Paul, London.
Arcilla, R.: 1991, 'Metaphysics in education after Hutchins and Dewey', *Teachers College Record* **93**, 281–289.
Aronowitz, S.: 1989, 'The new conservative agenda', in H. Holtz (ed.), *Education and the American dream*, pp. 203–215, Bergin and Garvey, Boston.
Astley, J.: 1993 (September), *Faith on the level? On teaching a Christian spirituality without God*, Paper presented at a National Conference on Moral and Spiritual Education at the University of Plymouth, Exmouth Campus, UK.
Astley, J.: 1994, *The philosophy of Christian religious education*, Religious Education Press, Birmingham, AL.
Augustine: 1961, *The confessions*, trans. R.S. Pine Coffin, Penguin, New York.
Austin, J.L.: 1962, *How to do things with words*, Oxford University Press, Oxford.
Ayer, A.J.: 1935, *Language, truth and logic*, Gollancz, London.
Ayer, A.J.: 1954, 'Can there be a private language?', *Proceedings of the Aristotelian Society*, Suppl. Vol. **28**, 63–76.
Ayer, A.J.: 1956, *The problem of knowledge*, Pelican Books, London.
Baker, G.P. & Hacker, P.M.S.: 1980, *Wittgenstein: Understanding and meaning. An analytical commentary on the philosophical investigations*, vol. 1, Basil Blackwell, Oxford.
Baker, G.P. & Hacker, P.M.S.: 1985, *Wittgenstein rules, grammar and necessity. An analytical commentary on the philosophical investigations*, vol. 2, Basil Blackwell, Oxford.
Bambrough, R.: 1993, 'Invincible knowledge', in A. Phillips Griffiths (ed.), *Ethics*, pp. 51–62, Cambridge University Press, Cambridge.
Bambrough, R.: 1991, 'Fools and heretics', in A. Phillips Griffiths (ed.), *Wittgenstein centenary essays*, pp. 239–250, Cambridge University Press, Cambridge.
Ball, T.: 1990, 'Review symposium: Richard Rorty', *History of the Human Sciences* **3**, 101–122.
Barrett, C.: 1991, *Wittgenstein on ethics and religious belief*, Basil Blackwell, Oxford.
Barrow, R. & White, P.: (eds.): 1993, *Beyond liberal education. Essays in honour of Paul H. Hirst*, Routledge, London.
Beccaria, C.B.: 1764, *An essay on crimes and punishment*, s.n., s.l.
Benn, S.F.: 1958, 'An approach to the problems of punishment', *Philosophy* **33**, 325–341.
Bennett, W.: 1984, 'To reclaim a legacy: Report on humanities in education', *The Chronicle of Higher Education* **29**, 16–22.
Berkeley, G.: 1954, *Three dialogues between Hylas and Philonous*, Library of the Liberal Arts, New York.
Bloom, A.: 1987, *The closing of the American mind: How higher education has foiled democracy and impoverished the souls of today's students*, Simon and Schuster, New York.
Bloor, D.: 1983, *Wittgenstein: A social theory of knowledge*, Columbia University Press, New York.
Bolton, D.: 1979, *An approach to Wittgenstein's philosophy*, Humanities Press, Atlantic Highlands.
Bourdieu, P. & Passeron, J-C.: 1977, *Reproduction in education, society and culture*, trans. R. Nice, Sage, London.
Bouwsma, O.K.: 1986, in L. Craft & R.E. Hustwit (eds.), *Wittgenstein: conversations 1949–1951*, Hackett, Indianapolis, IN.
Braine, D.: 1993, *The human person: Animal and spirit*, University of Notre Dame Press, Notre Dame.
Brandon, E.P.: 1982a, 'Radical children', *Access* **1**, 26–32.

Brandon, E.P.: 1982b, 'Rationality and paternalism', *Philosophy* **57**, 533–536.

Brandon, E.P.: 1982c, 'Quantifiers and the pursuit of truth', *Educational Philosophy and Theory* **14**, 50–58.

Brandon, E.P.: 1987, *Do teachers care about truth?*, Allen & Unwin, London.

Brose, K.: 1985, *Sprachspiel und Kindersprache: Studien zu Wittgensteins 'Philosophischen Untersuchungen'*, Campus, Frankfurt.

Brown, S.C.: 1969, *Do religious claims make sense?*, SCM Press, London.

Brummer, V.: 1993, 'Wittgenstein and the irrationality of rational theology', in J.M. Byrne (ed.), *The Christian understanding of God today*, pp. 88–102, Columba Press, Dublin.

Brubacher, J.S.: 1942, 'Introduction: Purpose and scope of the yearbook. N.S.S.E. Yearbook', in N.B. Henry (ed.), *Philosophies of education*, part 1, pp. 3–7, University of Chicago Press, Chicago.

Budd, M.: 1987, 'Wittgenstein on seeing aspects', *Mind* **96**, 1–17.

Burell, D.: 1986, *Knowing the Unknowable god: Ibn-Sina, Maimonides, Aquinas*, University of Notre Dame Press, Notre Dame.

Caputo, J.: 1982, *Aquinas and Heidegger: An essay on overcoming the tradition*, Fordham University Press, New York.

Carr, W.: 1989, 'The idea of an educational science', *Journal of Philosophy of Education* **23**, 29–37.

Cavell, S.: 1979, *The claim of reason*, Oxford University Press, Oxford.

Cavell, S.: 1988, 'Declining decline: Wittgenstein as a philosopher of culture', *Inquiry* **31**, 253–264.

Churchill, J.: 1989, 'Wittgenstein and the end of philosophy', *Metaphilosophy* **20**, 103–113.

Connolly, W.: 1990, 'Review symposium: Richard Rorty', *History of the Human Sciences* **3**, 101–122.

Cook, J.W.: 1988, 'Wittgenstein and religious belief', *Philosophy* **63**, 427–452.

Cooper, D.E.: 1993, 'Truth and liberal education', in R. Barrow & P. White (eds.), *Beyond liberal education. Essays in honour of Paul H. Hirst*, pp. 30–48, Routledge, London.

Cowdell, S.: 1988, *Atheist priest? Don Cupitt and Christianity*, SCM Press, London.

Cupitt, D.: 1980, *Taking leave of God*, SCM Press, London.

Cupitt, D.: 1984, *The sea of faith*, British Broadcasting Corporation, London.

Cuypers, S.E.: 1992, 'Is personal autonomy the first principle of education?', *Journal of Philosophy of Education* **26**, 5–17.

Dawes, H.: 1992, *Freeing the faith. A credible Christianity for today*, SPCK, London.

Dearden, R.F.: 1982, 'Philosophy of education, 1952–82', *British Journal of Educational Studies* **30**, 57–71.

De Dijn, H.: 1991, 'De kwestbaarheid van de ethiek. Woody Allen: Ethiek als een soort van trouw', *Onze Alma Mater* **45**, 334–350.

Dewey, J.: 1916, *Democracy and education*, Macmillan, New York.

Dewey, J.: 1938, *Logic: The theory of inquiry*, Holt, Rinehart, Winston, New York.

Dewey, J.: 1966, *Democracy and education*, The Free Press, New York.

Diamond, C.: 1989, 'Rules: Looking in the right place', in D.Z. Phillips & P. Winch (eds.), *Wittgenstein: Attention to particulars: Essays in honour of Rush Rhees*, pp. 12–34, Macmillan, London.

Dreyfus, H.: 1980, 'Holism and hermeneutics. Symposium with Richard Rorty and Charles Taylor', *Review of Metaphysics* **34**, 3–23.

Drury, M.O.C.: 1973, *The danger of words*, Humanities Press, New York.

Drury, M.O.C.: 1984, 'Some notes on conversations with Wittgenstein', in R. Rhees (ed.), *Recollections of Wittgenstein*, pp. 76–171, Oxford University Press, Oxford.

Eagleton, T.: 1982, 'Wittgenstein's friends', *New Left Review* **135** (Sept.-Oct.), 64–90.

Edel, A.: 1972, 'Analytic philosophy of education at the cross-roads', *Educational Theory* **22**, 131–152.

Edwards, J.: 1982, *Ethics without philosophy. Wittgenstein and the moral life*, University of Florida Press, Tampa.

Edwards, J.: 1990, *The authority of language. Heidegger, Wittgenstein, and the threat of philosophical nihilism*, University of Florida Press, Tampa.

Elliott, R.K.: 1986, 'Richard Peters: A philosopher in the older style', in D.E. Cooper (ed.), *Education, values and mind. Essays for R. S. Peters*, pp. 41–68, Routledge and Kegan Paul, London.

Elliott, R.K.: 1993, 'Wittgenstein's speculative aesthetics in its ethical context', in R. Barrow & P. White (eds.), *Beyond liberal education*, pp. 41–68, Routledge, London.

Elster, J.: 1979, *Ulysses and the sirens*, Cambridge University Press, Cambridge.

Engel, P.: 1987, 'Continental insularity: Contemporary French analytic philosophy', in A. Phillips (ed.), *Contemporary French philosophy*, pp. 1–19, Cambridge University Press, Cambridge.

Fenstermacher, G.D.: 1986, 'Philosophy of research on teaching: Three aspects', in M.C. Wittrock (ed.), *Handbook of research on teaching*, 3d ed., pp. 37–49, Macmillan, New York.

Finnis, J.M.: 1977, 'Scepticism, self-refutation, and the good of truth', in P.M.S. Hacker & J. Raz (eds.), *Law, morality and society: Essays in honour H.L.A. Hart*, pp. 247–267, Oxford University Press, Oxford.

Flew, A.: 1954, 'The justification of punishment', *Philosophy* **29**, 291–307.

Flitner, W.: 1952, 'Über die Macht der Erziehung', in W. Flitner (ed.), 1989, *Theoretische Schriften*, pp. 56–66, Schöningh, Paderborn.

Foot, Ph.: 1983, 'Peacocke on Wittgenstein and experience', *The Philosophical Quarterly* **33**, 187–191.

Foster, H.: (ed.).: 1985, *Postmodern culture*, Pluto Press, London.

Foucault, M.: 1975, *I, Pierre Rivière, having slaughtered my mother, my sister, my brother...*, trans. F. Jellinek, Pantheon, New York.

Foucault, M.: 1977, 'Truth and power', in C. Gordon (ed.), *Power/knowledge*, pp. 109–133, 1980, Harvester Press, Brighton.

Foucault, M.: 1978, 'The dangerous individual', in L.D. Kritzman (ed.), *Michel Foucault: Politics, philosophy, culture*, pp. 125–151, 1988, Routledge, London.

Foucault, M.: 1979a, *Discipline and punish: The birth of the prison*, trans. A. Sheridan, Vintage Books, New York.

Foucault, M.: 1979b, 'On governmentality', *Ideology and Consciousness* **6**, 5–26.

Foucault, M.: 1980, *The history of sexuality*, vol. 1, trans. R. Hurley, Vintage, New York.

Foucault, M.: 1984, 'Polemics, politics and problematisations', in P. Rabinow (ed.), *The Foucault reader*, pp. 381–390, Pantheon, New York.

Foucault, M.: 1987, *Mental illness and psychology*, trans. A. Sheridan, University of California Press, Berkeley.

Foucault, M.: 1989, 'How much does it cost for reason to tell the truth', in S. Lotringer (ed.), *Foucault live: Interviews, 1966–84*, pp. 233–256, Semiotext(e), New York.

Foucault, M.: 1992, 'Questions of method', in G. Burchell, *et al. (*eds.), *The Foucault effect: Studies in governmentality*, pp. 73–86, University of Chicago Press, Chicago.

Frankfurt, H.G.: 1971, 'Freedom of the will and the concept of a person', in H.G. Frankfurt, 1988, *The importance of what we care about*, pp. 11–25, Cambridge University Press, Cambridge.

Frankfurt, H.G.: 1988, 'Identification and wholeheartedness', in H.G. Frankfurt, *The importance of what we care about*, pp. 159–176, Cambridge University Press, Cambridge.

Frankfurt, H.G.: 1988, 'The importance of what we care about', in H.G. Frankfurt, *The importance of what we care about*, pp. 80–94, Cambridge University Press, Cambridge.

Freeman, A.: 1993, *God in us. A case for Christian humanism*, SCM Press, London.

Freinet, C.: 1978, *L'éducation du travail*, Delachaux et Niestlé, original work published 1946, Paris.

Fuller, T.(ed.): 1989, *The voice of liberal learning. Michael Oakeshott on education*, Yale University Books, New Haven.

Gardner, P.: 1988, 'Religious upbringing and the liberal ideal of religious autonomy', *Journal of Philosophy of Education* **22**, 89–105.

Gellner, E.: 1989, *Plough, sword and book: The structure of human history*, University of Chicago Press, Chicago.

Giesecke, H.: 1987, *Das Ende der Erziehung; neue Chancen für Familie und Schule*, Klett-Cotta, Stuttgart.

Goff, R.: 1969, 'Aphorism as *Lebensform* in Wittgenstein's' *Philosophical Investigations*, in J. Edie (ed.), *New essays in phenomenology: Studies in the philosophy of experience*, pp. 58–71, Quadrangle Books, Chicago.

Gordon, T.: 1975, *Parent effectiveness training: The tested new way to raise responsible children*, Wyden, New York.

Gordon, T.: 1981, 'Crippling our children with discipline', *Journal of Education* **163**, 228–243.

Grayling, A.C.: 1991, 'Wittgenstein's influence: Meaning, mind and method', in A. Phillips Griffiths (ed.), *Wittgenstein centenary essays*, pp. 61–78, Cambridge University Press, Cambridge.

Great Britain, Parliament, House of Commons: 1985, *Education for all*, The Report of the Committee of Inquiry into the Education of Children from Ethnic Minority Groups (Swann Report), cmnd 9453, HMSO, London.

Grene, M.: 1976, 'Life, death, and language: Some thoughts on Wittgenstein and Derrida', *Partisan Review* **46**, 265–279.

Guigon, C.: 1990, 'Philosophy after Wittgenstein and Heidegger', *Philosophy and Phenomenological Research* **50**, 649–672.

Haaften, A.W.: 1975/1976, 'Het "Principle of Expressibility"', parts 1 & 2, *Algemeen Nederlands Tijdschrift voor Wijsbegeerte* **67 & 68**, pp. 217–244, 1–33.

Habermas, J.: 1981, 'Modernity versus postmodernity', *New German Critique* **22**, 3–14.

Habermas, J.: 1990, *The philosophical discourse of modernity: Twelve lectures*, trans. F.G. Lawrence, The MIT Press, Cambridge, MA.

Hacker, P.M.S.: 1986, *Insight and illusion*, rev. ed., Clarendon Press, Oxford.

Hacker, P.M.S.: 1990, *Wittgenstein, meaning and mind. An analytical commentary on the philosophical investigations*, vol. 3, Basil Blackwell, Oxford.

Haldane, J.: 1989, 'Metaphysics in the philosophy of education', *Journal of Philosophy of Education* **23**, 171–184.

Haller, R.: 1988, *Questions on Wittgenstein*, Routledge and Kegan Paul, London.

Hamlyn, D.W.: 1970, *The theory of knowledge*, Macmillan, London.

Hamlyn, D.W.: 1978, *Experience and the growth of understanding*, Routledge, London.

Hamlyn, D.: 1989, 'Education and Wittgenstein's philosophy', *Journal of Philosophy of Education* **23**, 213–222.

Hanfling, O.: 1991, 'I heard a plaintive melody', in A. Phillips Griffiths (ed.), *Wittgenstein centenary essays*, pp. 117–134, Cambridge University Press, Cambridge.

Hardie, C.D.: 1942, *Truth and fallacy in educational theory*, Teachers College Press, Columbia University, New York.

Harris, C.K.: 1979, *Knowledge and education*, Routledge and Kegan Paul, London.

Harris, C.K.: 1982, *Teachers and classes*, Routledge and Kegan Paul, London.

Harris, R.: 1988, *Language, Saussure and Wittgenstein: How to play games with words*, Routledge and Kegan Paul, London.

Hart, H.L.A.: 1968, *Punishment and responsibility*, Clarendon Press, Oxford.

Hart, D.A.: 1993, *Faith in doubt. Non-realism and Christian belief*, Mowbray, London.

Hebblethwaite, B.: 1988, *The ocean of truth. A defence of objective theism*, Cambridge University Press, Cambridge.

Hellemans, M., Masschelein, J. & Smeyers, P.: (eds.): 1994, *The school: Its crisis*, Acco, Leuven.

Heller, E.: (ed.): 1959, 'Wittgenstein and Nietzsche', *The artist's journey into the interior and other essays*, pp. 199–226, Secker and Warburg, London.

Hepburn, R.W.: 1987, 'Attitudes to evidence and argument in the field of religion', in R. Straughan & J. Wilson (eds.), *Philosophers on education*, pp. 127–146, Macmillan, London.

Hepburn, R.W.: 1992, 'Religious imagination', in M. McGhee (ed.), *Philosophy, religion and the spiritual life*, pp. 127–144, Cambridge University Press, Cambridge.

Herbart, J.F.: 1965, *Pädagogische Schriften*, Band 2, Kupper, Düsseldorf.

Herrmann, U., Kaufmann, H.B., Flitner, W. & Bollnow, O.F.: 1987, *Kontinuität und Traditionsbrücke in der Pädagogik*, Comenius, Münster.

Hick, J.: 1993, *The metaphor of God incarnate*, SCM Press, London.

Hintikka, Merrill B. & Hintikka, J.: 1986, *Investigating Wittgenstein*, Basil Blackwell, Oxford.

Hirst, P.H.: 1970, 'Philosophy and religious education: A reply to D.Z. Phillips', *British Journal of Educational Studies* 18, 213–215.

Hirst, P.H.: 1972, 'Christian education: A contradiction in terms?', *Learning for Living* 11, 4, 6–11.

Hirst, P.H.: 1974a, *Knowledge and the curriculum. A collection of philosophical papers*, Routledge and Kegan Paul, London.

Hirst, P.H.: 1974b, *Moral education in a secular society*, Hodder and Stoughton, London.

Hirst, P.H.: 1981, 'Education, catechesis and the church school', *British Journal of Religious Education* 3, 85–93.

Hirst, P.H.: 1984, 'Philosophy of education', in J.M. Sutcliffe (ed.), *A dictionary of religious education*, pp. 259–260, SCM Press, London.

Hirst, P.H.: 1985, 'Education and diversity of belief', in M.C. Felderhof (ed.), *Religious education in a pluralistic society*, pp. 5–17, Hodder and Stoughton, London.

Hirst, P.H.: 1993, 'Education, knowledge and practices', in R. Barrow & P. White (eds.), *Beyond liberal education. Essays in honour of Paul H. Hirst*, pp. 184–199, Routledge, London.

Hobbes, T. : 1564, in W.G. Pogson Smith (ed.), *Leviathan*, Oxford University Press, Oxford.

Holley, R.: 1978, *Religious education and religious understanding. An introduction to the philosophy of religious education*, Routledge and Kegan Paul, London.

Hollis, M.: 1977, *Models of man*, Cambridge University Press, Cambridge.

Hudson, W.D.: 1973, 'Is religious education possible?', in G. Langford & D.J. O'Connor (eds.), *New essays in the philosophy of education*, pp. 167–196, Routledge and Kegan Paul, London.

Hudson, W.D.: 1975, *Wittgenstein and religious belief*, Macmillan, London.

Hudson, W.D.: 1982, 'Educating, socialising and indoctrination: A reply to Tasos Kazepides', *Journal of Philosophy of Education* 16, 167–172.

Hudson, W.D.: 1987, 'Two questions about religious education', in R. Straughan & J. Wilson (eds.), *Philosophers on education*, pp. 109–126, Macmillan, London.

Hull, J.M.: 1984, *Studies in religion and education*, Falmer, Lewes.

Husén, T. & Postlethwaite, T.H.: (eds.): 1994, *The international encyclopedia of education*, 2nd ed., Pergamon Press, Oxford.

Hunter, J.F.M.: 1981, 'Wittgenstein on seeing and seeing as', *Philosophical Investigations* 4, 33–49.

Jackson, R.: 1992, 'The misrepresentation of religious education', in M. Leicester & M. Taylor (eds.), *Ethics, ethnicity and education*, pp. 100–113, Kogan Page, London.

James, W.: 1982, *The varieties of religious experience*, Penguin, New York.

Jameson, F.: 1984, 'Foreword to Lyotard's' *The Postmodern Condition*, pp. vii–xxi, University of Minnesota Press, Minneapolis.

Janik, A.: 1985, *Essays on Wittgenstein and Weininger*, Rodopi, Amsterdam.

Janik, A.: 1989, *Style, politics and the future of philosophy*, Kluwer, Dordrecht.

Janik, A. & Toulmin, S.: 1973, *Wittgenstein's Vienna*, Simon and Schuster, New York.

Kaminsky, J.: 1985, *The first 600 months of philosophy of education: 1935–1985*, Paper presented at the Philosophy of Education Society of Australasia's 1985 Conference, Hobart, University of Tasmania.

Kant, I.: 1964, *Critique of pure reason*, trans. N. Kemp-Smith, Macmillan, London.

Kant, I.: 1966, *Critique of judgment*, trans. J.H. Bernard, Hafner, New York.

Kauffman, R.L.: 1991, 'Guest editor's introduction', *L'Esprit Créateur* 31 (Spring), 7–14.

Kazepides, T.: 1982, 'Educating, socialising and indoctrinating', *Journal of Philosophy of Education* 16, 155–165.

Kazepides, T.: 1991a, 'On the prerequisites of moral education: A Wittgensteinian perspective', *Journal of Philosophy of Education* 25, 259–272.

Kazepides, T.: 1991b, 'Religious indoctrination and freedom', in B. Spiecker & R. Straughan (eds.), *Freedom and indoctrination in education. International perspectives*, pp. 5–15, Cassell, London.

Keightley, A.: 1976, *Wittgenstein, grammar and God*, Epworth Press, London.

Kenny, A.: 1975, *Wittgenstein*, Penguin Books, Harmondsworth.

Kenny, A.: 1980, *Aquinas*, Mill and Wang, New York.

Kenny, A.: 1982, 'On the nature of philosophy', in B. McGuinness (ed.), *Wittgenstein and his times*, pp. 1–26, Basil Blackwell, Oxford.

Kerr, F.: 1986, *Theology after Wittgenstein*, Basil Blackwell, Oxford.

Kerschensteiner, G.: 1949, *Die Seele des Erziehers und das Problem der Lehrerbildung*, Von R. Oldenbourg, München.

Kleinig, J.: 1982, *Philosophical issues in education*, Croom Helm, London.

Kripke, S.A.: 1982, *Wittgenstein on rules and private language*, Oxford University Press, Oxford.

Kuhn, T.: 1962, *The structure of scientific revolution*, University of Chicago Press, Chicago.

Langeveld, M.-J.: 1946, *Beknopte theoretische pedagogiek*, Wolters-Noordhoff, Groningen.

Lawson, H.: 1989, 'Stories about stories', in H. Lawson & L. Appignesi (eds.), *Dismantling truth: Reality in the postmodern world*, pp. xi–xxvii, Weidenfield and Nicholson, London.

Lazerowitz, M.: 1977, *The language of philosophy. Freud & Wittgenstein*, D. Reider, Dordrecht.

Lazerowitz, M. & Ambrose, A.: 1984, *Essays in the unknown Wittgenstein*, Prometheus, Buffalo, NY.

Lecercle, J.J.: 1987, 'The misprision of pragmatics: Conceptions of language in contemporary French philosophy', in A. Phillips Griffiths (ed.), *Contemporary French philosophy*, pp. 21–40, Cambridge University Press, Cambridge.

Leicester, M. & Taylor, M.: (eds.): *Ethics, ethnicity and education*, Kogan Page, London.

Lévi-Strauss, C.: 1976, *Tristes tropiques*, trans. John & Doreen Weightman, Penguin, Harmonds worth.

Lloyd, D.I.: 1980, 'The rational curriculum: A critique', *Journal of Curriculum Studies* 12, 331–342.

Lloyd, I.: 1986, 'Confession and reason', *British Journal of Religious Education* 8, 140–145.

Luckhardt, C.G.: 1980, 'Wittgenstein and ethical relativism', in R. Haller & W. Grassl (eds.), *Language, logic, and philosophy: Proceedings of the Fourth International Wittgenstein Symposium*, pp. 316–320, Hölder-Pichler-Tempsky, Vienna.

Luhmann N. & Schorr, K.E.: (eds.): 1982, *Zwischen Technologie und Selbstreferenz: Fragen an die Pädagogik*, Suhrkamp, Frankfurt.

Lyotard, J-F.: 1983, 'Presentations', in A. Montefiori (ed.), *Philosophy in France today*, pp. 116–135, Cambridge University Press, Cambridge.

Lyotard, J-F.: 1984a, *The postmodern condition: A report on knowledge*, trans. G. Bennington & B. Massumi, University of Minnesota Press, Minneapolis.

Lyotard, J-F.: 1984b, 'Wittgenstein, "Après"', in J-F. Lyotard (ed.), *Tombeau de l'intellectuel et autres papiers*, pp. 57–66, Galilée, Paris.

Lyotard, J-F.: 1988, 'An interview with Jean-François Lyotard by W. van Reijen and D. Veerman', *Theory, Culture and Society* 5, 277–309.

Lyotard, J-F.: 1989, in A. Benjamin (ed.), *The Lyotard Reader*, Basil Blackwell, Oxford.

Lyotard, J-F.: 1991, 'Foreword: After the words', in J. Kosuth, *Art after philosophy and after: Collected Writings, 1966–1990*, G. Guercio (ed.), pp. xv–xviii, MIT Press, Cambridge, MA.

Lyotard, J-F.: 1992, in J. Pefanis & M. James (eds.), *The postmodern explained to children: Correspondence 1982–1985*, trans. D. Berry, Power Publications, Sydney.

MacIntyre, A.: 1981, *After virtue: A study in moral theory*, Duckworth, London.

MacIntyre, A.: 1990a, *Three rival versions of moral inquiry: Encyclopedia, genealogy and tradition*, University of Notre Dame Press, Notre Dame.

MacIntyre, A.: 1990b, *First principles, final ends and contemporary philosophical issues*, Marquette University Press, Milwaukee.

Mackie, J.L.: 1965, 'Causes and conditions', *American Philosophical Quarterly* 2, 245–264.

Mackie, J.L.: 1982, *The miracle of theism. Arguments for and against the existence of God*, Clarendon Press, Oxford.

Macmillan, C.J.B.: 1981, 'Wittgenstein and the problems of teaching and learning', in E. Leinfellner, *et al.* (eds.), *Language and ontology: Proceedings of the sixth International Wittgenstein Symposium*, pp. 483–486, Hölder-Pichler-Tempsky, Vienna.

Macmillan, C.J.B.: 1984, 'Love and logic in 1984', *Proceedings of the Philosophy of Education Society of the U.S.A.* 40, 3–16.

Macmillan, C.J.B.: 1985, 'Rational teaching', *Teachers College Record* 86, 411–422.

Macmillan, C.J.B.: 1989, 'Wittgenstein on not learning', in R. Haller & J. Brandl (eds.), *Wittgenstein – towards a re-evaluation: Proceedings of the 14th International Wittgenstein Symposium* (pp. 280–281). Vienna: Verlag Hölder-Pichler-Tempsky.

Malcolm, N.: 1981, *Wittgenstein: The relation of language to instinctive behaviour*, University College of Swansea, Wales.

Malcolm, N.: 1986, *Nothing is hidden. Wittgenstein's criticism of his early thought*, Basil Blackwell, Oxford.

Malcolm, N.: 1988, 'Subjectivity', *Philosophy* **63**, 147–160.

Malcolm, N.: 1993, *Wittgenstein: A religious point of view?*, Routledge, London.

Maloney, K.E.: 1985, 'Philosophy of education: Definitions of the field', *Educational Studies* **16**, 235–258.

Marples, R.: 1978, 'Is religious education possible?', *Journal of Philosophy of Education* **12**, 81–91.

Marshall, J.: 1975, 'Punishment and education', *Educational Theory* **24**, 148–157.

Marshall, J.: 1983, *What is education?*, Dunmore Press, Palmerston North.

Marshall, J.: 1984a, 'Punishment and moral education', *Journal of Moral Education* **13**, 79–85.

Marshall, J.: 1984b, 'John Wilson on the necessity of punishment', *Journal of Philosophy of Education* **18**, 97–104.

Marshall, J.: 1985, 'Wittgenstein on rules: Implications for authority and discipline in education', *Journal of Philosophy of Education* **19**, 3–11.

Marshall, J.: 1988a, *Why go to school*, Dunmore Press, Palmerston North.

Marshall, J.: 1988b, *Positivism or pragmatism: Philosophy of education in New Zealand*, New Zealand Association for Research in Education, Palmerston North.

Marshall, J. & Peters, M.: 1994, 'Postmodernism and education', in T. Husén & T.H. Postlethwaite (eds.), *The international encyclopedia of education*, 2nd ed., pp. 4639–4642, Pergamon Press, Oxford.

Martin, J.R.: 1982, 'The ideal of the educated person', *Philosophy of Education* **37**, 3–20.

Martin, D.M.: 1987, 'Learning to become a Christian', *Religious Education* **82**, 94–114.

Matthews, M.: 1980, *The Marxist theory of schooling*, Harvester Press, Brighton.

McAdoo, N.A.: 1987, '"Realization" in aesthetic education', *Journal of Philosophy of Education* **21**, 235–245.

McAdoo, N.A.: 1992, 'Can art ever be just about itself?', *The Journal of Aesthetics and Art Criticism* **50**, 131–138.

McCarthy, T.: 1990, 'Ironist theory as vocation: A response to Rorty's reply', *Critical Inquiry* **16**, 644–655.

McCarty, L. & McCarty, D.: 1991, 'Indoctrination as the face of knowledge: Endnotes for philosophy of education', *Philosophy of Education*, Proceedings of the Philosophy of Education Society of the U.S.A. **47**, 247–258.

McDonald, H.: 1990, 'Crossroads of scepticism: Wittgenstein, Derrida and ostensive definition', *The Philosophical Forum*, **21**, 261–276.

Mc Dowell, J.: 1994, *Mind and World*, Harvard University Press, Cambridge, MA.

McGuinness, B.: 1988, *Wittgenstein: A life. Young Ludwig 1889–1921*, Duckworth, London.

McLaughlin, T.H.: 1984, 'Parental rights and the religious upbringing of children', *Journal of Philosophy of Education* **18**, 75–83.

McLaughlin, T.H.: 1990, 'Peter Gardner on religious upbringing and the liberal ideal of religious autonomy', *Journal of Philosophy of Education* **24**, 107–125.

McLaughlin, T.H.: 1992, 'The ethics of separate schools', in M. Leicester & M. Taylor (eds.), *Ethics, ethnicity and education*, pp. 114–136, Kogan Page, London.

Miller, J.: 1993, *The passion of Michel Foucault*, Simon and Schuster, New York.

Mollenhauer, K.: 1968, *Erziehung und Emanzipation: Polemischen Skizzen*, Juventa, München.

Mollenhauer, K.: 1985, *Vergessene Zusammenhänge: Über Kultur und Erziehung*, Juventa, Weinheim.

Monk, R.: 1990, *Ludwig Wittgenstein: The duty of genius*, Vintage, London.

Moore, G.E.: 1903, *Principia ethica*, Cambridge University Press, Cambridge.

Moore, G.E.: 1955, 'Wittgenstein's lectures at Cambridge 1930–32', *Mind* **64**, 1–27.

Moore, G.: 1988, *Believing in God. A philosophical essay*, T and T Clark, Edinburgh.

Morawetz, T.: 1978, *Wittgenstein and knowledge: The importance of On Certainty*, University of Massachussetts Press, Amherst.

Nagel, T.: 1986, *The view from nowhere*, Oxford University Press, Oxford.

Neilsen, K.: 1971, *Contemporary critiques of religion*, Macmillan, London.

Neiman, A.: 1982, 'The Arguments of Augustine's *Contra Academicos*', *The Modern Schoolman*, Vol LIX, number 4, May 1982, 255–279.

Neiman, A.: 1984, 'Augustine's philosophizing person: The view from Cassiciacum', *The New Scholasticism* **58** (Spring), 236–255.

Neiman, A.: 1991, 'Ironic schooling: Socrates, pragmatism and the higher learning', *Educational Theory* **91**, 371–385.

Newman, J.H.: 1982, *The idea of a university*, University of Notre Dame Press, Notre Dame.

Nichols, K.: 1992, 'Roots in religious education', in B. Watson (ed.), *Priorities in religious education. A model for the 1990s and beyond*, pp. 113–123, Falmer, Lewes.

Nozick, R.: 1981, *Philosophical explanations*, The Belknap Press of Harvard University Press, Cambridge, MA.

Nyíri, J.C.: 1982, 'Wittgenstein's later work in relation to conservatism', in B. McGuinness (ed.), *Wittgenstein and his times*, pp. 44–68, Basil Blackwell, Oxford.

O'Connor, D.J.: 1957, *An introduction to the philosophy of education*, Routledge and Kegan Paul, London.

O'Hear, A.: 1984, *Experience, explanation and faith. An introduction to the philosophy of religion*, Routledge and Kegan Paul, London.

O'Hear, A.: 1991, 'Wittgenstein and the transmission of traditions', in A. Phillips Griffiths (ed.), *Wittgenstein centenary essays*, pp. 41–60, Cambridge University Press, Cambridge.

Oser F.: 1986, *Transformation und Entwicklung: Grundlagen der Moralerziehung*, Suhrkamp, Frankfurt.

Parfit, D.: 1971, 'Personal identity', *Philosophical Review* **80**, 3–27.

Parfit, D.: 1984, *Reasons and persons*, Clarendon Press, Oxford.

Parret, H.: 1983, 'Wittgenstein II bis', *Tijdschrift voor Filosofie* **45**, 261–290.

Patterson, Ch. J.: 1987, 'Wittgenstein, psychology, and the problem of individuality', in M. Chapman & R.A. Dixon (eds.), *Meaning and the growth of understanding. Wittgenstein's significance for developmental psychology*, pp. 167–185, Springer-Verlag, Berlin.

Peacocke, C.: 1982, 'Wittgenstein and experience', *The Philosophical Quarterly* **32**, 162–170.

Pears, D.: 1971, *Wittgenstein*, Fontana, London.

Pears, D.: 1989, 'The structure of the private language argument', *Revue Internationale de Philosophie* **43**, 264–278.

Peters, R.S.: 1964, *Education as initiation*, An Inaugural Lecture delivered at the University of London, Institute of Education, 9 December 1963, Institute of Education, London.

Peters, R.S.: 1966, *Ethics and education*, Allen & Unwin, London.

Peters, R.S.: 1967, *The concept of education*, Routledge, London.

Peters, R.S.: 1972, *Reason, morality and religion*, The 1972 Swarthmore Lecture, Friends Home Service Committee, London.

Peters, R.S.: 1973a, 'Introduction', in R.S. Peters (ed.), *The philosophy of education*, pp. 1–7, Oxford University Press, Oxford.

Peters, R.S.: 1973b, 'The justification of education', in R.S. Peters (ed.), *The philosophy of education*, pp. 239–268, Oxford University Press, Oxford.

Peters, R.S.: 1983, The philosophy of education, in P.H. Hirst (ed.), *Educational theory and its foundational disciplines*, pp. 30–61, Routledge and Kegan Paul, London.

Peters, M.: 1989, 'Techno-science, rationality and the university: Lyotard on the "Postmodern condition"', *Educational Theory* **39**, 93–105.

Peters, M.: 1991, 'Postmodernism: The critique of reason and the rise of the new social movements', *Sites: A Journal for Radical Perspectives on Culture* **22** (Autumn), 142–160.

Peters, M.: 1992, 'Performance and accountability in "post-industrial society": The crisis of British universities', *Studies in Higher Education* **17**, 123–139.

Peters, M.: (ed.): 1995, *Education and the postmodern condition*, Bergin and Garvey, New York.

Peters, M. & Marshall J.: 1993, 'Beyond the philosophy of the subject: Liberalism, education and the critique of individualism', *Educational Philosophy and Theory* **25**, 19–39.

Peukert, H.: 1993, 'Basic problems of a critical theory of education', *Journal of Philosophy of Education* **27**, 159–170.

Peukert, H.: 1994, 'Basic problems of a critical theory of education', in M. Hellemans, J. Masschelein & P. Smeyers (eds.), *The school: Its crisis*, pp. 111–123, Acco, Leuven.

Phillips, D.Z.: 1965, *The concept of prayer*, Routledge and Kegan Paul, London.

Phillips, D.Z.: 1970a, *Faith and philosophical enquiry*, Routledge and Kegan Paul, London.

Phillips, D.Z.: 1970b, 'Philosophy and religious education', *British Journal of Educational Studies* **18**, 5–17.

Phillips, D.Z.: 1971, *Death and immortality*, Macmillan, London.

Phillips, D.Z.: 1976, *Religion without explanation*, Basil Blackwell, Oxford.

Phillips, D.Z.: 1979, 'Is moral education really necessary?', *British Journal of Educational Studies* **18**, 42–56.

Phillips, D.Z.: 1980, 'Not in front of the children: Children and the heterogeneity of morals', *Journal of Philosophy of Education* **14**, 73–75.

Phillips, D.Z.: 1986, *Belief, change and forms of life*, Macmillan, London.

Phillips, D.Z.: 1988, *Faith after foundationalism*, Routledge, London.

Phillips, D.Z.: 1993, *Wittgenstein and religion*, Macmillan, London.

Phillips, D.Z. & Winch, P.: (eds.): 1989, *Wittgenstein: Attention to particulars*, Macmillan, London.

Phillips Griffiths, A.: (ed.): 1991, *Wittgenstein centenary essays*, Cambridge University Press, Cambridge.

Piaget, J.: 1971, *Insights and illusions of philosophy*, Meridean, New York.

Pieper, J.: 1952, *Leisure the basis of culture*, Faber and Faber, London.

Pieper, J.: 1957, *The silence of St. Thomas*, Pantheon Books, New York.

Pleines, J.E.: (ed.).: 1987, *Das Problem des Allgemeinen in der Bildungstheorie*, Königshausen und Neumann, Wurzburg.

Popper, K.R.: 1959, *The logic of scientific discovery*, Hutchinson, London.

Prado, P.W.: 1991, 'The necessity of contingency: Remarks on linkage', *L'Esprit Créateur* **33** (Spring), 90–106.

Proust, M.: 1972, *Remembrance of things past*, vol. 10, trans. C.K. Scott-Moncrieff, Chatto and Windus, London.

Putnam, H.: 1992, *Renewing philosophy*, Harvard University Press, Cambridge, MA.

Putnam, H.: 1994, *Words and Life*, Harvard University Press, Cambridge, MA.

Raulet, G.: 1983, 'Structuralism and post-structuralism: An interview with Michel Foucault', *Telos* **53**, 20.

Rhees, R.: 1969, *Without answers*, Routledge and Kegan Paul, London.

Rhees, R.: (ed.): 1984, *Recollections of Wittgenstein*, Oxford University Press, Oxford.

Rogers, C.: 1969, *Freedom to learn. A view of what education might become*, Merrill, Columbus, OH.

Rorty, R.: 1979, *Philosophy and the mirror of nature*, Basil Blackwell, Oxford.

Rorty, R.: 1980, 'A reply to Dreyfus and Taylor. Symposium with Hubert Dreyfus and Charles Taylor', *Review of Metaphysics* **34**, 3–23.

Rorty, R.: 1982a, *Consequences of pragmatism*, Harvester Press, Brighton.

Rorty, R.: 1982b, 'Hermeneutics, general education and teaching', *Synergos* **2**, 1–15.

Rorty, R.: 1983, 'Postmodern bourgeois liberalism', *Journal of Philosophy* **80**, 580–586.

Rorty, R.: 1985, 'Habermas and Lyotard on postmodernity', in R. Bernstein (ed.), *Habermas and modernity*, pp. 161–176, Polity Press, Cambridge.

Rorty, R.: 1989a, *Contingency, irony and solidarity*, Cambridge University Press, Cambridge.

Rorty, R.: 1989b, 'Education without dogma', *Dissent*, (Spring), 198–204.

Runzo, J.: (ed.): 1993, *Is God real?*, Macmillan, London.

Rusche, G. & Kirchheimer, O.: 1939, *Punishment and structure*, Columbia University Press, New York.

Russell, B.: 1912, *The problems of philosophy*, Oxford University Press, Oxford.

Russell, B.: 1916, *Principia mathematica*, Allen & Unwin, London.

Russell, B.: 1927, *An outline of philosophy*, Allen & Unwin, London.

Russell, B.: 1956, in R. Marsh (ed.), *Logic and knowledge, essays 1901–1950*, Allen & Unwin, London.

Ryle, G.: 1949, *The concept of mind*, Hutchinson, London.

Sayers, B.: 1987, 'Wittgenstein, relativism, and the strong thesis in sociology', *Philosophy of the Social Sciences* **17**, 133–145.

Scheffler, I.: 1960, *The language of education*, Thomas, Springfield.

Scheffler, I.: 1982, *Science and subjectivity*, Hackett, Indianapolis.

Scheffler, I.: 1985, *On human potential*, Routledge and Kegan Paul, London.

Schelling, T.C.: 1984, *Choice and consequence*, Harvard University Press, Cambridge, MA.

Schon, D.: 1983, *The reflective practitioner: How professionals think in action*, Basic Books, New York.

Schools Council: 1971, *Working paper 36: Religious education in secondary schools*, Evans/ Methuen, London.

Schweidler, W.: 1983, *Wittgensteins Philosophiebegriff*, Alber, Freiburg.

Scruton, R.: 1974, *Art and imagination*, Methuen, London.

Sealey, J.: 1985, *Religious education: Philosophical perspectives*, Allen & Unwin, London.

Sherry, P.: 1977, *Religion, truth and language games*, Macmillan, London.

Shields, P.R.: 1993, *Logic and sin in the writings of Ludwig Wittgenstein*, University of Chicago Press, Chicago.

Shulman, L.S.: 1987, 'Knowledge and teaching: Foundations of the new reform', *Harvard Educational Review* **57**, 1–22.

Sibley, F.: 1962, 'Aesthetic concepts', in J. Margolis (ed.), *Philosophy looks at the arts: Contemporary readings in aesthetics*, pp. 63–88, Charles Scribner's Sons, New York.

Sluga, H.: 1989, 'Thinking as writing', in B. McGuiness & R. Haller (eds.), *Wittgenstein in focus*, pp. 115–141, Rodopi, Amsterdam.

Smart, N.: 1968, *Secular education and the logic of religion*, Faber, London.

Smart, N.: 1973, *The science of religion and the sociology of knowledge. Some methodological questions*, Princeton University Press, Princeton.

Smeyers, P.: 1992, 'The necessity for particularity in education and child-rearing: The moral issue', *Journal of Philosophy of Education* **26**, 63–73.

Smeyers, P.: 1994, 'Philosophy of education: Western European perspectives', in T. Husén & T.H. Postlethwaite (eds.), *The international encyclopedia of education*, 2nd ed., pp. 4456–4461, Pergamon Press, Oxford.

Smeyers, P.: 1995a, 'Education and the educational project. I) In an atmosphere of postmodernism', *Journal of Philosophy of Education* **29**, 109–119.

Smeyers, P.: 1995b, 'Education and the educational project. II) Do we still care about it?', *Journal of Philosophy of Education* **29**, nr. 3.

Smith, P.: 1993, 'Critical notice: "Fact and meaning" by Jane Heal', *Philosophical Quarterly* **43**, 90–99.

Smith, R.: 1987, 'Learning from experience', *Journal of Philosophy of Education* **21**, 37–46.

Standish, P.: 1992, *Beyond the self: Wittgenstein, Heidegger, and the limits of language*, Publishing Group, Ashgate.

Staten, H.: 1985, *Wittgenstein and Derrida*, Basil Blackwell, Oxford.

Strawson, P.F.: 1962, 'Freedom and resentment', in P.F. Strawson 1974, *Freedom and resentment and other essays*, pp. 1–25, Methuen, London.

Suits, B.: 1978, *The grasshopper: Games, life and utopia*, University of Toronto Press, Toronto.

Sutton, C.: 1974, *The German tradition in philosophy*, Weidenfeld & Nicolson, London.

Taylor, C.: 1977, 'What is human agency?', in C. Taylor, 1985, *Human agency and language. Philosophical papers I*, pp. 15–44, Cambridge Universtity Press, Cambridge.

Taylor, C.: 1987, 'Overcoming epistemology', in K. Barnes, J. Bohman & T. McCarthy (eds.), *After philosophy: End or transformation?*, pp. 465–488, Cambridge University Press, Cambridge.

Taylor, C.: 1989, *Sources of the self: The making of the modern identity*, Cambridge University Press, Cambridge.

Taylor, C.: 1991, *The ethics of authenticity*, Harvard University Press, Cambridge, MA.

Thiessen, E.J.: 1993, *Teaching for commitment. Liberal education, indoctrination and Christian nurture*, McGill-Queen's University Press, Montreal & Kingston.

Tilghman, B.R.: 1991, *Wittgenstein, ethics and aesthetics*, Macmillan, London.

Tillmann, K.-J.: (ed.): 1987, *Schultheorien*, Bergmann-Hellig, Hamburg.

Trigg, R.: 1973, *Reason and commitment*, Cambridge University Press, Cambridge.

Ulmer, G.L.: 1985, 'The object of post criticism', in H. Foster (ed.), *Postmodern culture*, pp. 83–110, Pluto Press, London.

Von Wright, G.H.: 1972, 'Wittgenstein on certainty', in G.A. von Wright (ed.), *Problems in the theory of knowledge*, pp. 47–61, Nijhoff, The Hague.

Von Wright, G.H.: 1982, 'Wittgenstein and his times', in B. McGuiness (ed.), *Wittgenstein and his times*, pp. 108–120, Basil Blackwell, Oxford.

Waismann, F.: 1965, *The principles of linguistic philosopy*, Macmillan, London.

Walker, J.C.: 1983, 'Some recent developments in philosophy of education', in J.C. Walker (ed.), *Some new perspectives in philosophy of education*, Occasional paper 14, pp. 2–22, Department of Education, University of Sydney, Sydney.

Walker, J.C.: 1984, 'The evolution of the APE: Analytic philosophy of education in retrospect', *Access* **3**, 1, 1–16.

Ward, K.: 1982, *Holding fast to God. A reply to Don Cupitt*, SPCK, London.

Warehime, N.: 1993, *To be one of is: Cultural conflict, creative democracy and education*, SUNY Press, Albany.

Watson, G.: 1975, 'Free agency', in G. Watson (ed.), 1982, *Free will*, pp. 96–110, Oxford University Press, Oxford.

Webern, A.: 1963, *The path to the new music*, trans. L.Black, Theodore Presser, Pennsylvania.

White, S.R.: 1994, *Don Cupitt and the future of Christian doctrine*, Sun Press, London.

Williams, C.J.: 1979, 'Experiencing the meaning of a word', *Man and World* **12**, 3–12.

Wilson, J.: 1977, *Philosophy and practical education*, Routledge and Kegan Paul, London.

Wilson, P.S.: 1971, *Interest and discipline in education*, Routledge and Kegan Paul, London.

Winch, P.: 1958, *The idea of a social science*, Routledge and Kegan Paul, London.

Winch, P.: 1987, *Trying to make sense*, Basil Blackwell, Oxford.

Winch, P.: 1991, 'Certainty and authority', in A. Phillips Griffiths (ed.), *Wittgenstein centenary essays*, pp. 223–239, Cambridge University Press, Cambridge.

Winch, P.: 1993, 'Discussion of Malcolm's essay', in N. Malcolm (ed.), *Wittgenstein: A religious point of view?*, pp. 95–135, Routledge, London.

Wisdom, J.: 1963, *Problems of mind and matter*, Cambridge University Press, Cambridge.

Notes on Contributors

Edwin Philip Brandon, Programme Co-ordinator, Office of Academic Affairs, University of the West Indies, Barbados. Published two books and a number of articles including in such Journals as *Philosophical Quarterly, Educational Philosophy and Theory, Teaching Philosophy* and *Informal Logic*.

Dr. Stefaan Cuypers, Research Fellow and part-time Lecturer at the Higher Institute of Philosophy, University of Leuven, Belgium. Published several articles in Dutch and Anglo-Saxon Philosophy and Philosophy of Education Journals including in the *Journal of Philosophy of Education*.

Dr. A. Wouter van Haaften, Professor of Philosophy and History of Education, University of Nijmegen, The Netherlands. His major works include "Epistemologisch Relativisme" (In Dutch) (Epistemological Relativism) and "Ontwikkelingsfilosofie" (In Dutch) (Philosophy of Development). He published widely in Dutch and Anglo-Saxon Journals including in the *Journal of Philosophy of Education*.

Dr. Alven Neiman, Assistant Dean and Adjunct Assistant Professor in the College of Arts and Letters, University of Notre Dame, Indiana, U.S.A. He published a number of papers on Augustine, Wittgenstein and the Philosophy of Education in Journals such as *The Modern Schoolman, Teachers College Record, Educational Theory* and *Educational Philosophy and Theory*.

Dr. C.J.B. Macmillan, Professor of Philosophy of Education, Florida State University, U.S.A. Past-President of the Philosophy of Education Society of the U.S.A. in which he held besides the presidency, numerous other positions. Published widely within the area of Philosophy of Education (more then fifteen papers deal particularly with Wittgenstein's ideas as relevant to education) including in such Journals as *Educational Theory, Synthese* and *Teachers College Record*. He also contributed several times to the Wittgenstein Conferences in Kirchberg (Austria).

Dr. James D. Marshall, Professor, Dean, Faculty of Education University of Auckland, New Zealand, Author of six books and has published widely in International Journals in the areas of Social Theory and Education including *Journal of Philosophy of Education, Educational Theory* and *Educational Philosophy and Theory*. A book on Foucault is forthcoming and two other books are in press: one, with Michael Peters is entitled *The Individual and Community*, and the other co-authored with colleagues *Myths and Reality: Schooling in New Zealand*.

Dr. Nick McAdoo, Lecturer, Open University, United Kingdom. He is a member of the Executive Committee of the British Society of Aesthetics and

Studies in Philosophy and Education 14: 361–363, 1994.
© 1994 *Kluwer Academic Publishers. Printed in the Netherlands.*

published widely in this field. Recent publications include a chapter on "Mathematics and Art" in *Teaching Mathematics and Art* (ed.) Leslie Jones and papers in Journals such as the *British Journal of Aesthetics*, the *Journal of Philosophy of Education* and the *Journal of Aesthetics and Art Criticism*.

Dr. Luise McCarty and Dr. David McCarty respectively Assistant Professor, Department of Educational Leadership and Policy Studies and Visiting Assistant Professor, Department of Philosophy, both at Indiana University, U.S.A. She published among other articles a number of contributions in the *Proceedings of the meeting of the Philosophy of Education Society of the U.S.A.* He published more than 25 papers (the majority of which deal with issues relevant to Wittgensteinian philosophy) mainly within Philosophy Journals including such as *Journal of Philosophy Logic, The Notre Dame Journal of Formal Logic, The Journal of Pure and Applied Logic, The Journal of Philosophical Logic* and *Synthese*. He also contributed to the Wittgenstein Conferences in Kirchberg (Austria) and to the *Proceedings of the meetings of the Philosophy of Education Society of the U.S.A.* His article "Hintikka's Tractatus" appeared in the *Proceedings of the Wittgenstein Centenary* (1991) another has been anthologized in the volume *Wittgenstein in Florida* edited by Jaakko Hintikka (1991).

Dr. Terence H. McLaughlin, University Lecturer of Education and Fellow of St Edmund's College, Cambridge, United Kingdom. Published papers include articles in Journal such as the *Journal of Philosophy of Education*. He had recently held a Fellowship in the Centre for Philosophy and Public Affairs in the Department of Moral Philosophy at the University of St Andrews and was Visiting Scholar in Education at Harvard University. He is Secretary of the Philosophy of Education Society of Great Britian.

Dr. Michael Peters, Senior Lecturer, Education Department, University of Auckland, New Zealand. Publications include articles in *Educational Philosophy, Educational Philosophy and Theory, Policy Sciences, Journal of Education Policy, Studies in Higher Education, Pacific Education, Journal of Multilingual and Multicultural Development, Evaluation Review, Public Administration and French Cultural Studies*.

Dr. Paul Smeyers, Professor, Faculty of Psychology and Educational Sciences, University of Leuven, Belgium. Has published widely in Anglo-Saxon and European Journals on issues related to a Wittgensteinian Philosophy of Education, including in the *Journal of Philosophy of Education, Proceedings of the Philosophy of Education Society of Great Britain, Proceedings of the Philosophy of Education Society of the U.S.A.* and *Studies in Philosophy and Education*. He also contributed to the *Encyclopedia of Education* (Pergamon Press, 1994) and published more than 50 papers in Dutch Journals, books or conference proceedings. He was a Visiting Scholar at Harvard University.

Dr. Paul Standish, Lecturer, University of Dundee, United Kingdom. Published recently *Beyond the Self: Wittgenstein, Heidegger, and the Limits of Language* (Ashgate Publishing Group, 1992) and furthermore a number of articles in the *Journal of Philosophy of Education*.

AUTHOR INDEX

SUBJECT INDEX